THREE MODERN I

St Mary's College

A College of the University of Surrey

Waldegrave Road, Strawberry Hill
Twickenham TW1 4SX

020-8240 4000
http://www.smuc.ac.uk

Note on the Playwrights

Girish Karnad, one of India's foremost dramatists and actors, was born in Matheran, near Bombay, in 1938. A Rhodes scholar at Oxford, Karnad has directed films, served as the Director of the Film and Television Institute of India, and has been Chairman of the Sangeet Natak Akademi. He is the recipient of the Padma Bhushan, and was conferred the Bharatiya Jnanpith, India's highest literary prize, in 1999.

Badal Sircar is widely known in Bengal for his refreshing brand of Street Theatre. Famous playwright, actor, and director, he is the unofficial leader of experimental theatre in Kolkata, and his works have been translated into several Indian languages.

Vijay Tendulkar is regarded as one of India's best-known playwrights. He has more than fifty publications to his credit, and has received numerous prestigious awards such as the Padma Bhushan, the Vishnudas Bhave Memorial Award, and the Katha Chudamani Award, for successfully raising social issues through his plays.

THREE MODERN INDIAN PLAYS

TUGHLAQ
by Girish Karnad

EVAM INDRAJIT
by Badal Sircar

SILENCE! THE COURT IS IN SESSION
by Vijay Tendulkar

OXFORD
UNIVERSITY PRESS

OXFORD
UNIVERSITY PRESS

YMCA Library Building, Jai Singh Road, New Delhi 110 001

Oxford University Press is a department of the University of Oxford. It furthers the
University's objective of excellence in research, scholarship, and education
by publishing worldwide in

Oxford   New York

Auckland   Cape Town   Dar es Salaam   Hong Kong   Karachi   Kuala Lumpur
Madrid   Melbourne   Mexico City   Nairobi   New Delhi   Shanghai   Taipei   Toronto

With offices in

Argentina Austria Brazil Chile Czech Republic France Greece Guatemala
Hungary Italy Japan Poland Portugal Singapore South Korea Switzerland
Thailand Turkey Ukraine Vietnam

Oxford is a registered trademark of Oxford University Press
in the UK and in certain other countries

Published in India by Oxford University Press, New Delhi

© Oxford University Press 1989
Tughlaq first published 1972
Evam Indrajit first published 1974
Silence! The Court is in Session first published 1978

*All three plays are fully protected by copyright and all applications for
public performance have to be made in advance to the publisher*

The moral rights of the author have been asserted
Database right Oxford University Press (maker)

First published in Oxford India Paperbacks 1989
Eleventh impression 2005

ISBN 019 562372 X

Printed in India by Sai Printopack Pvt. Ltd., New Delhi 110 020
Published by Manzar Khan, Oxford University Press
YMCA Library Building, Jai Singh Road, New Delhi 110 001

Girish Karnad

TUGHLAQ
A play in thirteen scenes

to

KRISHNA BASRUR

*with affection
and admiration*

AUTHOR'S NOTE

This play was originally written in Kannada in 1964. I was persuaded to translate it into English by Alyque Padamsee, who later produced it for the Theatre Group, Bombay. This translation was first staged at the Bhulabhai Auditorium, Bombay in August 1970.

I should like to express here my thanks to Alyque Padamsee and the Theatre Group for the care and imagination with which they produced the play. My special thanks are also due to S. Gopalie, Madras, for his invaluable help with the translation.

Dharwar, 1971   G. K.

INTRODUCTION

Tughlaq, which was published in Kannada in 1964, is Girish Karnad's second play. His first play, *Yayāti,* was a self-consciously existentialist drama on the theme of responsibility. And those of us writing in the Kannada *Navya* movement of the time can still remember the excitement when we first read it in 1961. His interpretation of the familiar old myth on the exchange of ages between father and son baffled and angered many conventional critics but, for others, who were trying to root their contemporary concerns in old myths, Karnad's unheroic hero, Puru, was a great experience.

Tughlaq was an immediate success on the stage. It was first produced in Kannada in 1965 and was also done, about the same time, in Hindi by the National School of Drama. Bengali and Marathi productions followed, and in 1970 there was an English production in Bombay which was a major success.

It is not hard to account for the immediate response the play has received from Kannada as well as other audiences. One can enjoy the play on the stage without paying much attention to its rich and complex symbolism and the subtle weaving of its different motifs. The play has an interesting story, an intricate plot, scope for spectacle, and uses dramatic conventions like the comic pair, Aziz and Aazam (the *Akara* and *Makara* of *Natak* performances), to which theatre audiences respond readily.

Another reason for *Tughlaq's* appeal to Indian audiences is that it is a play of the sixties, and reflects as no other play perhaps does the political mood of dis-illusionment which followed the Nehru era of idealism in the country. Karnad himself has commented (*Enact*, June 1971) on this:

What struck me absolutely about Tughlaq's history was that it was contemporary. The fact that here was the most idealistic, the most intelligent king ever to come on the throne of Delhi . . . and one of the greatest failures also. And within a span of twenty years this tremendously capable man had gone to pieces. This seemed to be both due to his idealism as well as the shortcomings within him, such as his impatience, his cruelty, his feeling that he had the only correct answer. And I felt in the early sixties India had also come very far in the same direction—the twenty-year period seemed to me very much a striking parallel.

But the play is more than a political allegory It has an irreducible, puzzling quality which comes from the ambiguities of Tughlaq's character, the dominating figure in the play. All the other characters are dramatized aspects of his complex personality, yet they also exist in their own right. Kannada critics have made detailed analyses of the play, paying special attention to the symbolism of the game of chess, the theme of disguise, the ironic success of Aziz whose amazing story runs parallel to Tughlaq's, and the dualism of the man and the hero in Tughlaq, which is the source of the entire tragedy. Yet no critical examination of the play can easily exhaust its total meaning for the reader, because the play has, finally, an elusive and haunting quality which it gets from the character of Tughlaq who has been realized in great psychological depth. But it would be unjust to say that the play is about an 'interesting' character, for the play relates the character of Tughlaq to philosophical questions on the nature of man and the destiny of a whole kingdom which a dreamer like him controls.

Although the theme of the play is from history—there are many such plays in Kannada—Karnad's treatment of the theme is not historical. Take, for instance, the use Karnad makes of the leitmotiv of the play, 'prayer', in the scene where the Muslim chieftains along with Sheik Shams-ud-din, a pacifist priest, conspire to murder Tughlaq while at prayer. The use of prayer for murder is reminiscent of what Tughlaq himself did to kill his father. That prayer, which is most dear to Tughlaq, is vitiated by him as well as his enemies, is symbolic of the fact that his life is corrupted at its very source. The whole episode is ironic. It involves Shihab-ud-din, an idealist who has put great trust in Tughlaq's rule, and is himself ultimately betrayed by Ratansingh who masterminds the entire plan of murder for his own ends. The intrigue here not only enhances the theatrical interest of the play, but is a dramatized projection of Tughlaq's tortured, divided self. Thus, the external action throughout enacts the inner drama of Tughlaq. Both Tughlaq and his enemies initially appear to be idealists; yet, in the pursuit of the ideal, they perpetrate its opposite. The whole play is structured on these opposites: the ideal and the real; the divine aspiration and the deft intrigue. Tughlaq is what he is in spite of his self-knowledge and an intense desire for divine grace. He is aware of the irony of his life when Aziz, the only character in the play who has skilfully used all the schemes of Tughlaq for his own designs, kills Ghiyas-ud-din and comes in his guise as a holy messenger of peace to purify the land and revive the banned prayer. The irony is deeply tragic. In the end Tughlaq and his kingdom are one in their chaos, and he knows it.

There are some good single plays in Kannada like Masti's *Kākana Koṭe* and the plays of Adya Rangacharya who has kept the tradition of serious play-writing in Kannada alive; yet there is, perhaps, no play in Kannada comparable to *Tughlaq* in its depth and range. It is likely to become a classic in Kannada literature. The present translation, which has been ably done by Karnad himself, will be warmly welcomed by readers eager to know what is happening in the Indian languages.

It may not be out of place to mention here that many teachers of English in India have felt and still feel the need for English translations of literature in the Indian languages. Teachers like myself have often wished that along with Indian writing in English which we prescribe to our students, we should also be able to teach English translations of classics in the Indian languages which will engage our student's attention fully and meaningfully. Karnad's *Tughlaq* should be as rewarding an experience to teach and to study, as it has been to see on the stage all over India.

Mysore   U. R. Anantha Murthy
September, 1971

CHARACTERS

[In order of appearance]

ANNOUNCER
SULTAN MUHAMMAD TUGHLAQ
AAZAM
AZIZ
STEP-MOTHER
VIZIER MUHAMMAD NAJIB
ZIA-UD-DIN BARANI
SHEIKH IMAM-UD-DIN
SHIHAB-UD-DIN
SARDAR RATANSINGH
SHEIKH SHAMS-UD-DIN TAJUDDARFIM
GHIYAS-UD-DIN ABBASID

CROWD OF CITIZENS KAZI-I-MUMALIK AND RETINUE GUARD
DOOR-KEEPER SERVANT AMIRS SAYYID MUZZIN
SOLDIERS HINDU WOMAN REFUGEE FAMILY WATCHMEN KARIM

The action of the play takes place first of all in Delhi in the year 1327, then on the road from Delhi to Daulatabad, and lastly in and around the fort in Daulatabad five years later.

SCENE ONE

A. D. 1327

The yard in front of the Chief Court of Justice in Delhi. A crowd of citizens—mostly Muslims, with a few Hindus here and there.

OLD MAN: God, what's this country coming to!

YOUNG MAN: What are you worried about, grandfather? The country's in perfectly safe hands—safer than any you've seen before.

OLD MAN: I don't know. I've been alive a long time, seen many Sultans, but I never thought I would live to see a thing like this.

YOUNG MAN: Your days are over, old man. What's the use of Sultans who didn't allow a subject within a mile's distance? This King now, he isn't afraid to be human—

THIRD MAN: But does he have to make such a fuss about being human? Announce his mistakes to the whole world—invite the entire capital?

OLD MAN: And get kicked by an infidel too. It's an insult to Islam.

YOUNG MAN: That's good that! Insult to Islam! So you want to teach him Islam, do you? Tell me, how often did you pray before he came to the throne?

THIRD MAN: That isn't the point.

YOUNG MAN: That's precisely the point. Not even once a week, I bet. Now you pray five times a day because that's the law and if you break it, you'll have the officers on your neck. Can you mention one earlier Sultan in whose time people read the Koran in the streets like now? Just one?

OLD MAN: What's the use? One must act according to it . . .

THIRD MAN: All this about the Hindus not paying the

1

jiziya tax. That's against the Koran, you know.
A Mowlvi told me that—

HINDU: Now, now, don't look at *me* when you say that.
We didn't want an exemption! Look, when a Sultan
kicks me in the teeth and says, 'Pay up, you Hindu
dog', I'm happy. I know I m safe. But the moment
a man comes along and says, 'I know you are a Hindu,
but you are also a human being'—well, that makes
me nervous.

YOUNG MAN: Ungrateful wretch!

OLD MAN: But this wretch is our best friend, Jamal.
Beware of the Hindu who embraces you. Before you
know what, he'll turn Islam into another caste and call
the Prophet an incarnation of his god . . .

The PUBLIC ANNOUNCER *comes out and beats his drum.*
Silence.

ANNOUNCER: Attention! Attention! In the name of
Allah it is hereby announced that Vishnu Prasad, a
Brahmin of Shiknar, had filed a suit against His
Merciful Majesty, that his land had been seized illegally
by the officers of the State and that he should be given
just compensation for the loss of the land and the
privation resulting therefrom. The Kazi-i-Mumalik
having considered this matter carefully and in full
detail has declared . . .

He pauses for effect. The audience is tense and the
ANNOUNCER *looks pleased.*

. . . has declared that the Brahmin's claim is just. . .

Commotion in the crowd. The ANNOUNCER *silences them*
with a couple of drum beats and continues.

. . . that the Brahmin's claim is just and that His
Merciful Majesty is guilty of illegal appropriation of
land. The Kazi-i-Mumalik has further declared that
in return for the land and in compensation of the
privation resulting from its loss the said Vishnu Prasad
should receive a grant of five hundred silver dinars
from the State Treasury.

2

Scene One

Renewed commotion. But the ANNOUNCER *isn't finished yet.*
His Merciful Majesty has accepted the decision of the
Kazi-i-Mumalik as just and in addition to the grant of
five hundred silver dinars has offered the said Vishnu
Prasad a post in the Civil Service to ensure him a
regular and adequate income.

Beats the drums again and retires.

OLD MAN: What folly is this! May Heaven guide our
Sultan.

HINDU: I don't believe a word of it. There's something more
to this, that much is obvious—

The ANNOUNCER *comes out followed by* MUHAMMAD, *the*
KAZI *and the retinue.*

ANNOUNCER: Attention! Attention! The Warrior in the
Path of God, the Defender of the Word of the Prophet,
the Friend of the Khalif, the Just, His Merciful
Majesty, Sultan Muhammad Tughlaq.

CROWD: Victory—to the King.

MUHAMMAD: My beloved people, you have heard the
judgement of the Kazi and seen for yourselves how
justice works in my kingdom—without any
consideration of might or weakness, religion or creed.
May this moment burn bright and light up our path
towards greater justice, equality, progress and peace
—not just peace but a more purposeful life.
And to achieve this end I am taking a new step in which
I hope I shall have your support and cooperation.
Later this year the capital of my empire will be moved
from Delhi to Daulatabad.

The crowd reacts in bewilderment. MUHAMMAD *smiles.*

Your surprise is natural, but I beg you to realize that
this is no mad whim of a tyrant. My ministers and
I took this decision after careful thought and discussion.
My empire is large now and embraces the South and
I need a capital which is at its heart. Delhi is too near
the border and as you well know its peace is never
free from the fear of invaders. But for me the most

3

important factor is that Daulatabad is a city of the
Hindus and as the capital it will symbolize the bond
between Muslims and Hindus which I wish to develop
and strengthen in my kingdom. I invite you all to
accompany me to Daulatabad. This is only an
invitation and not an order. Only those who have
faith in me may come with me. With their help I
shall build an empire which will be the envy of the
world.

Exits with the retinue.

OLD MAN: You can go to the Kazi-i-Mumalik for small
offences. But who do you appeal to against such
madness?

THIRD MAN: This is tyranny. Sheer tyranny! Move the
capital to Daulatabad! Such things never happened
in his father's days—may his soul rest in peace. Now
he's got his father's throne. He isn't happy with
that and—

YOUNG MAN: What do you mean?

THIRD MAN: What?

YOUNG MAN: What did you mean by that—when you said
he had got his father's throne?

THIRD MAN: Don't try to threaten me, boy. The whole
capital saw it.

YOUNG MAN: Saw what?

THIRD MAN: You know what.

YOUNG MAN: Were you there?

THIRD MAN: There were others—my friends—

YOUNG MAN: Hang your friends! Were you there?

THIRD MAN: No!

YOUNG MAN: Well, I was. And I tell you it was an
accident.

THIRD MAN: I see.

YOUNG MAN: It was. The elephant suddenly went wild.
The crowds must have frightened it. It just ran and
dashed against the wooden pandal. And the pandal
collapsed.

OLD MAN: Very convenient.

4

THIRD MAN: And to think the procession had been arranged by the father in his honour!

YOUNG MAN: But the Sultan had gone to the mosque to pray! The old Sultan should never have had the procession at prayer time—You all know it was prayer time and the Sultan never misses a prayer!

HINDU: Yes, yes, we know that. But tell me. How did the elephant know it was time for prayer?

Laughter.

THIRD MAN: All right, don't trust my word. But do you think a man like Sheikh Imam-ud-din would lie? Well, he said in clear loud words that it was murder. And 'he said it publicly—I was there!

OLD MAN (*eagerly*): You've seen the Sheikh?

THIRD MAN: Why, of course. Only a week ago. In Kanpur. What a man! What a voice! The audience was spell-bound. And he said the Sultan's guilty of killing his father and brother, he said. He said so many other things too—about Islam and what's happening to it. It was the most inspiring speech I've ever heard. The audience went wild and burnt down half of Kanpur. You think he would talk like that if he wasn't sure?

OLD MAN: They say he looks like the Sultan.

THIRD MAN: No—not very much. People exaggerate, you know. But he has a certain resemblance—some gestures, you know, some mannerisms—

HINDU: Perhaps that's where he gets his habit of making speeches.

THIRD MAN: Watch your words, infidel. Don't you dare mock a saint like him.

The GUARD comes out of the Court.

GUARD: All right, all right. Go home! What are you waiting for? The show's over! Go home—

The crowd disperses. Only AAZAM remains, hanging around. Well, what do you want?

AAZAM: Nothing, I just wanted to see the Brahmin. He hasn't come out yet, has he?

GUARD: Oh, get away. Wants to see the Brahmin, if you please. Be off—

AAZAM retreats. The GUARD looks into the Court and shouts.

Come out—come out. Don't be scared, Your Highness.

The BRAHMIN comes out.

Perhaps Your Highness will want an escort to see you safely home! Complaining against the Sultan! Bloody Infidel! Get going, I'm already late.

BRAHMIN: Yes, yes. Certainly. Good-bye.

CUARD: Good-bye.

Goes in and shuts the door. The BRAHMIN starts to go. AAZAM follows him and then slowly taps him on the shoulder.

AAZAM: Ho . . . ooo . . .

The BRAHMIN whirls round and pulls out a dagger as he turns. AAZAM jumps back.

AAZAM: Oops. . .

They watch each other. AAZAM's jaw falls in surprise.

AAZAM: Who? Not . . . not . . .

BRAHMIN: Aazam?

AAZAM: Aziz? What on earth . . .

Gives a shout of joy, lifts AZIZ up and whirls him round and round ecstatically.

AZIZ: Let me down—let me down—

AAZAM lets him down.

And hold your tongue. If they find out, I'm finished, man.

AAZAM: But—I don't see you for years and then—this—this?

AZIZ: Shut up!

6

Scene One

They move off and sit under a tree.

AAZAM: I thought something was funny. I mean a man wins a case against the King himself—you would expect him to come out victoriously—I mean holding his head high? Not hide inside! Listen, Brahmins don't carry daggers around like that.

AZIZ quickly hides the dagger.

AZIZ: What are you doing here?

AAZAM: I am where there is a crowd. Look, today's earnings. And you won't believe me if I tell you where they hide their money—

AZIZ: So your bad habits continue, do they?

AAZAM: Not habit. Occupation. Anyway, I'm just a common pickpocket. But you are up to no good either. I can see that. A Muslim dhobi can't become a Brahmin that easily.

AZIZ: For God's sake, keep your voice down. Now look, if I tell you the truth, will you keep it to yourself?

AAZAM: Depends on what I get out of it—all right, you're an old friend. I'll keep quiet for nothing. So?

AZIZ: Did you hear the royal proclamation the other day?

AAZAM: Which one? There are so many.

AZIZ: You know, the one on the second anniversary of his coronation. (*Mimicking a public announcer.*) 'Henceforth people may file a suit against the Sultan himself for the misbehaviour of his officers. . . . No one need have any fear. . . . Justice will be done. . . Et cetera. Well, I was at the end of my tether then. There's no future in being a dhobi these days. So I did a bit of thinking. There's a Brahmin called Vishnu Prasad whose land had been confiscated recently. I shaved my head and went to him. I said I would buy the land.

AAZAM: Please a little slowly. I—you know I'm not very bright. But what's the point? I mean the land was confiscated, wasn't it?

AZIZ: Exactly, that's what he said too. But I said, 'Never mind about that.' So he sold me the land—back-

7

dating the contract. And I filed my suit. Well, here
I am. Five hundred silver dinars for nothing, and
a job in His Merciful Majesty's own Civil Service.

AAZAM: But what if he had cut off your head instead?

AZIZ *laughs.*

Anyway, why did you have to dress up in these
ungodly clothes? Couldn't you have come like a
proper Muslim?

AZIZ (*scandalized*): But then what would happen to the
King's impartial justice? A Muslim plaintiff against
a Muslim king? I mean, where's the question of
justice there? Where's the equality between Hindus
and Muslims? If on the other hand the plaintiff's a
Hindu. . . well, you saw the crowds.

AAZAM: Complicated!

AZIZ: It's a bit too subtle for you. Anyway here's my
offer. From tomorrow I join the Civil Service.
Why don't you come along too? I'll get you a job
under me. You know, a Brahmin with a Muslim
friend—the Sultan will like that.

AAZAM: No, thanks, I'm quite happy—

AZIZ: Come along. It won't be for long. I don't intend
to be a Brahmin all my life! There's money here and
we'll make a pile by the time we reach Daulatabad.

AAZAM: And then?

AZIZ: How should I know?

8

SCENE TWO

A room in the palace. MUHAMMAD *is bent over a chess-board, smiling with suppressed excitement. The* STEP-MOTHER *enters.*

STEP-MOTHER: Muhammad—

MUHAMMAD: Ah, there you are! Absolutely at the right moment. If you had come a minute earlier, the world would have been so much poorer.

STEP-MOTHER: Really? That sounds very important.

MUHAMMAD: But it is. I have just solved the most famous problem in chess. Even al-Adli and as-Sarakhi said it was insoluble. And it's so simple—

STEP-MOTHER: Who were they?

MUHAMMAD: Mother! How can you ask? They were the greatest chess players the world's ever seen.

STEP-MOTHER: What do I know about your chess? You'd better write to Ain-ul-Mulk about it. He'll love it!

MUHAMMAD: Funny you should mention him. I was just thinking of him—but not with reference to chess. You see, my dear friend Ain-ul-Mulk, the companion of my childhood, my fellow champion in chess, is at this very moment marching on Delhi.

STEP-MOTHER: What? What do you mean?

MUHAMMAD: Exactly what I said. He is marching on Delhi with an army of thirty thousand.

STEP-MOTHER: But why, Muhammad?

MUHAMMAD: I don't know. The last letter I wrote to him asked him to be the Governor of the Deccan. I need a strong man there and I thought he would like it.

STEP-MOTHER: But there must be some other reason! (*No reply.*) What are you going to do now?

MUHAMMAD: Do the best I can. But I don't even have six thousand soldiers—Look, I was so happy about this problem and now you've ruined it all. Anyway, you came for something?

9

STEP-MOTHER: It doesn't matter any more.

MUHAMMAD: But it does, certainly.

STEP-MOTHER: I was worried about your late nights.
These days you never seem to go to bed at all. I just
wanted to know why.

MUHAMMAD (*smiles*): And you think you've found the
answer? Look, if I was that worried about
Ain-ul-Mulk why would I waste my time on this?

Points to the chess-board.

STEP-MOTHER: Then what do you do all night?

MUHAMMAD (*theatrical*): I pray to the Almighty to save me
from sleep. All day long I have to worry about
tomorrow but it's only when the night falls that I can
step beyond all that. I look at the Pleiades and
I think of Ibn-ul-Mottazz who thought it was an
ostrich egg and Dur-rumma who thought it was a
swallow. And then I want to go back to their
poetry and sink myself in their words. Then again
I want to climb up, up to the top of the tallest tree in
the world, and call out to my people: 'Come, my
people, I am waiting for you. Confide in me your
worries. Let me share your joys. Let's laugh and
cry together and then, let's pray. Let's pray till our
bodies melt and flow and our blood turns into air.
History is ours to play with—ours now! Let's be
the light and cover the earth with greenery. Let's be
darkness and cover up the boundaries of nations.
Come! I am waiting to embrace you all!'
But then how can I spread my branches in the stars
while the roots have yet to find their hold in the earth?
I wish I could believe in recurring births like the
Hindu but I have only one life, one body, and my
hopes, my people, my God are all fighting for it.
Tell me, how dare I waste my time by sleeping?
And don't tell me to go and get married and breed
a family because I won't sleep.

STEP-MOTHER (*bursts into laughter*): I don't know what to do
with you. I can't ask a simple question without your

10

giving a royal performance. Even Ain-ul-Mulk
doesn't seem to stop you—

MUHAMMAD: Mother, suppose I die fighting Ain-ul-Mulk—

STEP-MOTHER: Stop it!

MUHAMMAD: No, really. Suppose I die in the battle.
What of it? Why should I waste my last few days
worrying? I am not worried about my enemies. I'm
only worried about my people.

STEP-MOTHER: Pompous ass! As though other kings didn't
do that.

MUHAMMAD: No, they didn't. Look at the past Sultans of
Delhi. They couldn't bear the weight of their crown.
They couldn't leave it aside. So they died senile in
their youth or were murdered.

STEP-MOTHER (*sharply*): Please, Muhammad—

MUHAMMAD: What?

STEP-MOTHER: Nothing—I can't bear to see you joking
about murder.

MUHAMMAD: Why not?

STEP-MOTHER: I can't. That's all.

Silence. They are both tense now.

MUHAMMAD: So you too believe that piece of gossip!

STEP-MOTHER: What gossip?

MUHAMMAD (*mocking*): What gossip? What scandal?
You know perfectly well what I mean.

STEP-MOTHER: Don't be silly. I didn't mean anything of
that kind.

MUHAMMAD: But you do believe it? And why shouldn't
you? After all my own mother believes it. The
whole court believes it. My Amirs believe it. Why
shouldn't my step-mother believe it?

STEP-MOTHER (*flaring up*): Shut up, fool! I've told you
I won't have you calling me that!

MUHAMMAD (*suddenly calm, but with deliberate viciousness*):
I know. But you are my step-mother!

Silence. Enter the DOOR-KEEPER.

DOOR-KEEPER: In the name of Allah. Vizier Muhammad

11

Najib and Zia-ud-din Barani to see you, Your
Majesty.

MUHAMMAD: Send them in.

> *The* DOOR-KEEPER *goes out. The* STEP-MOTHER
> *lowers the veil on her face.* NAJIB *and* BARANI *enter.*

NAJIB
BARANI } In the name of Allah.

MUHAMMAD: Come in, come in. I was just saying to
Mother. . .

STEP-MOTHER: Muhammad, why don't you tell them
about your chess?

MUHAMMAD: Because they aren't interested. Barani is a
historian—he's only interested in playing chess with
the shadows of the dead. And Najib's a politician—
he wants pawns of flesh and blood. He doesn't have
the patience to breathe life into these bones. One
needs Ain-ul-Mulk for that. So Najib, how far
have we reached?

NAJIB: I'm doing my best, Your Majesty. But I don't
think we'll get more than six thousand. The odds
against us are very heavy. . .

BARANI: May I know what odds, Your Majesty?

NAJIB: . . . but another equally important problem has
come up, Your Majesty. Sheikh Imam-ud-din is
in Delhi.

MUHAMMAD: Aha! Then we should take his blessings
before we leave.

NAJIB: Yes, Your Majesty, and get rid of him.

BARANI: What a terrible thing to say about a holy man
like that!

MUHAMMAD (*smiles to the* STEP-MOTHER, *explaining*): Najib
is upset because the Sheikh criticizes me publicly—
demands that I abdicate. The Sheikh thinks I'm
incompetent.

NAJIB: It's worse than that. He has become a backbone
of the rebels. As for what else he says, you may
ask Barani.

12

MUHAMMAD: So you've heard him, Barani. What's he
like? Is it true he looks like me?

BARANI (*flustered*): A little, Your Majesty. But—how did
Najib know I had heard the Sheikh? Forgive me,
Your Majesty, but I don't like being spied upon.

NAJIB: It's my job to know. That's why I asked you to
come here with me now.

MUHAMMAD: Surely a historian doesn't need an invitation
to watch history take shape! Come, Barani, what
does he say?

BARANI: It's as Your Majesty said. . . . He says the Sultan
is a disgrace to Islam.

MUHAMMAD: That's all? I could find worse faults in me.
What else?

Silence.

NAJIB: He says Your Majesty has forfeited the right to rule,
by murdering your father and brother at prayer time.

The STEP-MOTHER *and* BARANI *react sharply, but*
MUHAMMAD *is still. A short pause.*

MUHAMMAD (*quietly*): Did he say that?

BARANI (*almost in a whisper*): Yes, Your Majesty.

MUHAMMAD: So now they talk about it openly, do they?

BARANI: He said it in the heat of the moment, Your
Majesty. I'm sure he didn't mean it. Your Majesty
must ignore these little things.

MUHAMMAD: Do you really think parricide is a little thing?
And fratricide? And the pollution of prayer? It's
not what people say, Barani, it's their crooked minds
that horrify me. Look at my own mother—she
won't talk to me now—not because father died but
because my brother died in that accident. He was
more amenable to her whims and he would have made
a better king for her. So she believes I killed them.
Do you know, I've just found out that even this
step-mother of mine thinks I am a murderer.

Silence.

NAJIB (*quietly*): What about the Sheikh, Your Majesty?

MUHAMMAD (*in a tired voice*): Let him babble. He is a saint, it's his privilege.

NAJIB: But we must do something. In Kanpur, they're still rioting and he started it. Now he's here—in the capital.

BARANI: But His Majesty is right. The people have been told that they have a right to criticize the Sultan, to voice their grievances openly. Surely this is the time to show that the Sultan means it—that they were not empty words. The people will surely respond to His Majesty's courage, honesty and justice...

NAJIB (*groans*): Courage, honesty and justice! My dear Barani, we are dealing with a political problem!

BARANI: I know and that's where they count most. Because that's where the Kingdom of Islam which the Prophet has gifted us must blossom. Oh! You won't understand it. Your Hindu childhood has twisted your attitudes beyond repair.

NAJIB: Do you know why I gave up Hinduism? Because it didn't speak of salvation of society. It only talked of the soul—my individual soul—while a poor, frenzied world screamed in agony around. So I became a Muslim. Islam is worried about this world, I said, it'll bring the Kingdom of Heaven on earth. But I know now—it won't work. There's only the present moment and we must grasp it firmly.

MUHAMMAD (*ironic but affectionate*): So what does the present moment demand now?

BARANI: It's obvious, Your Majesty. He wants the Sheikh dead.

NAJIB: Nonsense! That'll make him a martyr. You can't kill the dead. If we kill him now, we're finished. We might as well surrender to Ain-ul-Mulk.

BARANI (*startled*): Surrender to whom?

MUHAMMAD: Ain-ul-Mulk. He is marching on Delhi.

BARANI: I don't believe it! (*Silence.*) But you mustn't act hastily, Your Majesty. There's obviously been some misunderstanding. (*Earnestly.*) You know Ain-ul-Mulk. He is a good man and he worships you.

He isn't the treacherous type. You know that!

MUHAMMAD (*in anguish*): But why *now*? Can't he see that I've no time for 'misunderstandings' now? He knows how important it is for me to concentrate on moving to Daulatabad.

BARANI: But there must be some way of finding out why he's doing this. Please send an envoy . . . send me . . . I'll go. . . .

NAJIB: What's the point? We can't waste our time on that. A traitor's a traitor, friend or saint, and he must be crushed.

BARANI: But don't you want to know why?

NAJIB: I do now why. It's obvious.

The rest look at him in surprise.

MUHAMMAD: It is?

NAJIB: Your Majesty, when you came to the throne, there was anarchy in Avadh and you made Ain-ul-Mulk the Governor then. He crushed the rebels, restored law and order, and the people in Avadh think him a God almost. He's happy there, secure. Then suddenly he gets your letter making him the Governor of the Deccan, asking him to leave immediately. Is it surprising he should suspect a knife in his back?

Silence.

MUHAMMAD: God, why didn't I think of that?

BARANI: But Najib did, Your Majesty, and didn't warn you.

NAJIB: Would His Majesty have listened to me if I'd warned then? His Majesty loved Ain-ul-Mulk— too much.

BARANI: And you hate him?

NAJIB: Dear Barani, not hate, just suspicion. It's my job to be suspicious and I can't exempt anyone from it.

STEP-MOTHER: No one?

NAJIB: No, Your Highness.

STEP-MOTHER: Not even the Sultan?

NAIJB (*senses a trap, but calmly*): No, not even the Sultan, Your Highness.

STEP-MOTHER (*flaring up*): Muhammad—

15

MUHAMMAD *silences her with a gesture of impatience.*

MUHAMMAD: So, Najib, what do you propose?

NAJIB: I can't think of anything right now, Your Majesty
—except that the Sheikh has a striking resemblance
to you.

MUHAMMAD, *startled, stares at* NAJIB.

BARANI: What has the Sheikh got to do with this?

MUHAMMAD (*slowly*): You are a devil, Najib! (*Pause.
Then briskly*). Good. We'll think about that. In the
meantime, the army should be ready to march. We'll
start for Kanauj the day after tomorrow in the evening.

STEP-MOTHER: And who'll look after the administration
here, Muhammad?

MUHAMMAD: Najib will be here.

The STEP-MOTHER *obviously doesn't like the answer.* NAJIB
smiles ironically but not too openly.

Besides I have invited Shihab-ud-din, the Prince of
Sampanshahr, to be here in my absence. You see,
the Amir there doesn't like me very much, so I
thought inviting his son would be a nice friendly
gesture.

BARANI: What's all this, Your Majesty? I can't follow
a thing. But my heart trembles for you.

MUHAMMAD: Forgive me if I let you down, Barani, but
I must play this game my own way. Come, Najib,
we must see the Commander-in-Chief. Mother, if
you'll excuse us (*Bows to her.*)

STEP-MOTHER: Can Barani stay for a while? I want to
talk to him.

MUHAMMAD: Why, yes, certainly.

MUHAMMAD *and* NAJIB *go out. Silence.*

STEP-MOTHER: I don't know what to say, Barani. I
mustn't complain against my own son—

BARANI: Your Highness may place full trust in me.

STEP-MOTHER: I know, that's why I asked you to stay. I am
worried about him. You know what he is like. He is

16

such an intelligent boy and he works so hard for the
people. He doesn't even go to bed these days.
(*Pause.*) But he is so impulsive—and when he gets
into one of his moods I don't know what he'll do next.
(*Pause.*) You are a sober man, Barani, level-headed
and honest, and he needs frineds like you. I just
wanted to ask you. . . . Oh, God! It all sounds so
stupid.

BARANI: I fully understand Your Highness's feelings.

STEP-MOTHER: It's not that. It's just that I don't like so
many of his advisers and friends. (*Suddenly.*) Please
promise me not to leave him—ever—whatever he does.

BARANI (*overwhelmed to the point of tears*): May God help me
to retain such confidence untarnished. I won't leave
His Majesty, Your Highness, I promise you. I love
him too much to do that.

STEP-MOTHER: Look at him now. He won't show it, but
Ain-ul-Mulk has hurt him. And this Sheikh Imam-
ud-din—I don't know what he's going to do.

BARANI: It's not for me to advise, Your Highness, but I
have to mention it. I am not jealous of Najib and I
admire his integrity. But sometimes I am bothered
by his influence on the Sultan.

STEP-MOTHER: I know. I am watching. I'll wait for a
few days. (*With sudden violence.*) If he goes on like
this, I won't wish his fate even on a dog!

> BARANI, *driven to tears by her maternal concern, looks up
> startled by the venom in her voice.*

The ANNOUNCER.

ANNOUNCER: Attention! Attention! The Slave of the Lord, the Merciful, the ever-Victorious Sultan Muhammad has declared that this evening after the prayer a meeting will be organized in the yard in front of the Big Mosque. Sheikh Imam-ud-din, who is revered all over India as a Saint and as one who stands in the Grace of Allah, will address the meeting. He will analyse His Merciful Majesty's administration and show where His Majesty has inadvertently taken wrong measures— measures harmful to the country and the Faith His Majesty himself will be present at the meeting to seek direction from the Revered Sheikh, and the citizens of Delhi are requested to attend the meeting in large numbers and do likewise Attention! Attention!

SCENE THREE

The yard in front of the Big Mosque. MUHAMMAD *and* SHEIKH
IMAM-UD-DIN *and a few odd servants of the palace. No one else.
There is a long silence.*

MUHAMMAD (*suddenly*): I can't bear this any longer!

IMAM-UD-DIN: Why Your Majesty? You should be happy
if no one turns up.

MUHAMMAD: Do you think I would have gone to the
trouble of arranging this meeting if I didn't want my
people to hear you? I don't want my people to be
dumb cattle, Sheikhsahib, and I do not claim to be
omniscient myself. I am quite willing to learn from
you—even eager.

IMAM-UD-DIN: Will you be as eager when you hear me,
I wonder? You know I am not the type to sweeten
my words because the Sultan himself is present.

MUHAMMAD: Don't I know it? The whole of Delhi has
heard of the courage and integrity of Sheikh Imam-
ud-din. I would not have taken so much trouble
for anyone else.

   Claps. A SERVANT *enters and bows.*

Go at once and tell the Vizier I want everyone here—
all the Khans, Amirs, Sardars—everyone—and at once!

IMAM-UD-DIN: But Your Majesty, I haven't come here to
speak to a collection of courtiers—

MUHAMMAD: And I'm afraid I can't go now from door to
door asking people to come. I should have given
orders at the Court today. We have been waiting for
over half an hour—and not a soul has come yet!

IMAM-UD-DIN: They say we look alike, but we don't think
alike, do we? What's the point in my addressing
a gang of bootlickers? I want to speak to the people
who are willing to act, who are willing to do something

19

for Islam and the country. If no one comes today,
well, no matter. I'll go to the market-place tomorrow
and speak there.

MUHAMMAD *signs to the* SERVANT *to go. He goes out.*

MUHAMMAD: Would you believe me if I told you I have
never consciously tried to go against the tenets of
Islam?

IMAM-UD-DIN: Please, Your Majesty, even you can't believe
that! I can quote scores of transgressions. If they
weren't wilful, they could only be results of ignorance.
But I can't believe that in a scholar of your eminence.
Perhaps you are sincere. But if one fails to understand
what the Koran says one must ask the Sayyids and
the Ulema. Instead you have put the best of them
behind bars in the name of justice.

MUHAMMAD: They tried to indulge in politics—I couldn't
allow that. I have never denied the word of God,
Sheikhsahib, because its my bread and drink. I need
it most when the surrounding void pushes itself into
my soul and starts putting out every light burning
there. But I am alone in my life. My kingdom has
millions—Muslims, Hindus, Jains. Yes, there is
dirt and sickness in my kingdom. But why should
I call on God to clean the dirt deposited by men?

IMAM-UD-DIN: Because only the Voice of God, the Holy
Word, can do it. Please listen to me, Your Majesty.
The Arabs spread Islam round the world and they
struggled and fought for it for seven hundred years.
They are tired now, limp and exhausted. But their
work must continue and we need someone to take the
lead. You could do it. You are one of the most
powerful kings on earth today and you could spread
the Kingdom of Heaven on earth. God has given you
everything—power, learning, intelligence, talent.
Now you must repay His debt.

MUHAMMAD: No one can go far on his knees. I have a long
way to go. I can't afford to crawl—I have to gallop.

20

IMAM-UD-DIN: And you will do it without the Koran to
    guide you? Beware, Sultan, you are trying to become
    another God. It's a sin worse than parricide.
MUHAMMAD (*refusing the bait*): Only an atheist can try to be
    God. I am God's most humble slave.
IMAM-UD-DIN: Yes. And slaves have often tried to replace
    their masters.
MUHAMMAD: My congratulations, Imam-ud-din Sahib.
    For a saint you are very good at innuendoes—I know
    all about slaves. My grandfather was one and he
    became a king. But that was in mundane politics.
    The analogy doesn't work here.
IMAM-UD-DIN: Religion! Politics! Take heed, Sultan, one
    day these verbal distinctions will rip you into two.
MUHAMMAD: Don't I know it? I still remember the days
    when I read the Greeks—Sukrat who took poison
    so he could give the world the drink of gods, Aflatoon
    who condemned poets and wrote incomparably
    beautiful poetry himself—and I can still feel the
    thrill with which I found a new world, a world I had
    not found in the Arabs or even the Koran. They tore
    me into shreds. And to be whole now, I shall have
    to kill the part of me which sang to them. And
    my kingdom too is what I am—torn into pieces by
    visions whose validity I can't deny. You are asking
    me to make myself complete by killing the Greek in
    me and you propose to unify my people by denying
    the visions which led Zarathustra or the Buddha.
    (*Smiles.*) I'm sorry. But it can't be done.
IMAM-UD-DIN: You are a learned man. You may be
    able to manage this delicate balance within yourself.
    But a kingdom needs not one king but a line of rulers.
    Will they manage this balance? Where are these bril-
    liant successors of yours? Where are these guarantors
    of your balanced future?
MUHAMMAD: There is none—yet. But I haven't lost hope.
    I shall find them and teach them to think like me.
    They are only cattle yet, but I shall make men out of
    a few of them. Look, Sheikhsahib, in Kanpur you

21

found so many honest men that they burnt down the whole of Kanpur. They are still on the rampage there and your words inspire them. Now you've come to Delhi and there isn't even a fly to listen to you. They are staying away—at home, safe and secure. They don't want you here. Do you know why?

Silence.

Because they suspect you now. The moment they heard that I, the Sultan, was organizing a meeting in which you, my severest critic, was going to speak— they became suspicious. Why should the Sultan sponsor his worst critic? They have smelt a trap. And wisely they have stayed away.

IMAM-UD-DIN (*stunned*): Was this a trap?

MUHAMMAD: No, I promise you.

IMAM-UD-DIN: But—you knew this would happen?

MUHAMMAD: I didn't *know*. But I half expected it. I know my people.

IMAM-UD-DIN: So they think I'm your spy—and you knew it when you arranged this meeting!

MUHAMMAD: Believe me, Sheikhsahib, I'm sorry I am not disappointed. Yes, they will now decide you are a spy—they'll greet you as a spy in the market-place tomorrow. But now you do see what I mean, don't you? You are known as a saint and you have risked your life by speaking out against the Sultan. Yet a trick—and they suspect you. It's futile to think of them as members of the *dar-ul-Islam*. Generations of devout Sultans have twisted their minds and I have to mend their minds before I can think of their souls.

There is a long silence. Then SHEIKH IMAM-UD-DIN *starts to move down slowly.*

IMAM-UD-DIN: My turn to congratulate you. Your experiment was a brilliant success. Yes, I have learnt my lesson. Thank you—and good-bye

MUHAMMAD: Good-bye? You are not going?

IMAM-UD-DIN: You have finished my work for me. You don't want me to wait longer, do you? For an

22

audience which won't turn up?

MUHAMMAD: I need your help, Sheikhsahib.

IMAM-UD-DIN: Don't play any more games with me—

MUHAMMAD: There's no time for games. I am desperate.
Ain-ul-Mulk of Avadh is marching on Delhi at this
very moment.

IMAM-UD-DIN: What? Your intimate friend and confidant?
Why? No, I don't wish to know why. That's
politics and you know your way there. But why tell
me this?

MUHAMMAD: Because I want peace. I am willing to make
peace but how can I do it? I don't even know why
he has turned against me. He won't even see my
official envoys. (*Pause*) But he will see you.

The SHEIKH *is about to speak. But* MUHAMMAD
goes on.

He respects you as every Muslim in India does. He
will trust your word. That's why I'm asking you—
will you please go as my envoy and dissuade him from
this folly? Please Sheikhsahib, I'm not asking you
only for my sake but for all the Muslims who will die
at the hands of Muslims if there is a war.

Pause.

IMAM-UD-DIN: I don't trust your motives.

MUHAMMAD: What do my motives matter? You can't
deny that this war will mean a slaughter of Muslims
at the hands of fellow-Muslims. Isn't that enough
for the great Sheikh Imam-ud-din? You have
attacked me for inaction. You can't turn away
now when you are offered a chance. You can't!

IMAM-UD-DIN: I know I can't.

MUHAMMAD: So you agree?

IMAM-UD-DIN: Do you leave me an alternative?

MUHAMMAD (*slowly*): I'll never be able to thank you
enough for this.

Claps his hands. A SERVANT *enters and bows.*

Bring the robes of honour for the royal envoy. At once!

23

The SERVANT *departs.*

IMAM-UD-DIN: You don't mean the robes are ready.

MUHAMMAD: Forgive me, Sheikhsahib, but I knew you wouldn't refuse.

IMAM-UD-DIN: But what about Ain-ul-Mulk? Won't he also think of me as your spy? It won't take long before he will know of this. (*Indicates the empty auditorium.*)

MUHAMMAD: He is not a fool. Besides he won't know. There isn't time. We have to start before nightfall. Ain-ul-Mulk has already started and we must meet him near the plains of Kanauj.

The SERVANT *brings the robes of honour and the head-dress on a golden plate.* MUHAMMAD *takes the robe and goes near the* SHEIKH.

IMAM-UD-DIN (*stopping him*): If you want peace, what does it matter where we meet him?

MUHAMMAD: I do want peace. But I can't leave anything to chance. If Ain-ul-Mulk refuses, I have to have my army in a safe place. I owe it to my soldiers.

Pause.

IMAM-UD-DIN: You know, Sultan, I'm just beginning to understand why they saw you are the cleverest man in the world.

MUHAMMAD: I am an incompetent fool—will you wear the robes now?

IMAM-UD-DIN: Very well.

He puts on the robes. MUHAMMAD *places the head-dress on his head. They stand facing each other. The dress makes them look even more alike.*

I wish I could be more sure of you. . .

SCENE FOUR

The Palace. SHIHAB-UD-DIN *is reading a few letters. There is an announcement.*

DOOR-KEEPER (*announcing*): Her Highness the Queen Mother.

> SHIHAB-UD-DIN *leaps up. The* STEP-MOTHER *enters and he bows to her.*

SHIHAB-UD-DIN: Welcome, Your Highness. I am most honoured by the visit but, had Your Highness sent for me, I would have come myself.

STEP-MOTHER: I suddenly felt frightened, Shihab-ud-din. I couldn't bear the tension any longer. Has there been any further news?

SHIHAB-UD-DIN: I'm afraid not, Your Highness. The last bulletin was received a week ago. Your Highness knows the contents. There has been nothing since then. I'm sorry but—

STEP-MOTHER: No, no, please don't apologize. I don't know what I should have done without you here. You know when Muhammad said he was inviting you to look after Delhi, I didn't understand him at all. I couldn't see why he had to ask you, rather than a local Amir. I know now—he couldn't have chosen a better man.

SHIHAB-UD-DIN: I am most grateful for Your Highness's trust. But I did very little. The credit should go to Vizier Muhammad Najib.

STEP-MOTHER: Oh! Don't talk to me about him. Thanks to you, I didn't have to deal with him.

SHIHAB-UD-DIN: Your Highness's most humble servant.

> *The* DOOR-KEEPER *enters.*

DOOR-KEEPER: In the name of Allah. Sardar Ratansingh.

SHIHAB-UD-DIN (*excited*): He is here? Send him in at once.

The DOOR-KEEPER *goes out.*

STEP-MOTHER: Who is that?

SHIHAB-UD-DIN: My adopted brother, Your Highness.

STEP-MOTHER: Him! He'll have news of the front then!

> RATANSINGH *enters.* SHIHAB-UD-DIN *goes to him in great excitement and embraces him.*

SHIHAB-UD-DIN: Welcome, Ratansingh. What happened?

RATANSINGH: His Majesty is back in Delhi. We arrived a few minutes ago.

STEP-MOTHER: Oh, then I must go.

RATANSINGH: Forgive me, Your Highness, but His Majesty has gone to see the Vizier. He has asked me to inform Your Highness that he will be here any minute.

> *The* STEP-MOTHER *doesn't like it. But she swallows it.*

STEP-MOTHER: But I can't understand it. Why didn't he send word he was coming? Why this secrecy?

RATANSINGH (*hesitates*): I don't think it was meant to be secret, Your Highness. It's just that His Majesty seems much affected by the death of Sheikh Imam-ud-din.

STEP-MOTHER: What? Sheikh Imam-ud-din dead?

RATANSINGH: Yes, Your Highness. He was killed in the battle.

> *Her face goes white.*

SHIHAB-UD-DIN: But what was the Sheikh doing in the battle?

DOOR-KEEPER (*off-stage*): The Warrior in the path of God, the Victorious, the Mighty, His Majesty the Sultan.

> MUHAMMAD *enters with* NAJIB *and* BARANI.

SHIHAB-UD-DIN (*bows*): In the name of Allah. May He shower greater successes on Your Majesty.

MUHAMMAD: That's no way to welcome, Shihab. Come—

> *They embrace.*

I am grateful to you for looking after my people in my absence.

SHIHAB-UD-DIN: Your Majesty's humble slave.
STEP-MOTHER: Muhammad, what's this about Sheikh
    Imam-ud-din?

    MUHAMMAD *freezes. Then slowly,*

MUHAMMAD: Did you have to mention it now? It was a
    terrible sight. They brought his body into my tent and
    I felt—as though it was I who was lying dead there
    and that he was standing above me looking at me.
    I should have been there—in his place.

    Pause.

BARANI: It's a great loss to Islam.
STEP-MOTHER: And what about Ain-ul-Mulk? I hope
    he's dead too.
MUHAMMAD: I let him go.

    General surprise.

STEP-MOTHER: You didn't! You couldn't have!
NAJIB: I hate to say it on this happy occasion, Your Majesty,
    but that would be really tossing another torch into
    the chaos at Avadh.
BARANI: Your Highness must forgive me, but His Majesty
    deserves congratulations on his courage. He has
    shown there are things more valuable then vengeance.
NAJIB: Not that again!
MUHAMMAD: I didn't just set him free, Najib. I gave him
    back the Kingdom of Avadh, *and* I promised not to
    send him to the Deccan.
NAJIB: We are helpless if Your Majesty insists on... (*Stops.*)
STEP-MOTHER: Why, Muhammad? Why did he deserve
    such special treatment?
MUHAMMAD: I'll tell you what happened. You remember
    the chess problem I solved the other day? Well,
    when they brought Ain-ul-Mulk before me, I said:
    'Look, I have solved the famous problem set by
    al-Adli!' He didn't say a word. I drew a sketch
    on the floor and showed him the solution. He said
    he liked it, then looked harder for a couple of minutes
    and said: 'No, there's a flaw here.' And he actually

showed me where I had gone wrong! Think of that!
I had spent days on that wretched problem and he
spots a flaw within half a minute. I had to forgive
him.

BARANI: You are a great man, Your Majesty, . . .

MUHAMMAD (*laughing*): And you are a good man, Barani,
and that's more important. Look at Najib—look
at the expression on his face! He can't even believe
I can be generous.

NAJIB: I am suspicious by nature, Your Majesty; fortunately
my duty also demands it of me.

MUHAMMAD: We must go now. Najib, Delhi will observe
a day of mourning tomorrow for Sheikh Imam-ud-din.
And there will be no festivities to celebrate the
victory. When men like him die, it's a sin to be
alive. Come, Mother. Good-bye, Shihab-ud-din
and many, many thanks.

> All except SHIHAB-UD-DIN *and* RATANSINGH *go.*
> *A brief silence.*

RATANSINGH: I have never seen an honest scoundrel like
your Sultan. He murders a man calmly and then
actually enjoys the feeling of guilt.

SHIHAB-UD-DIN: What are you talking about?

RATANSINGH: I'm silent!

SHIHAB-UD-DIN: I'm sorry. But you have never liked the
Sultan, I don't know why. After all that he has
done for the Hindus—

RATANSINGH: Yes indeed, who can deny that! He is
impartial! Haven't you heard about the Doab?
He levied such taxes on the poor farmers that they
preferred to starve. Now there's a famine there.
And of course Hindus as well as Muslims are dying
with absolute impartiality.

SHIHAB-UD-DIN: What's that got to do with Sheikh
Imam-ud-din?

RATANSINGH: I don't know. But I tell you I'm glad to
escape the Sultan's impartiality and be alive.

SHIHAB-UD-DIN: Must you spin riddles?

28

RATANSINGH: And do you really want to know the truth?
All right. Because you insisted, I went to fight
alongside the Sultan. I went and saw him in Kanauj.
He didn't seem too pleased to see me. He actually
scowled. A Sultan's scowl is a terrible thing.

SHIHAB-UD-DIN: So?

RATANSINGH: Next day I see what the scowl is doing.
Sheikh Imam-ud-din is to go and propose peace to
Ain-ul-Mulk. A platoon of soldiers is to accompany
him. And I am placed in the front rank of the
platoon. You know what that means. The front
rank never survives a battle

SHIHAB-UD-DIN: Go on.

RATANSINGH: The Sheikh is delighted about being the
Sultan's peace emissary. He looks gorgeous—all
dressed up in royal robes, a royal turban, even royal
slippers, and sitting on the royal elephant. In fact, he
looks exactly like the Sultan.

SHIHAB-UD-DIN (*suspicious*): And the Sultan? What was he
doing?

RATANSINGH: I didn't know it then, but he was hiding
behind some hills with the rest of the army. Laying
a trap.

SHIHAB-UD-DIN: A trap?

RATANSINGH: So we marched towards Ain-ul-Mulk's army,
led by the gorgeous Sheikh on the royal elephant.
The elephant halted about a hundred yards away
from the enemy. The Sheikh stood up on it and
tried to say something when a trumpeter on our side
sounded the charge! The battle was on—yes, my
dear Shihab, Ain-ul-Mulk didn't start the battle.
We did!

SHIHAB-UD-DIN: And the Sultan?

RATANSINGH: I couldn't understand what was happening.
Neither did the Sheikh, obviously. His face was
twisted with fear but he was shouting at the top of
his voice asking us to stop. He didn't stand a
chance. Arrows poured into him and within minutes
he looked a gory human porcupine.

SHIHAB-UD-DIN: And the Sultan? Didn't he do anything?

RATANSINGH: He did! The Sheikh plunged down from
the elephant and over his corpse we fled in confusion.
The enemy was convinced the Sultan was dead and
they pursued us. They walked right into the trap.
It was the bloodiest massacre I've ever seen. . . .
We won! (*Pause.*) Sheikh Imam-ud-din was murdered,
you know. In cold blood.

SHIHAB-UD-DIN: Oh my God!

RATANSINGH: This isn't all. There's a longer history to
all this. (*Pause.*) Do you want to hear it? (*Pause.*)
Listen, in a few days the nobles of the court and the
important citizens of Delhi are going to hold a secret
meeting to discuss. . . (*Stops.*)

SHIHAB-UD-DIN: What?

RATANSINGH: How should I know? I haven't attended
the meeting yet.

SHIHAB-UD-DIN: How do you know about it?

RATANSINGH: Ah! That's Delhi for you! They were
looking for recruits and the moment they realized the
Sultan had tried to kill me, off they discreetly
approached me and invited me. They have asked
you too, incidentally. They hope you won't be
too apathetic towards the attempted murder of your
adopted brother!

> *Silence.*

I have accepted the invitation, of course. Would
you like to come along too?

> *Silence.*

Why, Shihab, you look pale!

SCENE FIVE

A house in Delhi. A collection of Amirs, Sayyids, etc.,
SHIHAB-UD-DIN *and* RATANSINGH.

SHIHAB-UD-DIN: I'll be plain with you. If you don't like
the present administration, that's your problem.
I'm an outsider in Delhi. I've nothing to do with it.

AMIR I: But that's the whole point, don't you see? You're
the only man he won't suspect.

SHIHAB-UD-DIN: I hope that's not a point against him.

AMIR II: Besides, the people in Delhi never trust each
other. It's the climate. They have to have an
outsider to lead them!

SHIHAB-UD-DIN: Lead them in what?

AMIR I: Just consider this. Why is he taking us to
Daulatabad? Have you wondered about that?
I'll tell you. He wants to weaken the Amirs. You
see, we are strong in Delhi. This is where we belong.
But Daulatabad is a Hindu city and we'll be helpless
there. We'll have to lick his feet.

AMIR III: And it's no use his saying stay behind if you like.
We have to be in the capital!

AMIR II: Look at what's happening in Delhi. Just look
at it! You can't take a step without paying some
tax or another. There's even a tax on gambling.
How are we to live? You can't even cheat without
having to pay tax for it.

SHIHAB-UD-DIN: But he has done a lot of good work. Built
schools, roads, hospitals. He has made good use of
the money.

SAYYID: Then why can't he get it the right way? The
Koran sanctions only four taxes, but... (*Looks at*
RATANSINGH *and stops.*)

RATANSINGH (*smiles*): Carry on, sir. Don't mind me. I'm
here because Shihab's here; otherwise I am invisible!

31

SAYYID: Well . . . uhm, he could tax the Hindus. The jiziya is sanctioned by the Koran. All infidels should pay it. Instead he says the infidels are our brothers. . .

SHIHAB-UD-DIN (*getting up in disgust*): Come, Ratansingh, let's go. This is worse than I thought. They don't deserve to kiss the hem of the Sultan's dress.

The others are offended and retreat.

RATANSINGH: Ah, well. . .

Gets up. At this point an old man who has been sitting in a corner all along steps forward.

SHEIKH: Shihab-ud-din—

SHIHAB-UD-DIN: I said I am not going to associate. . .

SHEIKH: Shihab-ud-din, I have never asked anything of anyone but Allah. Today I implore you. In the name of Allah, help us.

SHIHAB-UD-DIN (*impressed by the old man's age and sincerity*): Who are you?

SAYYID (*contemptuously*): Don't you know? He is Sheikh Shams-ud-din Tajuddarfim?

SHIHAB-UD-DIN: Sheikh Shams-ud-din? Sir, what is a holy man like you doing in this company?

SHEIKH: Yes, you are right. I should shut myself up in a mosque and devote myself to Allah. I shouldn't get mixed up in the treacherous games of politicians. I know and I had hoped my life would be like that. But Allah isn't only for me, Shihab-ud-din; He's for everyone who believes in him. While tyranny crushes the faithful into dust, how can I continue to hide in my hole? Haven't you heard what's happening to the leaders of Islam today? Sheikh Haidari is in prison. Sheikh Hood in exile. . .

SHIHAB-UD-DIN: I know. But they dabbled in politics.

SHEIKH: Is it so reprehensible to worry about people? Is it a crime to speak out for oneself and one's family? What politics did Sheikh Imam-ud-din indulge in? That he was open, frank and honest?

SHIHAB-UD-DIN: I don't know enough about that. But,

32

to me it seems clear that if the Sultan is to be blamed
for that death, so are all the citizens of Delhi. I
sometimes feel the Sheikh must have almost wished
for death after what happened in Delhi.

AMIR I: What did happen in Delhi?

SHIHAB-UD-DIN: You know that better than me! He came
here to speak to the people and not a soul turned up
to hear him. Not one of you had the courage to
come to the meeting . . . and now you have the cheek
to blame the Sultan for his death.

The others whisper and chuckle in derision.

SHEIKH: So you don't know what actually happened
behind the scenes?

SHIHAB-UD-DIN: Behind the scenes?

More derisive laughter.

SHEIKH: Yes, behind the scenes. It's true the Sultan
invited the whole of Delhi to hear the Sheikh. Yet,
on that very afternoon, soldiers went from door to
door threatening dire consequences if anyone dared
to attend the meeting

Silence

SHIHAB-UD-DIN (*slowly*): Does the Sultan know this?

More laughter.

SHEIKH: They were his orders! And do you know,
while the Sultan stood in front of the Great Mosque
with the Sheikh and got more and more agitated
at the empty auditorium, his soldiers were hiding in
the streets around stopping those who tried to come?
You don't believe it? Look here. . .

(*Unbuttons his shirt and shows a wound on his shoulder.*)
I tried to force my way to the Big Mosque and this is
what I got for it. Who else would do this to an old
man like me?

RATANSINGH: There, you see! That explains why he
had to invite you from Sampanshahr to look after
Delhi in his absence. There's confidence for you!

SHIHAB-UD-DIN (*doggedly*): Perhaps. But it's done me no harm.

RATANSINGH: Of course not. Had he meant to harm you, you wouldn't be here to talk about it!

SHEIKH: Will you only think about yourself, Shihab-ud-din? You are the strong, the powerful in this country. You have the capacity to set things right. Won't you worry a little about the people? The citizens of Delhi don't wish to go to Daultabad, but they are weak. Will you do nothing for them? How many people like Sheikh Imam-ud-din have to die before you'll be ready to act?

No reply.

AMIR I: We have to act now—while the army here is still tired and disorganized. We have to do something while you're here. If you won't join us, will you at least promise not to fight against us?

SHIHAB-UD-DIN: I know too much now to remain neutral.

RATANSINGH (*with a sudden burst of anger*): Then why not join them? Even my infidel blood boils when I think of Sheikh Imam-ud-din and Sheikh Shams-ud-din here. You accuse the people of Delhi of cowardice and yet you won't raise a finger to correct an obvious wrong. (*Gets up.*) Come, let's go to the palace. The problem of justice won't bother us there.

AMIR I: You must help us, Shihab-ud-din.

SHEIKH: Islam needs your help.

SHIHAB-UD-DIN: What do you want me to do? You don't need me. You need my father. He is the strong man and even the Sultan is afraid of him. But you're in a hurry. I can only swell your numbers—little else.

RATANSINGH: Don't be stupid, Shihab. Don't tell me you still think the Amirs want to fight the Sultan in the open.

SHIHAB-UD-DIN *looks up at him sharply.* RATANSINGH *smiles and turns to the rest.*

You see what it is. Shihab is a clever young man

but he's just too nice! You see his father. . .

SHIHAB-UD-DIN: Don't, Ratansingh. . .

RATANSINGH: Come on, every one knows about it! His
father is supposed to have killed my father by
treachery and usurped the kingdom. Shihab can't
forget that. He wants to make up for it. That's why
I'm here, as his adopted brother. And that's why
he just can't stand the mention of treachery. (*To*
SHIHAB-UD-DIN.) Don't overdo it. You'll have to
face it some day. After all, what did the Sultan do
to Sheikh Imam-ud-din?

SAYYID: It's not going to be easy. We can't afford to
make mistakes.

AMIR II: I know. I have been trying to think of some way.
But it just gives me a headache.

A long silence.

RATANSINGH: I have a plan. It's perfect.

SHIHAB-UD-DIN: Yes?

RATANSINGH: Yes. The Sultan, as you know, is a fanatic
about prayer. He has made it compulsory for every
Muslim to pray five times a day.

SAYYID: That's his only saving grace.

RATANSINGH: Quite! Even the soldiers have to pray, and
while they pray they are not allowed to carry arms.
Which means that at the time of prayers, the whole
palace is unarmed.

Long pause.

AMIR II: It takes a Hindu to notice that! (*Half terrified
by the simplicity of it all.*) So?

RATANSINGH: Next Tuesday the Amirs here will be
seeing the Sultan for the Durbar-i-Khas. See that
you prolong the meeting till the prayer hour. Pray
with him. You'll only need an extra couple of
hundred soldiers outside the palace. The muezzin's
call to prayer will be the signal of attack!

There is an uncomfortable silence.

AMIR II (*quietly*): Fantastic!

35

SAYYID: But kill some one during prayer...

AMIR I: And a Muslim too...

RATANSINGH: Where's your Holy Koran? The tyrant doesn't deserve to be considered among the faithful. And then, he killed his own father during prayer time, after all.

AMIR I: That's true. But...

RATANSINGH: That's my plan Think of a better one if you can.

AMIR I: But we'll have to smuggle arms into the palace.

AMIR II: That can be arranged.

AMIR I: You are sure?

AMIR II: Of course, I'm sure. I think this is a brilliant plan.

AMIR III: It is simple.

They all talk animatedly.

SHEIKH: No, we can't have it!

Sudden silence as they all turn to SHEIKH SHAMS-UD-DIN.

SHIHAB-UD-DIN: Why, pray?

SHEIKH· You can't pollute the time of prayer. It's a sacred time. We can't stain it with the blood of a Mussulman.

AMIR II: Of come, we can always make up later. Do penance for it.

SHEIKH: But prayer isn't penance. Remember we are here to save Islam, not to insult it.

AMIR I: Don't get excited. Islam will benefit in the long run.

SHEIKH (*to* SHIHAB-UD-DIN, *pleading*): You can't agree to this, Shihab-ud-din. You are the only sensible person here. You can't agree to this sacrilege. You can't do this to Islam...

SHIHAB-UD-DIN: Does your Islam work only at prayer? You have persuaded me to do what I had sworn never to do—*you*, Your Holiness. I'm sure the Lord will not mind an interrupted prayer. (*To the others.*) All right, let's get down to the details. We have to work everything out carefully. (*Suddenly.*) Must we do this, Ratan? Must we?

SCENE SIX

The Palace. MUHAMMAD, NAJIB *and* BARANI. *Silence for a while.* MUHAMMAD *is restless and paces up and down.*

BARANI: Why are you both so quiet?

NAJIB: Oh, shut up!

MUHAMMAD: Please, Najib.

Silence again. The DOOR-KEEPER *enters.*

DOOR-KEEPER: In the name of Allah. The Amirs have come for the Durbar-i-Khas.

MUHAMMAD: Send them in.

The DOOR-KEEPER *goes out.* BARANI *and* NAJIB *stand up. The* AMIRS *enter along with* SHIHAB-UD-DIN. *They greet each other.*

AMIR 1: In the name of Allah.

NAJIB *smiles to himself.*

MUHAMMAD (*with obvious warmth*): Come in, come in. Please take your seats. I am glad you have all come on time. I want to finish the Durbar-i-Khas as soon as possible. I have promised the Imam I'll be at the mosque for today's prayer. That doesn't give us much time, I'm afraid. Are there any special problems any of you wish to raise?

No reply.

Excellent! I have only two topics myself. Not much to discuss there, but naturally I want to inform the Durbar-i-Khas before announcing to the public. First, I am very happy to inform you that Abbasid Ghiyas-ud-din Muhammad has accepted my invitation to visit our capital.

Silence.

AMIR 1: Who is he, Your Majesty?

37

AMIR II: I am afraid I have never heard of that name...

MUHAMMAD: Well, that's nothing to be ashamed of. Abbasid Ghiyas-ud-din Muhammad is not exactly famous. He is a member of the hallowed family of the Abbasid Khalifs.

Silence while the AMIRS *digest this bit of news which obviously makes no sense to them.*

BARANI: It's good news that a descendant of the last Khalif is visiting us, Your Majesty.

SHIHAB-UD-DIN: May I compliment His Majesty on his wisdom?

MUHAMMAD: Wisdom? What a strange word to use. Why wisdom? A visit by the descendant of the Khalif could show how faithful I am or how religious I am or even perhaps how modest. But why do you say 'wisdom'? Do you think I am inviting him to placate the stupid priests?

SHIHAB-UD-DIN: I didn't mean to...

MUHAMMAD: You know, since Sheikh Imam-ud-din died I have been asking myself just one question. I am a king. I wear the royal robes. I have honoured myself with the title of Sultan. But what gives me the right to call myself a King?

The AMIRS *are baffled.*

Am I a king only because I am the son of a king? Or is it because I can make the people accept my laws and the army move to my commands? Or can self-confidence alone justify it? I ask you— all of you—what would you have me do to become a real king in your eyes?

Silence.

NAJIB (*disapproving*): Your Majesty—

MUHAMMAD: You are all silent. The others only tell me what I should not do but not what I should. Until I know what else to do, Shihab-ud-din, I have to go on clutching the sceptre in my fist. But I am not happy and I am turning to tradition and history

38

now and seeking an answer there—in the blessings
of the Abbasid Khalif.

AMIR I: The sins of Delhi will be washed clean by the
visit of so great a man.

MUHAMMAD: You bring tears to my eyes. But the great
man isn't coming to Delhi. We shall be in Daulatabad
by then.

SHIHAB-UD-DIN: I implore Your Majesty not to move the
capital to Daulatabad. I am not from Delhi myself
and have no stake in it. But I know the people of
Delhi are very unhappy about the move. I have
seen—

MUHAMMAD: What am I to do, Shihab-ud-din? I have
explained every reason to them, shown how my
empire cannot flourish with Delhi as its capital.
But how can I explain tomorrow to those who haven't
even opened their eyes to the light of today? Let's
not waste more time over that. They'll see the
point soon. It's getting late and I must tell you the
more important news. From next year, we shall
have copper currency in our empire along with the
silver dinars.

AMIR I: Whatever for? I mean what does one do with a
copper coin?

MUHAMMAD: Exchange it for a silver coin! A copper coin
will have the same value as a silver dinar.

SHIHAB-UD-DIN: But I don't understand, Your Majesty.
How can one expect a copper coin to have the same
value as a silver one?

MUHAMMAD: It's a question of confidence. A question of
trust! The other day I heard that in China they
have paper currency—paper, mind you—and yet it
works because the people accept it. They have
faith in the Emperor's seal on the pieces of paper.

AMIR I (*whispers to the next man*): I told you he's mad!

MUHAMMAD: What was that?

AMIR I: I was just saying people here won't accept copper
currency.

MUHAMMAD: Then why not say it aloud? Because people

39

are afraid, will you mistrust me too? Laugh at me
if you like, criticize me, but please don't distrust me
I can order you all to obey me but tell me, how do
I gain your full trust? I can only beg for it.
(*Pleading.*) I have hopes of building a new future
for India and I need your support for that. If you
don't understand me, ask me to explain myself and
I'll do it. If you don't understand my explanations,
bear with me in patience until I can show you the
results. But please don't let me down, I beg you.
I'll kneel before you if you wish but please don't let
go of my hand.

> *He kneels before them. The* AMIRS *almost recoil at this
> sudden gesture.*

SHIHAB-UD-DIN (*embarrassed*): But, Your Majesty, it's
not for a king to beg. He must command. We
are your ever-willing servants.

MUHAMMAD: Is this your voice alone Shihab-ud-din, or
do the rest of the Amirs agree with you?

AMIRS: Of course we all do—no question of it—Your
Majesty should trust us. . .

MUHAMMAD: Thank you!

> *Gets up, walks up to the throne, picks up a copy of the
> Koran lying on it.*

Will you all then take an oath on the Koran to
support me in my measures?

> *A long tense silence.*

SHIHAB-UD-DIN: Does His Majesty distrust us so much
that he needs an oath on the Koran from us?

> MUHAMMAD *turns to him in a sudden burst of rage,
> then controls himself and replaces the Koran on the throne.
> Silence again. The* DOOR-KEEPER *enters.*

DOOR-KEEPER: In the name of Allah. It's the hour of
prayer, Your Majesty.

Scene Six

MUHAMMAD *stands silent for a while. The atmosphere is very tense.*

MUHAMMAD (*very. slowly*): We'll all pray here.

The DOOR-KEEPER *bows and exits. At the same moment, the* MUEZZIN'S *voice is heard calling the faithful to the prayer.*

MUEZZIN (*off-stage*): Alla-Ho-Akbar! Alla-Ho-Akbar!
Alla-Ho-Akbar! Alla-Ho-Akbar!
Ashahado La Elaha Illilah
Ashahado La Elaha Illilah
Ashahado Anna Muhammadur Rasool Illah
Ashahado Anna Muhammadur Rasool Illah
Haiyah Alis Salaat—Haiyah Alis Salaat
Haiyah Salil Falaa—Haiyah Salil Falaa
Alla-Ho-Akbar! Alla-Ho-Akbar!
La Elaha Illilah. . .

As soon as the MUEZZIN'S *call begins,* MUHAMMAD *unbuckles his sword and places it on the throne. About a dozen servants enter with pots of water, in which those on the stage wash their hands, faces, heads and feet. Another servant brings about a dozen mats on a plank and takes them round. Each person picks up a mat and spreads it facing west. They start praying.* MUHAMMAD *leads the prayer. Half way through the prayer a commotion is heard off-stage. Taking that as a cue,* SHIHAB-UD-DIN *and the* AMIRS *get up and pull out their daggers.*

BARANI (*frightened*): What's this? What's this?

The AMIRS *step towards the throne, near which* MUHAMMAD *is praying. Suddenly from behind the curtain near the throne about twenty Hindu soldiers rush in with spears and surround the* AMIRS. *One or two* AMIRS *try to run out but the soldiers bar their way. The* AMIRS *stand frozen in fear, then slowly throw down their daggers. The soldiers drag them away—all except* SHIHAB-UD-DIN. *While all this is going on,* MUHAMMAD *goes on praying unconcerned. Only after finishing the prayer does he*

41

*step down from the throne. Every one is silent for a
while.*

SHIHAB-UD-DIN: How did you guess?

MUHAMMAD: Do you really want to know?

SHIHAB-UD-DIN: You aren't worried about hurting my
feelings, are you?

MUHAMMAD: There was a letter in my letter-room today.
A strange letter—strange because, unlike all the others,
it didn't abuse me and it was signed. (*Pause.*)
By Ratansingh.

SHIHAB-UD-DIN (*smiles*): Do you really think I'll believe
that? It's the oldest trick in the world.

MUHAMMAD: Why should I lie to a dead man?

*Takes out the letter from his robe and holds it before
SHIHAB-UD-DIN. SHIHAB-UD-DIN looks crushed and
frightened.*

SHIHAB-UD-DIN (*almost to himself*): But does he say why he
is doing this to me?

NAJIB: He has disappeared—without a trace!

MUHAMMAD: Let me ask you something. Why did you
go against me? What wrong have I done you?

SHIHAB-UD-DIN: What's the point? You won't understand
it anyway.

MUHAMMAD: Won't I? Or could it be that you don't
know?

SHIHAB-UD-DIN (*suddenly violent*): Get on with your
killing, Muhammad. Or does your hand refuse to
rise against me? Beware! You won't be able to
trap me with your wiles. I am not Ain-ul-Mulk
to live crushed under your kindness.

*MUHAMMAD slowly takes out his dagger. SHIHAB-UD-DIN
is getting more and more frightened. He is almost
screaming now as he speaks.*

You want to solve all problems in the flash of a dagger,
don't you? But you can't stop this uprising now.
My father distrusts you and I've already written to
him, about everything here . . . everything . . .

42

NAJIB: Sorry, but Ratansingh has sent those letters to us.

SHIHAB-UD-DIN (*screaming*): Where will you hide my
corpse? How will you gag my voice? Kill me—
but you won't stop this—this will go on—

MUHAMMAD: I could have killed you with a word. But
I like you too much.

> *Stabs him. Then almost frenzied, goes on stabbing him.
> Hits out at* SHIHAB-UD-DIN's *dead body with a ferocity
> that makes even the soldiers holding the body turn away in
> horror.*

BARANI: Your Majesty—he's dead!

> MUHAMMAD *stops, then flings the dagger away in disgust.*

MUHAMMAD (*anguished*): Why must this happen, Barani?
Are all those I trust condemned to go down in history
as traitors? What is happening? Tell me, Barani,
will my reign be nothing more than a tortured scream
which will stab the night and melt away in the silence?

> *He is trembling all over. At a sign from* NAJIB, *the
> soldiers lay the body down on a mat and go away.*
> MUHAMMAD *stares at the body.*

Najib, see that every man involved in this is caught
and beheaded. Stuff their bodies with straw and
hang them up in the palace-yard. Let them hang
there for a week. No, send them round my kingdom.
Let every one of my subjects see them. Let every
one see what . . . (*Chokes.*)

BARANI: What will that achieve, Your Majesty? What's
the use?

> *Pause.*

NAJIB: We must do something about Shihab-ud-din's
father. He is a powerful man and he won't like this.

MUHAMMAD (*regaining control of himself*): Don't worry
about him. Make a public announcement that there
was a rebellion in the palace and that the nobles of
the court tried to assassinate the Sultan during prayer.
Say that the Sultan was saved by Shihab-ud-din

who died a martyr's death defending him. The
funeral will be held in Delhi and will be a grand
affair. Invite his father to it and see that he is treated
with the respect due to the father of a loyal nobleman.

BARANI: Oh God! Aren't even the dead free from your
politics?

NAJIB: Your Majesty, if this incident is to be kept a secret,
I'm afraid we'll have to hang everyone who was
here—even the Hindu guards. They remained
loyal to Your Majesty but they have seen it all and
are bound to talk. It does mean more corpses.
But then that'll only make the show more impressive.

MUHAMMAD: Najib, I want Delhi vacated immediately.
Every living soul in Delhi will leave for Daulatabad
within a fortnight. I was too soft, I can see that now.
They'll only understand the whip. Everyone must
leave. Not a light should be seen in the windows of
Delhi. Not a wisp of smoke should rise from its
chimneys. Nothing but an empty graveyard of
Delhi will satisfy me now.

BARANI: May Heaven protect us!

MUHAMMAD: Call on Heaven while you can, Barani—
you may not get another chance. What hopes I had
built up when I came to the throne! I had wanted
every act in my kingdom to become a prayer, every
prayer to become a further step in knowledge, every
step to lead us nearer to God. But our prayers
too are ridden with disease, and must be exiled.
There will be no more praying in the kingdom,
Najib. Anyone caught praying will be severely
punished. Henceforth let the moment of prayer
walk my streets in silence and leave without a trace.

NAJIB: But that would only be playing into the hands of
the Ulema, Your Majesty. I suggest we say there'll
be no more prayers till Ghiyas-ud-din Abbasid, the
descendant of the Khalif, visits us. God alone
knows when he'll come. Besides, it'll make such a
beautiful little paradox!

MUHAMMAD *does not reply.* NAJIB *goes out.* BARANI

44

sobs. MUHAMMAD *stands staring at* SHIHAB-UD-DIN'S *corpse.* BARANI *gets up, takes the silken cloth from the throne and starts spreading it on the corpse. But* MUHAMMAD *casts the cloth aside.*

MUHAMMAD: Don't cover him, Barani. I want my people to see his wounds.

The ANNOUNCER.

ANNOUNCER: Attention! Attention! The
Merciful Sultan Muhammad has declared—
that within the next month every citizen
of Delhi must leave for Daulatabad.
No one should remain behind in Delhi.
Anyone who attempts to stay behind or
to go elsewhere will be severely punished.
All arrangements have been made to
ensure the comfort of citizens on the
way to Daulatabad. All the needs of
the citizens, regarding food, clothing or
medicine, will be catered to by the State.
It is hoped that every citizen will use these
amenities to the full and be in Daulatabad
as soon as possible. Attention! Attention!

SCENE SEVEN

A camp on the Delhi-Daulatabad route. AZIZ *still dressed as a Brahmin, and* AAZAM. *A* HINDU WOMAN *is kneeling in front of* AZIZ.

HINDU WOMAN: Please let me go, sir . . . . My child. . .
please have mercy on it . . . only for a day, sir. . .
AZIZ: I told you I can't. No one can be allowed out of
sight until we reach Daulatabad. I'm sorry, but
I have my orders.
HINDU WOMAN: But I'll return tomorrow. . . . I swear
by my child I will. . . . It's dying, Your Excellency,
I have to take it to a doctor. . .
AZIZ: But what can I do? There's the hakim's tent.
Go to him. He'll give you some medicine. (*In a
low voice.*) I've told you what you can do. I
could try and bribe my senior officials, but you'll
have to pay for it.
HINDU WOMAN: But I haven't got a paisa on me, Your
Excellency. And what will I give the doctor?
My husband's also ill, sir, please, I hold your feet—
please let me go.
AZIZ: I can't waste any more time on you. There's a lot of
work here. Stop screaming and get back to your
tent—I said, get back to your tent!

The HINDU WOMAN *goes out weeping.*

AAZAM: Poor thing! Why don't you let her go?
The doctor may help her.
AZIZ: Have you seen the child? No witch-doctor can
save it now. My niece had that illness and went
out like a light. It's a waste of good money and
she's going to need every paisa of it. I'm doing her a
favour! And watch out for paise, Aazam; they're
going to cost a lot soon.

47

Footsteps are heard off-stage. AZIZ buries his head into his books. A family comes in. A man with a woman and six kids. They come and stand. AZIZ continues to read. AAZAM, embarrassed, wanders around without looking at them. The family waits patiently.

Three more families! They must be walking on their knees. (*Looks up and stares at the man.*) So you've come at last, have you? Perhaps you went to visit your in-laws on the way. Don't you know the orders? You were supposed to be here well before sunset.

MAN: What was I to do, Your Excellency? There were two corpses there on the road. Poor things! They must have walked till their hearts gave out. I thought, sinner that I am, I would at least give them a decent burial, Your Excellency.

AAZAM: Poor souls. From which camp were they, do you think?

AZIZ: I hope you checked whether they were Muslims before burying them.

MAN: Who's to do all that, Your Excellency? I did what I could.

AZIZ: And what if they were Hindus, pray? You know they don't bury their dead. You'll be in trouble if some one finds out. Actually I ought to send you back to dig them up again. It's against the orders to insult or cause harm to Hinduism—

MAN: I just didn't think of it, Your Excellency. Sinner that I am, I thought I would lighten the burden of my sins by giving them a resting place.

AZIZ: Leave the corpses alone in future. What did you do in Delhi, sinner that you are?

MAN: I am a Kafir, Your Excellency. I have to guard the dead bodies in the palace yard—those executed by the Sultan, you know. I have to guard them for a week, ten at a time, sir, and then carry them to the canal outside the city. There again I have to guard them against thieves.

AAZAM: Thieves? Ugh!

MAN: Isn't it terrible, Your Excellency? But there it is. That's what men have come to. The relatives of the dead have to pay us a fine before taking the bodies. Well, if the orders had been obeyed I would have built a house by now. But no, they won't pay— even for the dead! They come at night and steal them. Not just the poor. Even the rich folk—the most respectable people of Delhi! I could tell you a name or two and you wouldn't believe it. It is terrible. People won't stop at anything once they they get into the habit of thieving, that's certain.

AZIZ looks at AAZAM and laughs. AAZAM grimaces.

AZIZ: So this is your family. All eight here?

MAN: Yes, Sir.

AZIZ: Get on with you there. There's a tent kept for you. Yes! Whatever happens to the others, people like you mustn't die. The Sultan will need a lot more like you soon. So what are you going to do till the Sultan arrives in Daulatabad? Another couple of children?

MAN: Well, we have decided to get married first, Your Excellency.

AAZAM (*in disgust*): Oh God!

MAN (*apologetic*): Couldn't find time for it in Delhi, sir.

AAZAM: Go away. Go away!

The family goes off.

God, what a dirty man! I am feeling sick.

AZIZ: I like such people. They are the real stoics.

AAZAM: I just keep thinking of that poor woman. Why don't you let her see the doctor? I'm sure she'll come back. Look, if you want money, tell me. There are enough rich men in this camp. I'll get some in no time.

AZIZ: Don't you do anything of the kind! You'll ruin us both if they catch you.

AAZAM: We'll be ruined anyway ultimately. If not today, then tomorrow. What other future's there for us?

49

One day my fingers will slow down. I'll get caught.
Then, no arms! No legs! A torn mat and a begging
bowl, that's all.

AZIZ : You are a hopeless case, you know. Pathetic!
You've been in Delhi for so many years and you're as
stupid as ever. Look at me. Only a few months in
Delhi and I have discovered a whole new world—
politics! My dear fellow, that's where our future is—
politics! It's a beautiful world—wealth, success,
position, power—and yet it's full of brainless people,
people with not an idea in their head. When I think
of all the tricks I used in our village to pinch a few
torn clothes from people—if one uses half that
intelligence here, one can get robes of power. And
not have to pinch them either—get them! It's a
fantastic world!

The HINDU WOMAN *is heard wailing.*

AAZAM : That's that Hindu woman. Her child's dead.
She'll complain against you now. If you go on like
this, Aziz, we'll soon keep the Kafir company in
Daulatabad.

AZIZ : Don't call me Aziz. I've told you. As for her,
I've only obeyed my orders. Besides I'm a Brahmin
and she won't complain against a Brahmin to a Muslim
officer. That'll send her to hell straight. In any
case—and listen to this carefully—we won't stay in
the Sultan's service for long. I heard some rumours in
Delhi. The Sultan's going to introduce copper coins
soon. And a copper coin will have the same value
as a silver dinar. What do you say to that?

AAZAM (*making a face*): Eyah! There's no fun in stealing
copper coins.

AZIZ : Shut up! Just listen to what I'm telling you—
you are not going to pinch any coins, you are going
to make them. Make counterfeit coins, you understand?
If your fingers are getting restless, use them there.
(*Noise off-stage.*) Ha! There's the next lot!
  Buries his head in his books.

50

SCENE EIGHT

The fort at Daulatabad. Two watchmen—one young, the other past his middle-age. Night.

YOUNG MAN: What time do you think it is, grandfather?

OLD MAN: Must be just past midnight.

YOUNG MAN: Only that? Good God! When I was in the army, less than two seconds seemed to divide the lamp-lighting hour from the daybreak. Now the night scarcely moves.

OLD MAN: It's only when you wait for the morning that the night stands still. A good sentry must forget that morning even exists.

YOUNG MAN (*looking down the side of the fort*): What a fantastic fort! I have a good head but even my head goes round when I look down. And isn't that long white thing the road from Daulatabad to Delhi?

OLD MAN: Yes.

YOUNG MAN: They say it's the widest road in the world. But it looks no bigger than a thin snake from here.

OLD MAN: And four years ago that snake bit a whole city to death.

YOUNG MAN: What a fort! What a magnificent thing! I met a foreign visitor the other day and he said he has been round the world and not seen any fort as strong as this anywhere. No army could take this.

OLD MAN: No, if this fort ever falls, it will crumble from the inside.

YOUNG MAN: You don't love this fort very much, do you, grandfather?

OLD MAN: I am a man of the plains, son. I find it hard to breathe in this eagle nest.

YOUNG MAN: You are from Delhi?

51

OLD MAN: Yes.

YOUNG MAN: Was it hard, coming from Delhi to here?

OLD MAN: I survived. But my family was more fortunate. They all died on the way.

YOUNG MAN (*sympathetically*): I am sorry. The arrangements must have been very bad.

OLD MAN: Oh no. The merciful Sultan had made perfect arrangements. But do you know, you can love a city like a woman? My old father had lived in Delhi all his life. He died of a broken heart. Then my son Ismail. He was six years old—would have been ten now! The fine dust that hung in the air, fine as silk, it covered him like a silken shroud. After him, his mother.

Silence. The YOUNG MAN *is embarrassed.*

YOUNG MAN: Tell me more about this fort, grandfather. Is it true there is a strange and frightening passage within this fort? Dark, they say, like the new moon night.

OLD MAN: Yes, it's a long passage, a big passage, coiled like an enormous hollow python inside the belly of the fort. And we shall be far, far happier when that python breaks out and swallows everything in sight— every man, woman, child, and beast.

Footsteps off-stage.

YOUNG MAN (*raising his spear*): Who is that?

MUHAMMAD: Muhammad.

YOUNG MAN: Muhammad? What Muhammad?

OLD MAN: Shut up, fool. It's the Sultan.

MUHAMMAD *walks in—almost in a trance.*

BOTH: In the name of Allah!

MUHAMMAD (*to the old man*): Go and tell Barani I want to see him.

The OLD MAN *bows and retires.*

YOUNG MAN: I beg your Majesty's pardon for my impertinence. I didn't realize...

MUHAMMAD: Don't worry. You were doing your duty.

Goes to the edge of the wall and looks down.

YOUNG MAN: Your Majesty must forgive my impudence, but I beg Your Majesty not to go too near the edge of the fort. It's a very steep fall.

MUHAMMAD (*smiles*): You are new here, aren't you?

YOUNG MAN: Yes, I am, Your Majesty. I was in the army all these years. They sent me here yesterday. I am very sorry if I've said anything wrong, Your Majesty.

MUHAMMAD: Don't apologize at every word. If you stay here long enough you'll anyway learn to ooze spittle before everyone. Be yourself at least until then. How old are you?

YOUNG MAN: Nineteen, Your Majesty.

MUHAMMAD: Nineteen. Nice age! An age when you think you can clasp the whole world in your palm like a rare diamond. I was twenty-one when I came to Daulatabad first, and built this fort. I supervised the placing of every brick in it and I said to myself, one day I shall build my own history like this, brick by brick.

One night I was standing on the ramparts of the old fort here. There was a torch near me flapping its wild wings and scattering golden feathers on everything in sight. There was a half-built gate nearby trying to contain the sky within its cleft. Suddenly something happened—as though some one had cast a spell. The torch, the gate, the fort and the sky—all melted and merged and flowed in my blood-stream with the darkness of the night. The moment shed its symbols, its questions and answers, and stood naked and calm where the stars throbbed in my veins. I was the earth, was the grass, was the smoke, was the sky. Suddenly a sentry called from far: 'Attention!' Attention! And to that challenge the half-burnt torch and the half-built gate fell apart.

No, young man, I don't envy you your youth. All that you have to face and suffer is still ahead of you.

53

Look at me. I have searched for that moment since then and here I am still searching for it. But in the last four years, I have seen only the woods clinging to the earth, heard only the howl of wild wolves and the answering bay of street dogs. Another twenty years and you'll be as old as me. I might be lying under those woods there. Do you think you'll remember me then?

No answer.

Come, why are you silent?

YOUNG MAN (*scared*): Your Majesty must forgive me, Your Majesty. But I don't understand what Your Majesty is saying.

MUHAMMAD (*incensed*): You don't understand! You don't understand! Why do you live? Why do you corrupt the air with your diseased breath? (*Suddenly calm.*) I'm sorry. It's my turn to apologize. It isn't your fault. You are also one of them.

Uncomfortable silence. BARANI *enters.*

BARANI: In the name of Allah. Your Majesty sent for me?

MUHAMMAD *waves the sentries away.*

MUHAMMAD: I couldn't bear the walls any more. When I came here I felt I needed an audience—someone to confess my self-pity to. You were asleep?

BARANI: No, Your Majesty. I was reading a book by Imam Abu Hanifa.

MUHAMMAD: Fortunate! You can read when you don't feel sleepy. I can't sleep. I can't read. Even Rumi, who once used to transport me, has become simply a web of words. Do you know, five years ago I actually used to pray to God not to send me any sleep? I can't believe it now.

BARANI: Why don't you see a hakim, Your Majesty?

MUHAMMAD: What can a hakim do? You are a historian, Barani, you are the man to prescribe remedies for this.

54

Have you heard the latest news? Fakr-ud-din
has risen against me in Bengal.

BARANI: Oh, I'm . . .

MUHAMMAD: Yes. And there's been another uprising
in the Deccan. In Ma'bar Ehsanshah has declared
himself independent. Bahal-ud-din Gashtasp is
collecting an army against me. The drought in
Doab is spreading from town to town—burning up
the country. Only one industry flourishes in my
kingdom, only one—and that's of making counterfeit
copper coins. Every Hindu home has become a
domestic mint; the traders are just waiting for me to
close my eyes; and in my whole kingdom there are
only two people I can trust—Ain-ul-Mulk and
Shihab-ud-din's father. What should I do, Barani?
What would you prescribe for this honeycomb of
diseases? I have tried everything. But what cures
one disease just worsens another.

BARANI: I am a humble historian, Your Majesty; it's not
for me to prescribe. But since Your Majesty has
done me the honour of confiding in me, may I make
a suggestion? It is a difficult thing to suggest to a
king and I beg you to forgive me if it hurts. But
you are a learned man, Your Majesty, you are
known the world over for your knowledge of
philosophy and poetry. History is not made only
in statecraft; its lasting results are produced in the
ranks of learned men. That's where you belong,
Your Majesty, in the company of learned men. Not
in the market of corpses.

MUHAMMAD: You want me to retire from my throne?
(*Laughs.*) Barani, if you were capable of irony,
I would have thought you were laughing at me.
But as usual you mean it, which makes it harder.
I wish it was as easy as that. I have often thought of
that myself—to give up this futile see-saw struggle
and go to Mecca. Sit there by the Kaaba and search
for the peace which Daulatabad hasn't given me.
What bliss! But it isn't that easy. It isn't as easy
as leaving the patient in the wilderness because there's

no cure for his disease. Don't you see—this patient,
racked by fever and crazed by the fear of the
enveloping vultures, can't be separated from me?
Don't you see that the only way I can abdicate is by
killing myself? I could have done something if the
vultures weren't so close. I could have crawled
forward on my knees and elbows. But what can
you do when every moment you expect a beak to
dig into you and tear a muscle out? What can you
do? Barani, what vengeance is driving these shapes
after me?

BARANI: Your Majesty . . .

MUHAMMAD: You know what my beloved subjects call me?
Mad Muhammad! Mad Muhammad! (*Suddenly
pleading.*) How can I become wise again, Barani?

BARANI: Your Majesty, there was a time when you
believed in love, in peace, in God. What has
happened to those ideals? You won't let your
subjects pray. You torture them for the smallest
offence. Hang them on suspicion. Why this
bloodshed? Please stop it, and I promise Your
Majesty something better will emerge out of it.

MUHAMMAD: But for that I'll have to admit I've been
wrong all these years. And I know I haven't.
I have something to give, something to teach, which
may open the eyes of history, but I have to do it
within this life. I've got to make them listen to me
before I lose even that!

The OLD MAN *comes in running.*

OLD MAN: In the name of Allah—a calamity, Your
Majesty—the Nayab Vizier has sent word—

MUHAMMAD: What is it?

OLD MAN: Vizier Muhammad Najib is dead. His body
was found in his bed. The Nayab Vizier says it is
murder . . .

SCENE NINE

A hide-out in the hills. AZIZ *and* AAZAM *are stretched out on the floor.*

AAZAM: It's so hot—I'm fed up, I'm fed up of life, I'm
fed up of the whole bloody world.

AZIZ: Why don't you just go and commit suicide?

AAZAM: Tried once. Went and jumped into a well.
But the cold water cheered me up so much that
I had a good swim and went back home. I don't
think I could try again.

AZIZ: You'll never learn to do a thing properly.

AAZAM: But how come I steal properly? I have never
made a mistake while stealing. Why am I a thief,
Aziz? Why aren't we like other people? Have a
nice home, till a farm and live happily?

AZIZ: How many happy people have you met? Besides,
a man must commit a crime at least once in his life-time.
Only then will his virtue be recognized!

AAZAM: Aw, shut up!

AZIZ: No, truly. Listen. If you remain virtuous
throughout your life no one will say a good thing
about you because they won't need to. But start
stealing—and they'll say: 'What a nice boy he was!
But he's ruined now. . .' Then kill and they will
beat their breasts and say: 'Heavens! He was
only a petty thief all these days. Never hurt anyone.
But alas!' Then rape a woman and the chorus
will go into hallelujahs: 'He was a saint, a real
saint and look at him now. . .'

AAZAM: Well, you have robbed and killed. Now all you
have to do to become a saint is rape.

AZIZ: Presently, presently. No hurry. What's the
point in raping for sheer lust? That's a mug's game.
First one must have power—the authority to rape!
Then everything takes on meaning.

57

AAZAM (*giggles*): So you want power, do you? What do you want to be, a Sultan?

AZIZ: Laugh away, stupid. You'll soon see. It all depends on whether Karim will bring the goods.

AAZAM (*seriously*): But, no, Aziz, why are you so dissatisfied? We have such a nice establishment here. We take enough money from travellers and the other robbers are scared to death of you. There's no limit to what we can make here.

AZIZ: I am bored stiff with all this running and hiding. You rob a man, you run, and hide. It's all so pointless. One should be able to rob a man and then stay there to punish him for getting robbed That's called 'class'—that's being a real king!

AAZAM: May Allah shower His blessings on Your Majesty! Is there a post for your humble slave at the court?

AZIZ: Oh, yes! You are stupid. So you'll make a good nobleman—an Amir.

AAZAM (*in disgust*): Eah! I don't like that. I don't think I could be anything but a common pickpocket. What about a court thief?

AZIZ *bursts into laughter.*

AZIZ: That's beautiful, Aazam! A court thief! I'd never thought of that. It opens up all sorts of possibilities. . . . There's Karim now!

KARIM *comes in with a man, bound and gagged.*

You are late. Are you sure this is the right man?

KARIM: No need to worry.

AZIZ: Excellent. Here you are. (*Gives him a purse.*) I'll send for you if there's any more work.

KARIM *salaams and exits.*

AAZAM: Who is this animal?

AZIZ: Wait and see. Untie him first.

AAZAM *unties the man.* AZIZ *stares at him and an expresssion of horror spreads on his face.*

My God! I'll kill that ass Karim! He's brought the wrong man!

58

MAN: I told him so. I told him who I was. I told him
clearly. The rascal wouldn't listen. Tied me up.
Me! Let the Sultan hear of this outrage. He'll
whip you to death.

AZIZ ⎫
AAZAM ⎭ The Sultan?

AZIZ: We beg your pardon, Sir. There's been a mistake.
Karim was supposed to bring some one else—a Turk
merchant. But—may we know who you are?

MAN: You'll soon know, you scoundrels. I am Ghiyas-ud-din
Abbasid. The descendant of Khalif Abbasid. I am
the Guest of Honour of His Majesty.

AAZAM: Ya Allah!

AZIZ and AAZAM prostrate themselves in front of him.

GHIYAS-UD-DIN: You'll pay for this! I've come all the
way from Arabia and not a soul dared touch me.
They trembled at the mention of my name. And
now this outrage! You'll hear more about this—

AZIZ: Forgive us, Your Worship. It was a mistake.
There's been a slip somewhere. It's just that you
are alone—I mean the Sultan's Guest of Honour—
from the Holy Family of the Khalifs—

GHIYAS-UD-DIN: Mind your own business, slave. I'll
soon have an entourage, as soon as the Sultan knows
I've arrived. He is sending a special entourage from
Daulatabad.

AZIZ: Then perhaps Your Worship will allow us to make
amends for this sacrilege by following you? We'll
be your slaves till you reach Daulatabad.

GHIYAS-UD-DIN: Hm! You may redeem yourself that
way. Get up. No need to prostrate yourself so
long. Yes, I do need guides. It's an unfamiliar
country and the people here are treacherous. The
moment they know you are a foreigner they're out
to rob you. Yes, you'll do till the entourage arrives.

AZIZ: But haven't you been here before, Your Worship?
Haven't you seen the Sultan?

GHIYAS-UD-DIN: I haven't. But I shall soon.

59

In the mean time, AAZAM *has spread a mat on which* GHIYAS-UD-DIN *sits imperially.* AAZAM *offers him some fruits to eat.*

AZIZ: Forgive me if I am talking beyond my station, Your Worship. But I must warn you that the Sultan is in a suspicious frame of mind, we hear. There have been a lot of deaths since he came to Daulatabad.

GHIYAS-UD-DIN: Yes, I've heard all that. I'm not worried.

AZIZ: Recently he flogged a man to death, had his body filled with straw and strung up in the market place— all because the man claimed to be a descendant of the Prophet.

GHIYAS-UD-DIN: For a common thief you talk too much. What's your name?

AZIZ: Aziz, Your Worship and this is Aazam. I realize I sound impertinent, Your Worship. We are happy to follow you to Daulatabad, be your slaves to make up for our sacrilege. But Your Worship will forgive us for being worried about our necks—

GHIYAS-UD-DIN: You don't need to worry. I have got the Sultan's letters with me—and the ring he sent as a mark of recognition. (*Shows the ring.*) I know there are no precious stones in it. But that would have attracted too much attention.

AZIZ: The Sultan is a wise man. But Your Worship has no friends or acquaintances in Daulatabad?

GHIYAS-UD-DIN (*irritated*): You ask too many questions for a slave. No, no friends there. You just hold your tongue and follow me.

AZIZ *laughs.* GHIYAS-UD-DIN *looks at him, suddenly suspicious.* AZIZ *bursts into loud laughter and jumps up.*

AZIZ: Caught him, Aazam! He fell into my trap like a mouse. This is the goods, Aazam, this is it! I had heard he was here—without a paisa on him but boasting of his good fortune—

GHIYAS-UD-DIN: What do you mean?

AZIZ: In five minutes, you won't need to know any meanings.

AAZAM (*frightened*): Don't kill him, Aziz, please don't!
He's the Khalif's grandson—

GHIYAS-UD-DIN (*frightened*): Kill me? But why? What'll
you gain by killing me? I've nothing—you know
that—I'll get nothing till I reach Daulatabad—
I'm a poor man. Why kill me?

AAZAM: He is right, Aziz.

GHIYAS-UD-DIN: It's the truth, I swear. That's how
I've come here alive—no one could get anything
out of me. What do you want from me? Look,
if you come with me to Daulatabad, I'll see you'll get
something too—

AZIZ: I am not going with you. I am going in your place.

AAZAM: Aziz, listen—

AZIZ: Shut up! Don't waste your stupid breath!
We'll never get an opportunity like this again. Arabia
must be full of the Khalif's descendants. They were
a fertile lot, the Khalifs. Now the Sultan's picked
this rat up from the gutters for some game of his
own. Who will worry about this fool when people
are dying without food in Daulatabad? Get out
now. Get out. You'll just make things worse.

AAZAM *goes out.*

GHIYAS-UD-DIN: Don't kill me, please. I'll kiss your feet.
Take everything—my ring, letters, everything.
I'll go back. I'll go back to my village. I won't
bother you. Please don't kill me. I'll kiss your
feet. Please let me go. (*Embraces his legs.*)

AZIZ: No!

GHIYAS-UD-DIN: No? No! No! I knew it. I knew
something like this would happen. It was too good
to be true—to grow up in filth, live in filth—and
then a letter from nowhere. A hope—a ray of
light. Now my fate will change, I thought, now
I'll be happy. Now things will start afresh. So
I started. But I knew it was too good—good things
don't come like that—they don't stay—

He gives AZIZ *a sudden push.* AZIZ *falls down on the floor.* GHIYAS-UD-DIN *runs out.*

AZIZ (*shouts without getting up*): Stop him, Aazam. Stop him.

Jumps up and runs out. Noise of a scuffle.

AZIZ (*off-stage*): That's it, Aazam! Bravo!

GHIYAS-UD-DIN (*off-stage*): Don't kill me, please.

A scream. Then silence. AAZAM *comes in running. He is covered with blood. He is sweating, trembling and weeping. After a while* AZIZ *comes in, with* GHIYAS-UD-DIN's *turban on his head.*

AZIZ: Why are you crying, you clown?

AAZAM: Don't talk to me—God! God! Why did I stop him? Why didn't I let him go?

AZIZ opens GHIYAS-UD-DIN's *bundle.*

AZIZ: You are a funny creature. You have seen enough corpses to last you seven lives. You have stuffed them with straw, practised obscenities on them. And still you can't see a man die. (*Takes out a robe and puts it on.*) How do I look, eh? The great-grandson of the Khalif!

AAZAM *looks away.* AZIZ *slaps him on the back.*

Laugh, you fool, laugh. Celebrate! What are you crying for? Look, look at the palace doors. They are opening for us. Dance, dance, you son of an ass—

Sings.

Grandson of the Khalif! Great-grandson of the Khalif! Great-great-great-grandson of the Khalif!

Sings and dances in a circle, clapping his hands. AAZAM *looks at him angrily. Then slowly his face breaks into a smile and soon he is laughing.*

62

SCENE TEN

The Palace. MUHAMMAD *is looking out of the window. The*
STEP-MOTHER *comes in.*

STEP-MOTHER: Muhammad, do you know what's happening
  outside?

MUHAMMAD: Yes.

STEP-MOTHER: Why are you doing it?

MUHAMMAD: What else can I do? I said the new copper
  coins would have the same value as the silver dinars.
  Now I can't go against my own orders

STEP-MOTHER: But this is sheer folly! The Vizier says
  there are five hundred carts out there and they are
  all full of counterfeit coins. Are you going to
  exchange them all for silver?

MUHAMMAD: There's nothing else for it. I should have
  expected this but didn't—that was my fault. If I
  don't withdraw the coins now, the whole economy
  will be in shambles. It's in a bad enough state
  already.

STEP-MOTHER: Five hundred carts on the first day!
  And what about tomorrow and the day after?
  You are just legalizing robbery—

MUHAMMAD: It's all their wealth. I can't let my whim
  ruin them.

STEP-MOTHER: And how is a treasury full of counterfeit
  coins going to help them? Will that revive your
  economy?

MUHAMMAD: Don't worry, Mother. The coins aren't
  going into the treasury. They'll all be heaped in
  the new rose garden.

STEP-MOTHER: What's wrong with you? You spent
  years planning that rose garden and now—

MUHAMMAD: Now I don't need a rose garden. I built it
  because I wanted to make for myself an image of

63

Sadi's poems. I wanted every rose in it to be a poem.
I wanted every thorn in it to prick and quicken the
senses. But I don't need these airy trappings now;
a funeral has no need for a separate symbol.

STEP-MOTHER: Then why don't you stop the funeral?
Why this unending line of corpses? Muhammad,
I have been hearing rumours lately. The Amirs
and Khans are apparently getting upset because
you are hounding them about Najib.

MUHAMMAD: I am not hounding them. I merely want
to find out who murdered Najib.

STEP-MOTHER: Is it true five of them have fled?

MUHAMMAD: Not five—four. The fifth committed
suicide. Amir Jalal-ud-din.

STEP-MOTHER: Oh God!

MUHAMMAD: He told his wife he knew who had killed
Najib. One of his servants overheard the
conversation.

STEP-MOTHER (*alarmed*): Please, don't go on like this.
Please. Najib's dead. Finished. You can't drive
the nobles to rebellion for his sake?

MUHAMMAD: Don't you think it strange that an Amir like
Jalal-ud-din should kill himself to save the murderer?
It must be someone very special.

STEP-MOTHER: I'm glad Najib's dead. He was leading
you astray. It's because you wouldn't trust anyone
as much as him that the kingdom's in this state!
The Ulema are against you; the noblemen are
against you; the people hate you. It's all his work.
I'm glad he's dead. He should have died a long
time ago.

MUHAMMAD: Najib wasn't loyal to me; he was loyal to
the throne. The day he turned against me I would
have known I'd made a mistake.

STEP-MOTHER: Why not forget him? What good is it to
the throne—

MUHAMMAD: I must know who killed him and why.

STEP-MOTHER: Muhammad, how long are you going to
torture yourself like this?

MUHAMMAD: Not for long. The Amirs will return. If they
don't, I'll be sorry for their families.

STEP-MOTHER: You frighten me, Muhammad, you really do.
Please stop this. Muhammad—please—for my sake.

No reply.

Won't you? I appeal to you.

No reply.

All right. I killed him. I had him murdered.

MUHAMMAD (*exploding*): For God's sake, don't joke
about it! And don't try to be noble and save me
from the stupid Amirs and Khans. This isn't a
small thing.

STEP-MOTHER: I am perfectly serious. I had him
poisoned.

MUHAMMAD: Stop it! Why are you torturing me now?
Don't you see how you're burning out my guts with
your silly jokes?

STEP-MOTHER: Why shouldn't I have killed him? It was
easier than killing one's father or brother. It was
better than killing Sheikh Imam-ud-din.

MUHAMMAD: I killed them—yes—but I killed them for
an ideal. Don't I know its results? Don't you
think I've suffered from the curse? My mother
won't speak to me—I can't even look into a mirror
for fear of seeing their faces in it. I had only
three friend, in the world—you, Najib and Barani.
And now you want me to believe you killed Najib.
Why are you doing this to me?

STEP-MOTHER: It's only seven years ago that you came
to the throne. How glorious you were then, how
idealistic, how full of hopes. Look at your
kingdom now. It's become a kitchen of death—
all because of him. I couldn't bear it any longer.

MUHAMMAD: But you don't know that for the past few
months he had been advising me against violence,
do you? He wanted me to hold back my sword
for the stability of the throne.

STEP-MOTHER: Then why didn't you?

MUHAMMAD: Because I couldn't. Not now. Remember Shihab-ud-din of Sampanshahr? He was the first man I killed with my own hands. And I had a glimmer then of what now I know only too well. Not words but the sword—that's all I have to keep my faith in my mission. Why should Najib be sacrificed for that?

STEP-MOTHER: You had your share of futile deaths. I have mine now.

MUHAMMAD (*shouting*): No, they were not futile. They gave me what I wanted—power, strength to shape my thoughts, strength to act, strength to recognize myself. What did your little murder give you?

Suddenly freezes. Stares at her. Then quietly,

Woman, woman, so you are also one of them! So that's what you too wanted! Mother is annoyed she can't control me. And now you too are trying the same game, aren't you? Get rid of Najib, so you could control me?

STEP-MOTHER: I want nothing for myself. You are my life, Muhammad. You know that. If I had wanted power, I wouldn't have confessed.

MUHAMMAD: You needn't have confessed. I would have found out on my own. Or else, the Amirs would have rebelled. And then, what power? Clever you. You thought I wouldn't punish you, didn't you? Because I love you more than I have loved anyone in my life. That was the price of your love, wasn't it? (*Suddenly in agony.*) Why did you have to do it?

STEP-MOTHER (*puts her hand on his shoulder*): Listen to me—

MUHAMMAD: Don't touch me! There's only one punishmen for treachery—death!

Claps twice.

STEP-MOTHER: Don't be a fool, Muhammad. I'm telling you for your own sake. My death won't make you happy. You have enough ghosts to haunt you. Don't add mine to it.

66

MUHAMMAD: The others died unjustly. You deserve
to die—
> *Two soldiers enter.*

You are worse than an adulteress. But I can't think
of a worse punishment for you. Take her to prison.
> *The* STEP-MOTHER *stands petrified. The soldiers are
> also baffled.*

(*Screaming.*) Take her away!
> *The soldiers hold her. She tries to break away.*

Tell the Nayab Vizier I want her stoned to death
publicly tomorrow morning.

STEP-MOTHER (*finding her voice*): Not that, Muhammad,
don't do that to me—please.

MUHAMMAD: That's how an adulteress dies. Take her away.

STEP-MOTHER: Muhammad, please—
> *She is dragged away.* MUHAMMAD *stands looking
> stunned. Then suddenly he falls to his knees and
> clutches his hands to his breast.*

MUHAMMAD: God, God in Heaven, please help me.
Please don't let go of my hand. My skin drips with blood
and I don't know how much of it is mine and how
much of others. I started in Your path, Lord,
why am I wandering naked in this desert now?
I started in search of You. Why am I become a
pig rolling in this gory mud? Raise me. Clean me.
Cover me with Your Infinite Mercy. I can only
clutch at the hem of Your cloak with my bloody
fingers and plead. I can only beg—have pity on me.
I have no one but You now. Only You. Only
You . . . You . . . You . . . You . . .
> *Enter* BARANI.

BARANI: In the name . . .
> *Stops.* MUHAMMAD *raises his head.*

MUHAMMAD: Come in, Barani. You've come at the right
moment. You have saved me from treachery, you

know. I was trying to pray! Think of that—no one
in my kingdom is allowed to pray and I was praying.
Against my own orders! But what else could I do,
Barani? My legs couldn't hold me up any longer.

BARANI (*smiles*): You needn't worry, Your Majesty.
I'm here because I insisted on bringing the joyful
tidings myself—

MUHAMMAD: Joy? It's such a long time since I heard
that word.

BARANI: We have just received a letter from your
Governor. Ghiyas-ud-din Abbasid, the descendant
of the Khalif's is arriving here—within the next month
or so. We can all pray now, Your Majesty.

MUHAMMAD: What's the use? I was trying to pray—but
I could only find words learnt by rote which left
no echo in the heart. I am teetering on the brink
of madness, Barani, but the madness of God still
eludes me. (*Shouting.*) And why should I deserve
that madness? I have condemned my mother to
death and I'm not even sure she was guilty of the
crime. . .

The ANNOUNCER.

ANNOUNCER: Attention! Attention! Muhammad
   Tughlaq who craves only for the mercy of
   Allah and for the blessings of the Khalifs,
   hereby announces that His Worship Ghiyas-
   ud-din Muhammad, son of His Worship
   Abdul Kahir, grandson of His Worship Yusuf,
   great-grandson of His Worship Abdul Aziz,
   great-great-grandson of His Imperial
   Holiness Abbasid Al-Mustansir, the Khalif
   of Baghdad, will bless and purify Daulatabad
   by arriving here tomorrow afternoon.
   And Muhammad is sure that the citizens
   of this city will collect in large numbers to
   welcome this Saviour.
   This is a holy day for us—a day of joy!
   And its glory will be crowned by the fact
   that the Public Prayer, which has been
   mute in our land these five years, will be
   started again from next Friday. Henceforth every Muslim will pray five times
   a day as enjoined by the Holy Koran
   and declare himself a Faithful Slave of
   the Lord. Attention! Attention!

SCENE ELEVEN

A plain outside the fort of Daulatabad. Crowds of citizens.

FIRST MAN: Prayer! Prayer! Who wants prayers now?

SECOND MAN: Ask them to give us some food.

FIRST MAN: There's no food. Food's only in the palace. It's prayers for us.

SECOND MAN: The Amirs have food.

FIRST MAN: We starve and they want us to pray. They want to save our souls.

THIRD MAN: Is it true the Sultan has opened up his granary

SECOND MAN: There was not a grain in it! Not a skin of paddy.

FIRST MAN: And they want us to pray.

THIRD MAN: The other day my younger brother came here from our village. He says it's much worse there. We are better off here, he says. They have to pay twenty grains of silver for a fistful of wheat. And the scenes he saw on his way here! Ugh!

SECOND MAN (*getting annoyed*): Hm...

THIRD MAN: He says the roads are lined with skeletons. A man starved to death right in front of his eyes. In Doab, people are eating barks off the trees, he says. Yes, and women have to make do with skins of dead horses.

SECOND MAN: Shut up.

THIRD MAN: In Baran—that's where Barani, the Sultan's friend, comes from you know—they have to eat burnt strips of skin, he says. No one knows what animals—

SECOND MAN: Why don't you shut up?

The crowd listens, tensely.

THIRD MAN: He says we are much better off here. Not them. On his way here he saw people crowding

70

round a butcher's shop. You know why? To catch
the blood spurting from the slaughtered beasts and
drink it!

SECOND MAN: Shut up, you butcher—

He attacks the THIRD MAN. *There's a fight. The*
SECOND MAN *throws the* THIRD MAN *down, sits on his
chest and beats him. He is crying even as he beats.
The others watch.*

FIRST MAN: Why do they need prayer?

*Music and the announcers are heard from the two sides of
the stage.*

ANNOUNCER I: Attention! Attention! The Slave of the
Lord, the Upholder of the Word of the Prophet, the
Friend of the Khalif, the Faithful, Sultan Muhammad
Tughlaq—

ANNOUNCER II: Attention! Attention! The Protector of
the Faith, the Descendant of the Holy Khalif
al-Mustansir, Amir-ul-Mominin Ghiyas-ud-din
Muhammad—

AZIZ, AAZAM *and their entourage enter from one side.
Exactly at the same moment,* MUHAMMAD *and his
entourage step down from the fort. There is tense
silence.* MUHAMMAD *stares at* AZIZ *as though he is not
quite sure what is happening. The* HINDU WOMAN *of
Scene Seven steps out of the crowd and stares at* AZIZ.
Her husband pulls her back. MUHAMMAD *steps forward
and embraces* AZIZ.

MUHAMMAD: Welcome to our city, Your Holiness, welcome
to our poor land. My kingdom rejoices at the
arrival of your gracious presence. We have waited
for years for this joyful moment. Our streets have
waited in silence for the moment when the call to the
holy prayer will ring in them again. And each year
has been a century. We have waited long, Your
Holiness, and our sins have become shadows that
entwine round our feet. They have become our

71

dumbness and deprived us of prayer. They have
become the fiery sun and burnt up our crops. Now
the moment has come for me and my people to
rejoice. Only you can save me now, Your Holiness,
only the dust of your feet on my head can save me
now—

*Falls to his feet. The crowd gasps. Then everyone
kneels.*

AZIZ: Amen.

*MUHAMMAD gets up. They embrace again. They
depart to the accompaniment of the announcements.*

HINDU WOMAN: It's him! It's him—
THIRD MAN: Who?
HINDU WOMAN: He killed my child! Those eyes—I'll
never forget them—he killed my child ... (*Screams.*)
He killed my child ... (*Keeps on screaming.*)
FIRST MAN: What's it?
SECOND MAN: I didn't hear. Something about a child—
ANOTHER: She says someone killed her child—
FIRST MAN: Who killed the child?
SECOND MAN: I didn't hear properly. Probably the
Sultan—
FIRST MAN: Who else will kill her child?
THIRD MAN: It's murder, that's what it is. To ask us to
live without food. My daughter died without food.
She was murdered.
FIRST MAN: How long are we going to starve like this?
SECOND MAN: Just a fistful of rice—a piece of meat would be
enough—
FIRST MAN: We don't want any prayer. We want food—
SEVERAL VOICES: Yes, food—we want food—not prayer—
A SOLDIER: Quiet! Quiet!
FIRST MAN (*shouting*): Kill us, kills us. Don't starve us to
death. Kill us quickly. . .
SECOND MAN: They'll kill us, will they? Let's see who
kills whom? Bring them down.
ALL: Bring him down—let's see—so they'll give us

poison instead of food, will they—kill him—kill him—
show him what we can do—

Confusion. Some of them mob the SOLDIER *and beat him.
A group of soldiers arrives and starts beating them,
ordering them to keep quiet. The riots begin.*

SCENE TWELVE

The Palace. AZIZ *is eating some fruit.* AAZAM *enters.*

AAZAM: Aziz—

AZIZ: Shut up! I've told you not to call me by that name.

AAZAM: I'm fed up of these games, Aziz, I'm going.

AZIZ: Going? Where?

AAZAM: I don't know. But I've bribed two servants of
the palace. They are to bring two horses. They'll
be here with the horses inside of half an hour. So
hurry up.

AZIZ: Fool, now you've probably made them suspicious.
I've told you a hundred times nothing can happen
to us here. You're asking for the butcher's block.

AAZAM: Have you seen the city? The people are like
mad dogs. They have been screaming, burning
houses, killing people for a whole week now. Have
you ever stepped out of the palace?

AZIZ: Of course not.

AAZAM: I have. Twice.

AZIZ: Twice! Is your skull filled with dung? Twice!
How did you go out?

AAZAM: There's a secret passage. I discovered it the day
we came here. I have been through it. Twice.
And do you know what the city is like? In the
northern part, the houses are like forts and the streets
are like little fingers. And they are full of dead
bodies. Corpses and flies. It stank so much I almost
fainted—I can't stand it any longer, Aziz. Today
the people are a little quieter. They are tired;
besides, they have to dispose of the bodies. Tomorrow
they'll start again. . .

AZIZ: Now look. Why don't you think? Just once—
once in your life time? How do you know the
servants won't betray you? Listen to me. Stay in

74

the palace. It's the safest place now.

AAZAM: Safe? This palace? Ha! The Sultan's mad.
How can you trust him? Don't you know how he can
slaughter people? How can you trust this lord of
skins? It's better to trust servants. Listen. You
know there are those heaps of counterfeit coins in the
garden outside my window?

AZIZ: I hope they haven't scared you. After all, quite a
lot of them are our handiwork.

AAZAM: On the night we came here, I was so nervous
I couldn't sleep. So I was standing by the window,
looking at those heaps. They looked like giant
ant-hills in the moonlight. Suddenly I saw a shadow
moving among them. I stared. It was a man
wandering alone in the garden. He went to a heap,
stood there for half an hour, still as a rock. Then
he dug into the heaps with his fists, raised his fists
and let the coins trickle out. It was frightening.
And you know who it was? Your Sultan. He does
that every night—every single night—it's like
witchcraft—

AZIZ: So you are running away because the Sultan has
insomnia? What about all that you were hoping
to get? And what happens to me if you go?
How will Ghiyas-ud-din Abbasid explain the
disappearance of his disciple?

AAZAM: You come with me too, Aziz. I can't go alone.
I've tied all our presents in a bundle. It's a huge
bundle. Will last us for ever. You are a clever man,
Aziz. I know I am a fool. I can't survive without
you. . . . It's time. The horses will probably have
come. Let's go. Come on. . .

AZIZ: I order you to stay, Aazam.

AAZAM: I can't. I can't. I'll die of fright here.

AZIZ: All right then. Go. Get out, you traitor.

AAZAM: What else can I do? I wish you would come too.
Look. We'll forget all this wealth, these courts,

this luxury and live in peace. Please come . . . please, Aziz, I'll kiss your feet—

No reply.

I'm going, Aziz. . .

No reply.

Good-bye.

Goes out.

AZIZ: Idiot!

SCENE THIRTEEN

Another part of the Palace. MUHAMMAD *and* BARANI.

MUHAMMAD: May I know why, Barani?

BARANI: It's as I said, Your Majesty, I have just received
a letter from Baran and it says my mother's dead.
I couldn't be by her side in the last moments of her
life. I must be there at least for her funeral.

MUHAMMAD: What did she die of, do you know?

BARANI: I don't know, Your Majesty. The letter didn't
say anything more.

MUHAMMAD: I see. (*Pause.*) And you will return to the
court after the funeral, won't you?

BARANI (*frightened*): I don't know, Your Majesty.

MUHAMMAD: If you are only going for the funeral, why
shouldn't you be able to come back?

BARANI (*desperately*): I don't know.

MUHAMMAD: Don't you? Because I do. She died in the
riots, didn't she, when my soldiers butchered everyone
in sight—old men, women, children, everyone?
So you see, even I know what is happening in my
kingdom. I may be responsible for that massacre,
I accept. But have I really fallen so low that even
you have to lie to me?

BARANI (*almost crying*): I don't know. I don't know.
Please don't ask me. I beg of you.

> *Silence. A* SOLDIER *enters running.*

SOLDIER: In the name of Allah. A terrible thing—
Your Majesty, I don't know how to—

MUHAMMAD: What is it now?

SOLDIER: Your Majesty, Aazam Jahan, the friend of His
Holiness Ghiyas-ud-din Abbasid, is dead.

BARANI: Dead?

SOLDIER: Murdered, Your Majesty. I was on sentry duty
at the mouth of the secret tunnel from the palace.

77

I heard a scream. I ran to the spot. It was Aazam
Jahan. He was lying in a pool of blood.

BARANI: Heaven have mercy on us!

MUHAMMAD: Was anyone else there?

SOLDIER: Two horsemen, Your Majesty. They had a big
bundle with them. But before I could even shout,
they were gone I didn'ι even see their faces—

MUHAMMAD: Did he say anything before he died?

SOLDIER: No, Your Majesty. He was alive ιor a while.
When I went near I thought—J thought—

MUHAMMAD: Yes?

SOLDIER: I thought he was laughing—giggling. But of
course it could be just—his dying breath—

> *There is a long silence.* MUHAMMAD *stares at the*
> SOLDIER, *stunned and incredulous.*

MUHAMMAD: Not a word of this to anyone. Not even to
His Holiness Ghiyas-ud-din Abbasid. No one in the
palace must know. You understand?

SOLDIER: Yes, Your Majesty.

MUHAMMAD: Go back to your place. And ask the doorman
to fetch His Holiness—at once.

SOLDIER: Yes, Your Majesty.

> *Goes out.*

MUHAMMAD (*almost to himself*): Don't you think it's ironic
that a man who has just come from Arabia should
prefer the bloody streets to the palace?

BARANI: But I don't understand, Your Majesty, I can't
understand how—

MUHAMMAD: You wanted to see history formed in front of
your eyes, didn't you? Just wait a few moments,
and you'll see not just the form but the coiled
intestines of it.

BARANI (*wounded*): Your Majesty is a learned man and
has every right to laugh at a poor fool like me.
But I implore Your Majesty to understand I am not
going because my life here has been fuιile. I have
spent seven years here and the greatest historians of
the world would have given half their lives to see a

year in it. Your Majesty has given me a gift——

MUHAMMAD: Must there be a farewell speech before you go?
You want to go. Go. That's all there is to it.

Silence.

BARANI (*suddenly remembering*): But the public prayer!
It's to start within half-an-hour! It wouldn't be
right to start it when the palace is in mourning.
Your Majesty must——

MUHAMMAD: No, no, no! This is the first public prayer
in my kingdom after a silence of five years! We are
praying because a holy man like Ghiyas-ud-din
Abbasid has come to our land and blessed us! We
can't let anything stop that! (*Laughs.*) Oh Barani,
Najib should have been here now. He would have
loved this farce.

> AZIZ *enters with soldiers.* BARANI *and* MUHAMMAD
> *bow. The soldiers bow and retire.*

AZIZ (*blessing them*): May Heaven guide Your Majesty.

MUHAMMAD: I hope Your Holiness is well.

AZIZ: Who would have grounds for complaint when the
generosity of Your Majesty looks after him?

MUHAMMAD: I hope Your Holiness has not been too
inconvenienced by the riots. I was busy and couldn't
attend to your needs personally. And now that I
see you, I stand a bearer of evil tidings. We have
just received some tragic news. (*Pause.*) Aazam
Jahan's body was found outside the palace. He
was murdered.

AZIZ: May Allah save our souls. What's happening to
this world? What's man coming to if even an
innocent like Aazam Jahan isn't to be spared the
sword?

MUHAMMAD: Who are you?

> *Silence. For a moment no one speaks.* AZIZ *is obviously
> frightened.*

Who are you? How long did you hope to go on
fooling us with your masquerade?

BARANI: But your Majesty—

MUHAMMAD: Answer me. Don't make me lose my temper.

AZIZ: I am a dhobi from Shiknar. My first name was
Aziz. There have been many others since then.

BARANI: But—what about His Holiness?

MUHAMMAD: Do you know the punishment for killing a
saint like Ghiyas-ud-din Abbasid? And for deceiving
me and my subjects?

AZIZ (*bolder*): No, Your Majesty, though I have never
underestimated Your Majesty's powers of imagination
But it would be a grave injustice if I were punished,
Your Majesty.

BARANI: What's happening here?

AZIZ: 'Saint' is a word meant for people like Sheikh
Imam-ud-din. I doubt if your Majesty would have
used it for Ghiyas-ud-din. I know I am a dhobi
and he was a descendant of the Khalif. But surely
Your Majesty has never associated greatness with
pedigree.

MUHAMMAD: Be careful, dhobi. Don't overreach yourself.

AZIZ: I daren't. But since Your Majesty came to the
throne, I have been your most devout servant.
I have studied every order, followed every instruction,
considered every measure of Your Majesty's with the
greatest attention. I insist I am Your Majesty's
true disciple.

MUHAMMAD: Don't try to flatter me. I am accustomed
to it.

AZIZ: It's hardly flattering you, Your Majesty, to say
I am your disciple. But I have watched Your
Majesty try to explain your ideas and acts to the
people. And I have seen with regret how few have
understood them.

BARANI (*who is just beginning to comprehend*): Your Majesty,
this scoundrel is trying to spread a net of words
around you. It's dangerous even to talk to him.
He must be punished at once.

AZIZ: Come, sir, let's be sensible. You know His Majesty
will never do that to me.

MUHAMMAD: Won't I?

AZIZ: Forgive me. But Your Majesty has publicly welcomed me as a saint, started the public prayers after a lapse of five years in my honour, called me a Saviour. Your Majesty has even—forgive me for pointing it out, but I wasn't responsible for it—fallen at my feet, publicly.

BARANI: Villain—

AZIZ: But I am not a common blackmailer, Your Majesty. I stand here on the strength of my convictions and my loyalty to you.

MUHAMMAD: What do you want to say?

AZIZ: I was a poor starving dhobi, when Your Majesty came to the throne and declared the brotherhood of all religions. Does the Sultan remember the Brahmin who brought a case against him and won? I was that Brahmin.

MUHAMMAD: Was the disguise necessary?

AZIZ: I think o. (*Pause.*) Soon after that Your Majesty introduced the new copper currency. I succumbed to its temptation.

BARANI: God... God...

AZIZ: There was enough money in that business, but too much competition. Soon it became unprofitable, so we took the silver dinars and went to Doab and bought some land there for farming.

BARANI: But this is nonsense! There has been a famine there for five years...

MUHAMMAD: That's exactly his point. They got the land dirt-cheap and collected the State subsidy for farmers. When they were discovered, they ran into the hills and became robbers. (*With mock humility to* AZIZ.) Am I right?

AZIZ: Dare I contradict what the whole world knows about His Majesty's wisdom? But Your Majesty missed out an important stage in my life. Your officers track down criminals with the zest of a tribe of hunters and there was only one way to escape them. We joined them as servants. We had to

81

shift the corpses of all the rebels executed by the
State and hang them up for exhibition.

Such famous kings, warriors and leaders of men
passed through our hands then! Beautiful strong
bodies and bodies eaten-up by corruption—all, all
were stuffed with straw and went to the top of the
poles.

One day, suddenly I had a revelation. This was all
human life was worth, I said. This was the real
meaning of the mystery of death—straw and skin!
With that enlightenment I found peace. We left
the camp and headed for the hills.

MUHAMMAD: Yes, that was a rather important stage.

AZIZ: One day I heard about a beggar who claimed to be
Ghiyas-ud-din Abbasid and was on his way to the
capital—I couldn't resist the temptation of seeing
my master in person.

I admit I killed Ghiyas-ud-din and cheated you.
Yet I am Your Majesty's true disciple. I ask you,
Your Majesty, which other man in India has spent
five years of his life fitting every act, deed and thought
to Your Majesty's words?

BARANI: This man should be buried alive this minute!

AZIZ: I only acted according to His Majesty's edicts.

MUHAMMAD (*exploding*): Hold your tongue, fool! You
dare pass judgement on me? You think your
tongue is so light and swift that you can trap me by
your stupid clowning? Let's see how well it wags
when hanging from the top of a pole. I haven't
cared for the bravest and wisest of men—you think
I would succumb to you? A dhobi, masquerading
as a saint?

AZIZ (*quietly*): What if I am a dhobi, Your Majesty?
When it comes to washing away filth no saint is a
match for a dhobi.

> MUHAMMAD *suddenly bursts into a guffaw. There is a
> slight hysterical tinge to the laughter.*

MUHAMMAD (*laughing*): Checkmate! Checkmate!
I don't think I have ever seen such insolence. This

man's a genius—all right, tell me. What punishment
should I give you for your crimes?

AZIZ: Make me an officer of your State, Your Majesty.

MUHAMMAD: That would be punishing myself—not you.

AZIZ: All these years I have been a beggar wasting my
life and I'm not proud of that. I beg Your Majesty
to give me a chance to show my loyalty. I'm ready
to die for my Sultan.

MUHAMMAD: I don't know why I am acting like a fool.
Yet perhaps a State office really would be the best
punishment for you. You'll have to return to Arabia
after Aazam Jahan's funeral, and disappear on the way.
Can you do it?

AZIZ: It certainly won't be the first time I've done that.

MUHAMMAD: Good. Then go to the Deccan. I'll give
you a letter to Khusrau Malik appointing you as an
officer in his army. He'll look after you.

AZIZ: What can I say? How can I express my gratitude?
In the name of the Prophet, I swear—

MUHAMMAD: Don't overdo it. It's time for the prayer.
Remember, you are still His Holiness Ghiyas-ud-din
Abbasid and you have to be there to lead the prayer.
Be off now.

AZIZ: Your Majesty's most faithful servant.

> *Bows and retires.* MUHAMMAD *slowly moves to the
> throne. He looks tired, dispirited. There is silence
> for a while.* BARANI *can't contain himself any longer.*

BARANI: But why? Why?

MUHAMMAD: All your life you wait for someone who
understands you. And then—you meet him—
punishment for wanting too much! ... As he said,
'One day suddenly I had a revelation.'

BARANI: By all the history I know, I swear he'll stab you
in the back. This is sheer folly. He is a thief and a
murderer and Your Majesty knows he won't keep
trust. Once he has power in the Deccan, his
ambition will know no barriers. He is bound to find
unlimited scope for his villainy there. He is bound to

rebel against the Sultan. How can you not see that,
Your Majesty?

MUHAMMAD: I forgave Ain-ul-Mulk once, and you were
on my side then.

BARANI: But how can one mention Ain-ul-Mulk in the
same breath as this rascal?

MUHAMMAD: Last week I received a letter from Ain-ul-Mulk.
He has invited me and my subjects to his capital to
stay there until the famine here subsides.

BARANI: He is a great man, a great friend of yours—

MUHAMMAD: A friend? How are you so sure it's his
friendship that invites us to his capital? You know
that, since the day he killed Sheikh Imam-ud-din,
he has lost his hold on people. His maulvis won't
support him, his people don't trust him. He needs
my support now. How do you know he isn't
inviting me to strengthen himself?

BARANI: Then ... Your Majesty isn't accepting the
invitation?

MUHAMMAD: There is only one place to go back to now.
Delhi. Back to Delhi, Barani, I have to get back to
Delhi with my people.

BARANI: But why—why are you doing this to yourself and
your people? Your subjects starve for you—struggle
for you—die for you—and you honour this murderer?
What's the logic in it? It's criminals like him that
deserve to die. Death would be too simple a
punishment for him. It wouldn't be enough if you
flogged the skin off his back. It wouldn't be enough
if you had his tongue pulled out. It wouldn't even
be enough if you had him put in a sack and tied to a
running horse—

MUHAMMAD: Bravo! I doubt if even that dhobi could
have thought of so many tortures—

> BARANI *shudders as though he were slapped in the face.*

If justice was as simple as you think or logic as beautiful
as I had hoped, life would have been so much clearer.
I have been chasing these words now for five years and
now I don't know if I am pursuing a mirage or

fleeing a shadow. Anyway what do all these subtle distinctions matter in the blinding madness of the day? Sweep your logic away into a corner, Barani, all I need now is myself and my madness—madness to prance in a field eaten bare by the scarecrow violence. But I am not alone, Barani. Thank Heaven! For once I am not alone. I have a Companion to share my madness now—the Omnipotent God! (*Tired.*) When you pass your final judgement on me, don't forget Him.

BARANI: Who am I to pass judgement on you, Your Majesty? I have to judge myself now and that's why I must go and go immediately. I am terrified when I think of all the tortures I recommended only a moment ago. I am a weak man, Your Majesty. I don't have your strength to play with violence and yet not be sucked in by it. Your Majesty warned me when I slipped and I am grateful for that. I ask Your Majesty's permission to go while I'm still safe.

Waits for an answer. There's no answer. MUHAMMAD *is sitting on the throne with his eyes closed.*

Your Majesty—

No answer.

Your Majesty—

MUHAMMAD (*opening his eyes*): Yes?

BARANI: Is Your Majesty not feeling well?

MUHAMMAD: I am suddenly feeling tired. And sleepy. For five years sleep has avoided me and now suddenly it's coming back. Go, Barani. But before you go—pray for us

Closes his eyes again. BARANI *bows and exits, obviously in tears. There is silence on the stage for a while, and then a* SERVANT *comes in.*

SERVANT: In the name of . . .

He sees that MUHAMMAD *is asleep and goes out.* MUHAMMAD's *head falls forward on his chest in deep sleep. The* SERVANT *re-enters with a shawl which he*

carefully wraps round the Sultan. He is about to go out when the MUEZZIN'S *call to prayer is heard. The* SERVANT *turns to wake the Sultan, then after a pause goes out without doing so.*

MUEZZIN *(off-stage)*: Alla-Ho-Akbar! Alla-Ho-Akbar!
Alla-Ho-Akbar! Alla-Ho-Akbar!
Ashahado La Elaha Illilah
Ashahado La Elaha Illilah
Ashahado Anna Muhammadur Rasool Illah
Ashahado Anna Muhammadur Rasool Illah
Haiyah Alis Salaat—Haiyah Alis Salaat
Haiyah Salil Falaa—Haiyah Salil Falaa
Alla-Ho-Akbar! Alla-Ho-Akbar!
La Elaha Illilah......

As the MUEZZIN'S *call fades away,* MUHAMMAD *suddenly opens his eyes. He looks around dazed and frightened, as though he can't comprehend where he is.*

Badal Sircar

EVAM INDRAJIT

Translated by
Girish Karnad

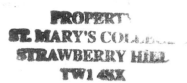

INTRODUCTION

WRITING about Badal Sircar's *Evam Indrajit* (literally, 'and Indra-jit') is like going on a sentimental journey; a nostalgic foray into the recent past of the Indian theatre; an encounter with the bitter-sweet memories of a struggling sensibility trying to strike roots in a barren land; because, after all, it is only in relation to Indian theatre history that *Evam Indrajit* really makes its presence felt; otherwise it is just a very good, sensitively written play, like many others written in the last decade in India.

The year 1962 is important to India for many reasons. 1962 was a year of great political turmoil. But it was also the year when Dharamvir Bharati's Hindi play *Andha Yug* was performed by Theatre Unit (Bombay). *Andha Yug* was a small beginning but the seeds of creative pride had been sown and a determined effort at looking at one's surroundings was to become an imperative which went beyond the platitudinous slogan of seeking one's roots. This imperative found its first fully conscious expression the same year in Calcutta, where a lean and balding Bengali architect was fulfilling his assignment as an urban designer and also writing a play, later to be recognized as a milestone in the history of modern Indian drama. The play was *Evam Indrajit*, written in Bengali by Badal Sircar.

Immediately after Independence, the concept of a composite Indian culture had taken birth. While on one level it prodded Indian artists to compete with the best in the world and assert their Indian identity, on another level it served to instil in the mind of the artist the almost pitiable craving for a sanction from the West. The measure of omniscience and superiority granted to the cultural palate of the West was ridiculous and humiliating, but even this humiliation ultimately contributed to the idea of a composite Indian culture.

In the theatre, the Indian People's Theatre Association (the cultural front of the Communist Party of India) had been very active in the pre-Independence era. But some of its political deci-sions in the late forties led to the disillusionment of many creative talents hitherto associated with the IPTA. With the coming of Independence, the IPTA lost its hold on many of its stalwarts. One of the major breakaways was Sombhu Mitra who was primarily responsible for major developments in the theatre in the early fifties. His production of Tagore's *Raktakarabi* in 1954 and his adaptations of Ibsen's plays shaped the future of the 'minority' theatre in India, and Indian theatre of the sixties drew its inspiration directly from Mitra. The fact that he travelled all over the country with his plays helped in shaping the talent of the sixties.

With the performance of Sircar's *Evam Indrajit* in Bengali in Calcutta in September 1965, theatre practitioners all over India became aware of a major talent and a major play. The play provided for them the shock of recognition. It was about the Indian reality as they knew it; it was a theatrically effective and crystallized projection of all the prevalent attitudes, vague feelings and undefined frustrations gnawing at the hearts of the educated urban middle class.

The intellectually alive urban middle class regards itself as the backbone of the country. Their so-called middle class values have been glorified and yet their genuine and deeper values have always been attacked by those who swear by fashionable Marxist dogmas. The middle classes have been made to feel guilty for opting for stability, aspiring for culture and believing in a national identity. In Bengal, the contradiction was resolved at a certain level with the middle classes aligning themselves with the left forces. In other parts of the country, the best elements in the middle classes were opting for the armed forces or the administrative services. *Evam Indrajit* is in some ways about the residue; the residue consists of those who have failed to adjust, align, and ceased to aspire, and also those who are enmeshed in the day to day struggle for survival.

The play starts with the Writer in search of a play. As he furiously tears up his manuscripts, his inspiration appears as a woman whom Sircar calls Manasi—'the creation of the mind' and perhaps an Indian counterpart of Jung's *anima*. The Writer's dilemma is related to what he considers the limitedness of his experience. He does not know 'people', he has not experienced life at its primitive and basic reality; and he is goaded to write only about those who at that moment are sitting in the auditorium (incidentally, the middle classes in Calcutta and Bombay are known for their addiction to theatre in spite of the inroads it makes into their budget). The Writer finds them undramatic (Sircar hitting at the traditional concept of the dramatic in relation to subject matter). Meanwhile The Mother, eternal and typical, keeps popping in to deliver her homilies. There is a totally bewildered incomprehension on her part of The Writer's need to write at the cost of neglecting important human functions like eating and sleeping. Throughout the play we shall find The Mother and Manasi counterpointing each other.

The Writer suddenly turns towards the audience and calls out to four latecomers and asks them to come on-stage. As the four give their names, The Writer does not accept the name of the fourth. The fourth ultimately confesses to having shied away from giving his real name. He is not Nirmal, but Indrajit (the name of the mythical rebel Meghnad who defeated Indra, the Indian Zeus). Fear prompted him to practise this minor deception—the fear of the consequence of deviating from the social code (its rules are never defined, but they range from social inhibitions to deep-rooted social taboos). From this point in the play The Writer takes over like an ubiquitous and omniscient presence, probing the lives of Amal, Vimal, Kamal and Indrajit.

The humdrum existence of Amal, Vimal and Kamal is made theatrically captivating, and we laugh at them, sympathize with the monotony of their existence, and then like Indrajit (because everybody in the audience identifies himself with Indrajit), start aspiring for a life harnessed to definite worries and cares because the 'anguish' of being aware has become an impossible burden.

The yearnings and dissatisfactions of an adolescent Indrajit or his insistence on an existence beyond geography, are feelings that the educated middle class mind has known often. His love for Manasi, the taboo attached to it (she is his first cousin on the mother's side), his wanting to break the taboo and failing to accomplish it, his anger at the state of affairs and his total inability to do anything are again common experiences in India. His failure to fulfil his love makes him see his own existence through the wrong end of the microscope. He finds our mean little world ridiculous because it can be blown up by the flick of a switch, because it is so small when placed against the vastness of the cosmos. Then comes a stage when he realizes that even the fulfilment of his love would not have provided the answer. A visit to London (a onetime Mecca for Indians) proves disappointing. He contemplates suicide as an act of faith, but finds himself incapable of the act.

At this point Sircar suddenly changes 'scale' (a feat in which he is very accomplished and which he employs as his major technique throughout), with Manasi intruding upon Indrajit's cogitation to ask him to eat some food—which has been the function of The Mother so long. The Writer feels betrayed, and Manasi is shocked at what she has said, and reverts to her original role to ask, 'Have you written anything yet?'

The Writer insists that Indrajit does not have a core, a commitment; he is too elusive to be contained within the structural framework of the play, because he denies reality and questions its very base. But Manasi insists that Indrajit is good material because he can still dream, and it does not matter whether his dreams accomplish anything or not. The Writer asks her, 'But how do you know?' Manasi does not know, she only believes, and that is all she can do.

The Writer asks himself: Belief? In What? Belief in *pataal*, in the Nether World, in the circle for condemned souls? At this point a bolder shift in scale is effected with the entrance of Indrajit, slightly cynical and married to a giggling wife. She is also introduced as Manasi, because Indrajit has concluded that distinctive individual qualities are a fiction of the mind.

But the real Manasi is still there at the same old place. Indrajit still meets her from time to time, but it is no longer the same. For Indrajit finds himself looking at parallel railway tracks on either side—tracks with an illusory meeting point: the train does not come on these tracks any more; if it had, it could have provided an opportunity of total surrender and release from human bondage. He does not believe in his dreams any more, for he has now come to the bitter awareness that they were just dreams dreamt by a person who thought that he had the potential but in fact is a very ordinary person—he is Nirmal.

The scenes with the real Manasi, in terms of real time, have taken place in the past. But Sircar's fondness for Indrajit and what he stands for forces him to indulge in a sleight of hand: and in terms of theatrical presentation Indrajit is taken out of a vivid emotional past (the last scene with the real Manasi) straight into a sort of limbo, a no man's land in unreal time, for a final confrontation with The Writer.

The Writer now asserts his belief in a travel towards no defined goal, knowing for certain that the road is meaningless, the journey futile and irrational. Indrajit is quick to see the Sisyphus analogy, and the play ends with an assertion that goes beyond logic and reaches out to us like a cry for help from a drowning man with a sense of the essential and inescapable sadness of life. A political commitment on the part of Indrajit would not have shaped his destiny differently; it would have only dissipated his complexity because Indrajit is the eternal question mark, and he still seeks an answer.

Structurally Sircar anticipates and captures the hybridization of the period; for the complexity of Indrajit's situation is such that stylistic punctiliousness must give precedence to what needs to be expressed with uncompromising honesty.

When Indrajit unwittingly emerges almost a decade later, as a character in Satyajit Ray's *Pratidwandi*, then in spite of his real 'feel' in cinema, one finds that his wings have been clipped. An Indrajit so totally circumscribed by the realism of cinema never achieves the evocative richness of his original theatrical framework.

SATYADEV DUBEY

EVAM INDRAJIT was first presented in English by the Madras Players at the Museum Theatre, Madras in April 1970. It was directed by Girish Karnad and Ammu Matthew, with decor by Vishalam Ekambaram, music by K. S. Narayanan and lights by S. V. Krishnamurty and Adi Dalal. The cast was as follows:

THE WRITER	Bruno Castelino
AUNTIE	Yamuna Prabhu/Lakshmi Krishnamurty
MANASI	Bhagirathi Narayanan
AMAL	S. Gopalie
VIMAL	Ambi Harsha
KAMAL	A. C. Krishna Kumar
INDRAJIT	A. V. Dhanushkodi

ACT ONE

A table with a huge pile of papers on it. Sitting on the chair in front of it is the Writer, his back to the audience. He is writing. Perhaps he has been writing for some time.

'Auntie' enters. She is called 'auntie' here only for convenience. She could be 'mother', 'elder sister', anything. She is frantic because she can't make any sense of her boy's behaviour. But then, not being able to make sense is the prerogative of 'aunties'.

AUNTIE. I just can't understand you!

[*No response from the Writer.*]

I'm asking you...are you coming in to eat or aren't you? You are the limit! I can't put up with this any longer...

[*No response.*]

Why don't you speak?

WRITER. I'll have finished in a moment.

AUNTIE. You have already said that three times—I am *not* going to call you again.

WRITER. You have said that three times too, Auntie.

AUNTIE. Do what you want. Night and day—scribble, scribble, scribble. No food, no drink, just scribble. Only God knows what will come out of all this scribbling...

[*She goes out grumbling. The 'scribbling' has of course come to a stop already. The Writer gets up and walks downstage reading what he has written so far. A girl comes in. She will be called 'Manasi'.*]

MANASI. Finished?

WRITER. No.

MANASI. Won't you read out what you have written so far?

WRITER. Haven't written a thing.

[*Tears up the papers.*]

MANASI. Why did you do that?

WRITER. It's no good. I have nothing to write about.

MANASI. Nothing?

WRITER. What shall I write? Who shall I write about? How many people do I know? And what do I know about them?

MANASI. [*Pointing to the audience.*] There are all these people. Don't you know any of them? Don't you know anything about any one of them?

WRITER. Them? Oh yes. I do know a couple of them. A few like us. But they won't make a play.

MANASI. Try.

WRITER. I have tried.

[*He throws away the bits of paper and goes back to the table. After a brief pause Manasi goes out. The Writer turns round suddenly and advances towards the audience. At exactly this moment four gentlemen are looking for their seats in the auditorium. The Writer calls out to them.*]

Listen....My dear sir....You there...

FIRST MAN. Eh! Are you addressing us?

WRITER. Yes, please. Would you mind stepping over here for a moment?

SECOND. All of us?

THIRD. On stage?

WRITER. Yes, if you don't mind. There's some important work.

[*The four advance towards the stage.*]

FIRST. How do we get on there?

WRITER. This way....Here. Up these steps.

[*The four go up.*]

WRITER. May I know your name?

FIRST. Amal Kumar Bose.

WRITER. And...yours, please?

SECOND. Vimal Kumar Ghosh.

[*The Writer turns to the third man.*]

THIRD. Kamal Kumar Sen.

WRITER. And...?

FOURTH. Nirmal Kumar...

WRITER. [*Suddenly shouts.*] No....It can't be!

[*Silence. The four look at him in surprise, and freeze.*]

Amal, Vimal, Kamal and Nirmal? No, it can't be. You must have another name. You have to have. Tell me truly, what's your name?

[*The stage is plunged into darkness. Amal, Vimal and Kamal withdraw leaving the fourth man centre-stage. The Writer's voice is heard in the dark.*]

What's your name?

FOURTH. Indrajit Ray.

WRITER. Then why did you call yourself Nirmal?

INDRAJIT. I was scared.

WRITER. Scared? Of what?

INDRAJIT. Scared of unrest. One invites unrest by breaking the norm.

WRITER. Have you always called yourself Nirmal?

INDRAJIT. No, but I do now.

WRITER. Why?

INDRAJIT. I'm older now. Age is afraid of joy, of happiness. It only wants comfort. Peace. Now Indrajit only wants the comfort of a dark, cloudy sky.

WRITER. How old are you?

INDRAJIT. A hundred. May be two hundred. I don't know. According to the Matriculation Certificate, thirty-five.

WRITER. Where were you born?

INDRAJIT. In Calcutta.

WRITER. Education?

INDRAJIT. In Calcutta.

WRITER. Work?

INDRAJIT. In Calcutta.

WRITER. Marriage?

INDRAJIT. In Calcutta.

WRITER. Death?

INDRAJIT. Not dead yet.

WRITER. Are you sure?

INDRAJIT. [*After a long pause.*] No, I'm not sure.

[*The stage lights up slowly, but not fully. The four stand like statues staring at the rear wall of the auditorium. The Writer turns to the audience, looks at them and then speaks in the tone of a tired teacher.*]

WRITER. According to the census of 1961, the population of Calcutta is 2,92,12,891. Of them about two and a half

per cent are graduates. They are known by different names.
They are the middle-income group, although within that group
there is enough disparity of income. They are the intellectuals,
although if they really relied on their intellect, they would
die of starvation. They are the educated minority, if a degree
is indeed a mark of education. They are the élite, because they
are well aware of their difference from the rest. They are Amal,
Vimal, Kamal.

[*The three go out.*]

And Indrajit.

[*Indrajit looks at the Writer and goes out. There is anguish in his
eyes, exhaustion in his movements.*]

It's possible that there is drama in their lives. Enough drama
to make short scenes—any number of them. It's even possible
that one day a great playwright will make a play out of them.

AUNTIE. [*Enters.*] Aren't you going to eat tonight?

WRITER. No.

[*Auntie goes out. Manasi comes in.*]

MANASI. Written anything?

WRITER. No.

[*Manasi goes out.*]

I've written many plays. I want to write many more. But...I
know nothing about the suffering masses. Nothing about the
toiling peasants. Nothing about the sweating coal-miners.
Nothing about the snake-charmers, the tribal chieftains or the
boatmen. There is no beauty in the people around me, no
splendour, no substance. Only the undramatic material—
Amal, Vimal, Kamal and Indrajit.

[*Slow darkness on the stage.*]

I am...Amal, Vimal, Kamal and Indrajit.

[*A chorus of voices whispers in the dark.*]

VOICES. Amal, Vimal, Kamal and Indrajit.

Vimal, Kamal and Indrajit.

Kamal and Indrajit.

And Indrajit.

Indrajit.

Indrajit.

Indrajit.

[*Suddenly loud music drowns the voices. White, shadowless glare on the stage. The stage is empty. The music stops suddenly. A college bell rings. Indrajit comes in. His movements are those of a man much younger than thirty-five, though there is no special make-up on his face. He is followed by Amal, who looks serious as befits a Professor. Amal, Vimal and Kamal take on appropriate voices and gestures although there is a hint of puppet-show in their movements.*]

AMAL. Roll Number Thirty-four!

INDRAJIT. Yes, Sir.

AMAL. Every body continues in its state of rest or of uniform motion in a straight line unless it is compelled by an external impressed force to change that state.

[*The bell rings. Amal goes out. Indrajit stands up. Vimal enters.*]

VIMAL. Roll Number Thirty-four!

INDRAJIT. Yes, Sir.

VIMAL. Poetry, in a general sense, may be defined to be 'the expression of imagination'.

[*The bell again. Exit Vimal, Kamal enters.*]

KAMAL. Roll Number Thirty-four!

INDRAJIT. Yes, Sir.

KAMAL. The fundamental elements of the essay are logical development, expressive language, lucidity of thought and a balanced combination of theory and facts.

[*The bell. Exit Kamal.*]

INDRAJIT. A balanced combination of theory and facts. A balanced combination of theory and facts. Expression of the imagination. Expression of the imagination. State of rest or of uniform motion. State of rest or of uniform motion. State of rest or of uniform motion.

[*Amal, Vimal, Kamal come in noisily and surround Indrajit. They are all young now.*]

AMAL. Not a cricketer? Just because he was out for two you don't call him a cricketer?

VIMAL. But is that the way to bat? What the hell is he going to do in the Second Test?

KAMAL. But look, cricket is a game of glorious uncertainty. What do you say, Indrajit?

INDRAJIT. True enough.

AMAL. You mean there is no skill in it? What are you saying?

INDRAJIT. But who's saying that?

VIMAL. I don't care what you say, but cricket isn't half as exciting as football.

INDRAJIT. That's true.

KAMAL. But then, Texas style films are exciting. So why see good films?

VIMAL. Amal, have you seen any film of Yul Brynner?

AMAL. Every one of them! Brother, can he act! You know you can praise Marlon Brando as much as you like. But he isn't a patch on Yul Brynner. Have you seen them, Indrajit?

INDRAJIT. A couple!

KAMAL. Oh, go on.... That skin-head!

AMAL. Yes, yes, but it's because he has such a marvellous head that he can keep it skinned.

VIMAL. But a 'marvellous head' means something quite different!

KAMAL. Einstein's head, for instance.

INDRAJIT. The other day I saw a book on Einstein's theory. Couldn't understand a word.

AMAL. Einstein says there are four dimensions, not just three.

VIMAL. And the fourth dimension is Time. Right?

KAMAL. Search me! I can't even understand college physics! That reminds me, Amal, is your practical book ready?

AMAL. I have got my brother's book. Will just have to copy that. What's the date of submission?

VIMAL. Thirteenth, I think. I haven't even started yet. And how far have you got, Indrajit?

INDRAJIT. I started again yesterday. The first time I started I found an excellent book to read and couldn't put it down—

KAMAL. Which one?

INDRAJIT. *The Complete Plays of Bernard Shaw.*

AMAL. Shaw! Oh, he is fantastic! A real whip, I tell you. Have you read *Man and Superman*?

VIMAL. I've only read the *Plays Pleasant*.

KAMAL. You know, our Pramatha Nath Bishi has also started writing plays like Shaw?

AMAL. Come on! Where's G.B.S. and where's P.N.B.?

VIMAL. Bishi loads his plays with politics.

KAMAL. And why not? There'll always be politics in literature. There should be!

AMAL. Come, come. Literature should embody all that's true, good and beautiful. It has nothing to do with politics. Politics is dirty.

VIMAL. Look, Brother, I object to 'dirty'. If Truth is dirty, ignoring it would be sheer escapism. Literature should be a reflection of life. Realistic. Don't you agree, Indrajit?

INDRAJIT. I'm not very clear actually. True, literature should be realistic. But to say it should be a naked reflection of life...

KAMAL. God! Do you know what time it is? Half past seven.

AMAL. Oh My God! My practical book! Come on, come on...

VIMAL. We are going that way.

KAMAL. Come on, Amal.

[*Amal and Kamal go out.*]

VIMAL. Aren't you coming home?

INDRAJIT. I, I've to finish some work first.

VIMAL. Where?

INDRAJIT. Just...[*Points after Amal and Kamal.*]

VIMAL. Then why didn't you go with them?

INDRAJIT. Didn't strike me then.

VIMAL. Well, *I'll* have to foot it alone now.

[*Exit Vimal. This entire dialogue has been accompanied by a slow, repetitive pattern on the tabla. Now the rhythm gets faster and more complex. The Writer enters.*]

WRITER. Hello! You still there?

INDRAJIT. Yes.

WRITER. What are you doing?

INDRAJIT. Nothing.

WRITER. Didn't they come today?

INDRAJIT. They did.

WRITER. Who?

INDRAJIT. Amal, Vimal and Kamal.

WRITER. What did you do?

INDRAJIT. Nothing. Just gossiped.

WRITER. About what?

INDRAJIT. Nothing in particular.

WRITER. Cricket, cinema, physics, politics, literature?

INDRAJIT. Eh? Yes, cricket, cinema, physics, politics and literature. How did you guess?

[*The Writer takes out a few monkey-nuts from his pocket.*]

WRITER. Have one.

INDRAJIT. What should one do, do you think?

WRITER. About what?

INDRAJIT. I'm tired of being a student.

WRITER. What do you want to do?

INDRAJIT. I don't know. Sometimes I just want to run away.

WRITER. Where to?

INDRAJIT. Don't know. Some place, you know, somewhere far away. I don't know what'll be there—jungle probably, or desert, or iceberg. Birds—penguins, ostriches. Wild animals—kangaroo, jaguar. Strange people—Bedouin, Eskimo, Maori....

WRITER. In a nutshell, The Simple School Geography. The textbook prescribed by the D.P.I. for Standard Six.

INDRAJIT. There must be a world outside geography. It's not here. But it'll be somewhere far away—outside—beyond.

WRITER. Beyond cricket, cinema, physics, politics and literature?

INDRAJIT. Yes, beyond all that.

WRITER. Good. Let's go.

INDRAJIT. Where?

WRITER. Well, you said you wanted to go away.

INDRAJIT. Now?

WRITER. Why not?

INDRAJIT. Don't be stupid. I shouldn't have talked to you about it.

WRITER. How much do you have in your pocket?

INDRAJIT. About eight annas. Why?

WRITER. I have about a rupee and a quarter. Let's start from Howrah Station and go as far as a rupee and twelve annas will take us. After that, we can walk.

INDRAJIT. If I knew you were going to make fun of me, I wouldn't have talked to you about it.

WRITER. I am damned serious.

INDRAJIT. [*Watches the Writer for any trace of a smile. But the Writer is really serious.*] What about Mother?

WRITER. True, there is Mother.

INDRAJIT. And the exams are just round the corner.

WRITER. O.K. We'll talk about it after the exams. [*Offering him some more nuts.*] Here. There are a few left.
  [*Goes out.*]

AUNTIE. [*From inside*] Indrajit...

INDRAJIT. I am coming.
  [*But doesn't move. Auntie enters.*]

AUNTIE. Aren't you going to eat tonight? How long do you want me to wait?

INDRAJIT. Look, Mother...

AUNTIE. What?

INDRAJIT. Suppose...I have to go away...somewhere.

AUNTIE. I can never make any sense of what you say. Come and eat. The food is getting cold.
  [*Goes out, followed by Indrajit. A chorus of voices is heard singing the following song. Slowly at first, then faster.*]

VOICES. One–two–three
  One–two–three–two–one–two–three
  One–two–three–two–one–two–three
  Four–five–six
  Four–five–six–five–four–five–six
  Four–five–six–five–four–five–six
  Seven–eight–nine
  Seven–eight–nine–eight–seven–eight–nine
  Seven–eight–nine–eight–seven–eight–nine

Nine–eight–seven–six–five–four–three–two–one

[*The Writer enters half-way through the song. At the last line of the song, he joins in with the chorus and walks down-stage.*]

WRITER. Undramatic. It's all totally undramatic. You can't make a play out of these people. It isn't possible. You there—Amal, Vimal, Kamal...

[*They come in giggling and surround the Writer.*]

AMAL. How are things, Poet?

WRITER. All right.

VIMAL. Any new epics?

WRITER. Nothing special.

KAMAL. Come, come, Brother, don't hide it. Afraid we will copy it? Don't worry, *baba*, we can't! We have forgotten our spelling.

[*They burst out laughing.*]

WRITER. I have written only a short poem.

AMAL. There, you see. That's more like it. All right. Let's hear it.

VIMAL. Sing, Heavenly Muse...

KAMAL. If we understand it, tear it up. If we don't, send it to a literary journal.

[*Laughter again.*]

WRITER. Do you want to hear it?

ALL THREE. Yes, yes, of course.

WRITER. One–two–three
One–two–three–two–one–two–three
Four–five–six
Four–five–six–five–four–five–six
Seven–eight–nine
Seven–eight–nine–eight–seven–eight–nine

AMAL. Then?

WRITER. Nine–eight–seven–six–five–four–three–two–one

VIMAL. Carry on.

WRITER. That's all.

KAMAL. That's all?

WRITER. Yes, that's all.

[*A short silence. Then the three burst out laughing.*]

AMAL. Bravo! Marvellous!

VIMAL. You are a genius!

WRITER. Did you understand that?

KAMAL. I would have in the Arithmetic Class. But this is a poem, after all. Not so easy!

[*Laughter again.*]

WRITER. Actually I want to write a play.

AMAL. And give up poetry? Just like that?

WRITER. Not just like that. I have been thinking about it for quite a while.

VIMAL. Write it. Write it down. Get hold of Bishu and ask him to produce it at the College Reunion.

KAMAL. But Bishu is so particular. Do you know Sanat Choudhury of the Fourth Year? Well, he had written a play...quite a good play really, but Bishu didn't like it. Said it didn't have a proper dramatic climax.

AMAL. What sort of a play do you want to write? Social?

WRITER. What do you mean—Social?

VIMAL. You don't even know what Social means? Then what are you going to write?

KAMAL. Social means—about this day and age—about our time, you know...

WRITER. Yes, of course, I'll write about our times.

AMAL. What's the plot?

WRITER. There isn't one.

VIMAL. I see...what about the theme?

WRITER. The theme? Well..., us!

KAMAL. Who 'Us'?

WRITER. Well, all of you, Indrajit, me...

AMAL. Us? Good luck to you then.

VIMAL. What drama is there in our lives, mate?

KAMAL. Look, Brother, a play about us will have no female characters in it.

[*Laughter.*]

AMAL. Don't talk nonsense, Kamal. What about that heroine in your street?

VIMAL. That's right. I had forgotten all about her. How far has that affair progressed, Kamal?

KAMAL. Brother, it isn't going beyond window-poetry. The real Romeo here is Amal. You know what happened during the last Pooja festival at Puri! Ask him. Ask him.

VIMAL. This is news to me. Amal, you've been hiding it from me...

AMAL. Oh, go away...

KAMAL. Come on now, darling boy, tell him. Tell him. Why so shy?

[*The three talk in whispers. The Writer listens from a distance. Manasi crosses the stage. The three stare after her. Then talk in whispers. Then laugh. Manasi comes out again—as another girl, with a bag in her hand and a different gait. The same response. Again, Manasi enters, but dressed simply and with Indrajit. The three stare, curious and jealous. Indrajit and Manasi go out talking.*]

AMAL. Did you see that?

VIMAL. Well, well! I had been wondering why our darling Indrajit was acting so strange!

KAMAL. Sinking—Sinking—Drinking water! Did you see, Poet?

WRITER. Yes.

AMAL. And what did you understand?

WRITER. The play won't be without female characters.

VIMAL. Make Indrajit the hero. We'll be the soldiers.

KAMAL. And do you know the heroine?

AMAL. How should I? Indrajit hasn't said a word about her.

VIMAL. He is very secretive.

KAMAL. He isn't secretive...he is just bloody vain. Thinks he is a superior being. I know that type.

AMAL. Do you know her, Poet?

WRITER. Who?

VIMAL. What's happened? Inspired? He means the heroine of your play.

WRITER. She is called Manasi.

KAMAL. There, you see, he knows her! Perhaps he has been introduced to her by Indrajit.

WRITER. No.

AMAL. Come, Poet, don't try that on us.

WRITER. Honestly, I have seen her for the first time today.

VIMAL. All right, we'll believe you. Now tell us, what has Indrajit told you about her?

WRITER. Nothing.

KAMAL. So you've seen her for the first time, Indrajit hasn't told
you anything, and yet you know her name is Manasi.

WRITER. I don't know her name at all. I just felt it should be
Manasi.

AMAL. Terrific! God alone knows when he is normal and when
he is 'inspired'!

WRITER. What shall we call the play?

VIMAL. A title even before you write it?

KAMAL. Yes, yes, of course, one starts with the name. All right,
Poet. You tell us. We know you have a real knack for christen-
ing.

WRITER. I was thinking of calling it 'Amal, Vimal, Kamal,
Indrajit and Manasi'.

AMAL. No, no. That won't fit into the title-page.

VIMAL. Why do you want to shove us in? We are only the
soldiers, after all!

KAMAL. Call it 'Indrajit and Manasi'. That's best! Look, we had
better move...

AMAL. Where shall we go?

VIMAL. What about giving us some tea, Kamal?

KAMAL. O.K.

  [*They go.*]

WRITER. Indrajit and Manasi. Indrajit and Manasi. [*To the audience, pontificating.*] As you all know, different conditions, different cultures, different countries have produced plays about
Indrajit and Manasi. Mythical plays, histories, social plays,
comedies, tragedies...all kinds. Hordes of Indrajits and
Manasis have appeared from all levels of society, in all forms,
with all possible names...and it's difficult to say what joys and
sorrows, what meetings and partings, what pride and hatred,

what mental blows and reactions have shaped their plays. The love of Indrajit and Manasi. An immortal dramatic theme...
Indrajit!

[*Indrajit enters. After the Writer's rhetoric, his voice sounds flat and bored.*]

INDRAJIT. What are you shouting for?

WRITER. [*Theatrically.*] Speak, Indrajit...

INDRAJIT. What about?

WRITER. Narrate your tale...that tale which is ever old and ever new, which started in the age of the *Mahabharata*...

INDRAJIT. Can't you put it more simply? What do you want?

WRITER. [*Deflated.*] Your and Manasi's story.

INDRAJIT. Manasi? Which Manasi?

WRITER. That girl I saw you with that day.

INDRAJIT. Oh! Her! But she isn't Manasi. Her name is...

WRITER. I don't want her name. I have named her Manasi.

INDRAJIT. What do you mean you have named her? Her parents call her...

WRITER. Listen, what does it matter what they call her? You just tell me...

INDRAJIT. What?

WRITER. About yourself and Manasi. What is she to you?

INDRAJIT. Sister!

WRITER. [*Pause.*] Sister?

INDRAJIT. Well, cousin then.

WRITER. Cousin? Why?

INDRAJIT. What do you mean why? Her mother is my aunt, that's why.

WRITER. I mean why were you with her?

INDRAJIT. She had to come to our house. I was seeing her home. I do that often.

WRITER. I see—so she isn't called Manasi.

INDRAJIT. No, I've already told you that.

WRITER. I thought you two were discussing something.

INDRAJIT. Yes, we were.

WRITER. Very seriously.

INDRAJIT. [*Laughs.*] Did you think so? Yes, probably that's how it looked. But I like talking to her. We often take a long way round to her house.

WRITER. Good, so you like talking to her. Why?

INDRAJIT. Well—It's difficult to say. Perhaps because it's so different from all the daily chatter.

WRITER. I see. So there's no cricket, politics, literature.

INDRAJIT. No, no cricket, politics or literature. Not every time, anyway.

WRITER. Then what do you talk about?

INDRAJIT. All sorts of things. About me, my friends and acquaintances. She talks about her family, her friends and her college...

WRITER. And then?

INDRAJIT. And *then*? Well, what sort of things do you and I talk about?

WRITER. Cricket, cinema, literature...

INDRAJIT. No, not every time. We talk about other things besides. About your writing, for instance, people, the future... Things one wants and doesn't want...

WRITER. I see. Penguins, Kangaroos, Eskimoes...

INDRAJIT. And why not? I can't talk about them to everyone.

WRITER. But you can to Manasi.

INDRAJIT. Her name isn't...

WRITER. I know her name isn't Manasi. But would you mind terribly if I called her Manasi?

INDRAJIT. [*Laughs.*] Not really. Besides I like your name. Her real name doesn't have the same poetry.

WRITER. All right then. Answer my question.

INDRAJIT. What question?

WRITER. Could you talk to her about things you discuss with me?

INDRAJIT. Not only could I but I have already done so. I have told her a lot of things I wouldn't tell you.

WRITER. Really?

INDRAJIT. Not that I couldn't. But I haven't anyway. It's not as though they were something special—just tit-bits from here and there. Some thoughts. Problems. Some things I like. Some which

2

I don't. Mostly very ordinary, very minor things.

WRITER. She is a friend of yours, isn't she?

INDRAJIT. I suppose so. I like talking to her, that's all. I feel happy after talking to her. Light. You know—all this that goes on all day, every day, unchanging...Well, don't you feel that?

WRITER. What?

NDRAJIT. That all these minutiae—they are all meaningless. There is just a large wheel going round and round. And we go round and round with it.

WRITER. One–two–three–one–two–three–two–one–three.

NDRAJIT. What did you say?

[*The song 'One–two–three' begins. Amal comes in as a professor.*]

AMAL. Roll Number Thirty-four!

INDRAJIT. Yes, Sir.

AMAL. What is the specific gravity of iron?

INDRAJIT. Eleven point seven, Sir.

[*A bell rings. Exit Amal. Vimal enters.*]

VIMAL. Roll Number Thirty-four!

INDRAJIT. Yes, Sir.

VIMAL. Who was Mazzini?

INDRAJIT. One of the founders of modern Italy.

[*A bell rings. Exit Vimal. Kamal enters.*]

KAMAL. Roll Number Thirty-four!

INDRAJIT. Yes, Sir.

KAMAL. How has the ancient Indian Literature been influenced by the essential asceticism of the Indian spirit?

INDRAJIT. The influence of the asceticism of the Indian spirit on ancient Indian Literature can be seen in the profusion of inter-polations and the way descriptions, theoretical analyses and unrelated tales continually hamper the flow of the main story.

[*Exit Kamal. Loud music drowns Indrajit's voice. Enter Amal, young and boisterous.*]

AMAL. Indrajit, will you please answer the roll call for me? I'm going to a film.

INDRAJIT. All right.

[*Exit Amal. Enter Vimal.*]

VIMAL. Indrajit, can you lend me your chemistry notebook next Saturday?

INDRAJIT. O.K.

[*Exit Vimal. Enter Kamal.*]

KAMAL. Can you lend me a rupee, Indrajit? I'll return it on Monday.

INDRAJIT. I'm afraid I can't today. Tomorrow perhaps?

[*Exit Kamal. Enter Auntie.*]

AUNTIE. Shall I put the plate away then?

INDRAJIT. Just a moment, Mother.

AUNTIE. How long do you want me to wait? Just finish your supper, son, and give me my release!

[*Exit Auntie. Music gets louder and comes to an end with the refrain, 'Nine–eight–seven–six–five–four–three–two–one!'*]

INDRAJIT. We are all just going round and round and round...

AUNTIE. [*From inside.*] Indrajit...

INDRAJIT. Coming.

[*Exit. Auntie enters.*]

AUNTIE. Are you eating tonight or aren't you?

WRITER. No.

[*Exit Auntie. Enter Manasi.*]

MANASI. Finished writing?

WRITER. No.

[*Exit Manasi.*]

WRITER. One–two–three! Amal, Vimal, Kamal. And Indrajit. And Manasi. From home to school. From school to college. From college to the world. They are growing up. They are going round. Round and round and round. One–two–three–two–one. Amal, Vimal, Kamal. And Indrajit.

[*Amal, Vimal, Kamal and Indrajit are taking an exam. A table and a stool. Papers and answer books. The Writer acts as the invigilator. The bell rings.*]

WRITER. Time up. Stop writing please.

[*They continue to write hurriedly. The Writer snatches away the papers. They go out discussing in low, depressed voices.*]

WRITER. From school to college. College and examinations.

Examinations and results. And then the world.

[*Amal, Vimal, Kamal and Indrajit enter. The Writer arranges tables and chairs in the background.*]

AMAL. What will you do after passing the exam?

VIMAL. Let me pass first. I'll worry about it then.

KAMAL. Well, whether I pass or fail, I'll have to look out for a job. Father is retiring this year.

AMAL. Just looking out won't get you a job, you know. I scan the papers every morning. There just aren't any good ones going.

VIMAL. What are *you* grumbling about? I have three unmarried sisters to look after.

KAMAL. It was all good fun till now. As the results get nearer I can't even swallow my food.

WRITER. Amal Kumar Bose.

[*Amal screams with joy. The others congratulate him.*]

Vimal Kumar Ghosh.

[*As before.*]

Kamal Kumar Sen. Indrajit Ray.

[*As before in every case. Auntie comes in. They all touch her feet one after another. She blesses them. They go out noisily.*]

WRITER. Right. Now the world. On these chairs sit men of great virtue and intellect. They examine others. Judge them. Decide who is worth what. And on that long bench outside the door sit Amal, Vimal, Kamal, and Indrajit.

[*Amal, Vimal, Kamal and Indrajit enter.*]

Not yet! Not yet! One moment, please!

[*They all go out.*]

WRITER. Oh, yes! I had forgotten all about it. Before we come to that there is something more. Imagine that these chairs aren't here. Forget this bench. There's green grass here. That's a tree. And there beyond, an orange sky. The sun which rises every morning rose today as usual, and he is now setting. And in that corner, there between the branches, is the orange moon.

[*Indrajit and Manasi enter. She has a new book in her hand.*]

MANASI. Why are you giving me this present? I should give you one.

INDRAJIT. Why?

MANASI. After all, you are the successful candidate.

INDRAJIT. But where does it say that just because I've passed the examination, you have to give me a present? Why not the other way round?

MANASI. I don't know why. But that's the rule.

INDRAJIT. You always go by rules, don't you?

MANASI. [*Laughs.*] Whenever you allow me to.

INDRAJIT. You like it?

MANASI. Girls have to.

INDRAJIT. Girls have to! How often have I heard you say that about girls! Girls must follow the rules. Men can do what they like, but women must be obedient.

MANASI. But isn't that so?

INDRAJIT. I don't know. I accept several rules too. One has to study—that's a rule. One has to take exams—that's a rule. One must take up a job—that's one too. I accept them all. Of course I would have taken a job even if there was no rule about it.

MANASI. Why?

INDRAJIT. There are reasons. One is that I want to stand on my own feet. I don't like making my people pay for my education.

MANASI. And then?

INDRAJIT. There are others. Tell me one thing.

MANASI. Yes?

INDRAJIT. Is there a rule that one has to abide by rules?

MANASI. What else can one do?

INDRAJIT. One can hate rules. Why should they be there at all?

MANASI. What would be the point of hating them?

INDRAJIT. What's the point of worshipping the rope that binds you?

MANASI. I'm not asking you to worship it.

INDRAJIT. But you are! If the rope is a rule and you accept it happily—that is worshipping it.

MANASI. What else would you do with it?

INDRAJIT. Perhaps—tear it into shreds. Bring down all these walls which surround us.

MANASI. And who are you supposed to be fighting?

INDRAJIT. The world! The people around us! What you call society. Have I told you about Leela?

MANASI. Her husband died of TB, didn't he?

INDRAJIT. Yes. That's the girl. He died a few months ago. Now her in-laws have thrown her out.

MANASI. Thrown her out?

INDRAJIT. They kept her at home for a few days. Took all the Provident Fund and Insurance money they could get. Took her ornaments and threw her out.

MANASI. Then?

INDRAJIT. Apparently she is staying with a second cousin of hers. This gentleman has a small shop, which is famous for stolen and smuggled goods.

MANASI. What will happen to Leela, do you think?

INDRAJIT. Nothing more to happen. Everything that could happen has already happened. I heard about it yesterday, though it happened three months ago. Tell me what sort of a rule is that?

[*No answer.*]

You know, one day at the bus-stop a boy of about seven started pestering me. Wanted to polish my shoes, he said. But he had a child on his waist and it was playing with the polishing rag.

[*No answer.*]

I didn't get my shoes polished. I didn't give him any money either. I chased him away. If he had bothered me more, I would probably have beaten him.

MANASI. [*Clutching his hand.*] But why?

INDRAJIT. I don't know. I don't know who should be beaten. I know I shouldn't hit him—still I would have. I could not accept him. I can't accept the rule either—the rule by which a boy of eight with a child in his arms has to go polishing shoes.

MANASI. But that's a different thing.

INDRAJIT. But how? It's the same sort of thing as in your home —where you observe every rule and then say, 'I have to!'

MANASI. [*Softly.*] Are you going to scold me?

INDRAJIT. You know I am not trying to scold you. [*Manasi doesn't reply.*] Don't you?

MANASI. Yes, I do.

INDRAJIT. Then why do you say such things?

MANASI. When I see you like this I feel scared.

INDRAJIT. Like this? Like what?

MANASI. All this—this anger. Anger against rules.

INDRAJIT. [*Laughs.*] It's a pointless anger. It's blind. Powerless. It only beats its head against the wall.

MANASI. Then why do you want to hurt yourself?

INDRAJIT. You know about the Tree of Knowledge, don't you?

MANASI. Yes, I do.

INDRAJIT. If I hadn't tasted the fruit of knowledge I could have gone on living in this paradise of your blessed society of rules. Now I can only batter my head against the wall.

[*A pause.*]

MANASI. Indra!

INDRAJIT. Yes?

MANASI. You know I'm stupid.

INDRAJIT. [*Laughs.*] What's the matter?

MANASI. I can't understand all that. I see things too. But I become sad; I feel a sense of pity. I can't be angry like you.

INDRAJIT. [*After a pause.*] Do you want me not to be angry?

MANASI. No, I want you to be as you are. It's only that I'm... I'm scared.

INDRAJIT. When this anger is gone, I'll be finished.

MANASI. [*Softly.*] I know Indra. [*Pause.*] Be what you are. Don't accept. Don't accept my fear either.

[*Silence.*]

MANASI. Sometimes I wonder...What would happen to me if you weren't there?

INDRAJIT. Why?

MANASI. You'll probably get annoyed if I tell you. I can accept a lot because you are there. If you weren't there—probably I should get very angry too.

INDRAJIT. So—I'm depriving you.

MANASI. Don't say that! Don't ever say that. [*Pause.*] How can I explain it? Don't you know what you mean to me? I feel stronger because of you. Strong enough to live. Otherwise I would have just gone in. [*Pause.*] But I can't get angry. I don't want to be angry. I like life. I accept a lot of things. I have to, but it doesn't worry me. Because you are there—I can take life more easily —more... [*Suddenly.*] I can't explain!

INDRAJIT. Go on. Tell me.

MANASI. No. I can't analyse things. Let's talk of something else.

INDRAJIT. We were talking of something else.

MANASI. If I don't understand this book will you explain it to me? [*He stares at her.*] Why aren't you saying anything?

INDRAJIT. The day I get a job—I'll marry you.

MANASI. No!

INDRAJIT. Just watch.

MANASI. But don't you see—I'm your first cousin.

INDRAJIT. How could I not see? You've reminded me every time I've talked of marriage. How could I forget?

MANASI. And every time you say the same old thing again—that you won't accept it!

INDRAJIT. Of course I won't. Why should I? I shan't abide by anything...

MANASI. Not even me?

INDRAJIT. I like you, but not your rules.

MANASI. I'll soon get on your nerves.

INDRAJIT. Yes, that's another thing you go on about...

MANASI. Truly. I'm a very ordinary girl.

INDRAJIT. And I am extraordinary!

MANASI. I don't know. I think you are.

INDRAJIT. I am delighted to hear that!

MANASI. Well, then. You are *not* extraordinary.

INDRAJIT. Then there's no problem.

MANASI. What do you mean?

INDRAJIT. There should be no problem if an ordinary boy marries an ordinary girl.

MANASI. Of course, there is. Come, let's go home.

INDRAJIT. I don't want to go.

MANASI. We'll be late.

INDRAJIT. Let us.

MANASI. Yes, let us! At home I get told off every day because of you.

INDRAJIT. Home—Home—Home be damned...

MANASI. No. We won't start on that again. Get up. Let's go.

INDRAJIT. [*Gets up.*] All right.

MANASI. Oh! Angry again! And I'll be scared!

INDRAJIT. Look, you are getting late. You'll be told off at home... ·

MANASI. I am not going...

INDRAJIT. All right. Let's sit down.

MANASI. No, no, no! Let's go.

    [*Indrajit puts his hand on her shoulder. She hurriedly removes it.*]

    Indrajit! This is a public park!

INDRAJIT. So?

MANASI. [*Whispering as she points to the Writer who has just entered and is sitting in a corner.*] There—there's someone there under the tree.

INDRAJIT. So what?

MANASI. He'll see.

INDRAJIT. He will? Well, let him.

    [*Puts his hand on her shoulder. Again she removes it hurriedly and walks out. He smiles and follows her.*]

WRITER. Indrajit and Manasi. They've come a long way. A long way? Have they really come? Or are they just going round and round? Round and round? They can get married. Then the same round again. They may not get married. Again the same round. One–two–three–four–three–two–one. It's all a question of going round and round. The answer is a circle—a zero. That's why no one asks the whole question. They cut it to suit their size. The answer they get is—life. A different sort of life for each man....

    [*Enter Amal, Vimal and Kamal.*]

    Wait! Not now. Not yet.

[*Amal, Vimal and Kamal go out.*]

One moment, one single moment. Deny that circle. Deny that going round and round. Deny the whole question. One moment, one moment in the present. Life. And let's not add this life to other lives. For that will lead us to the whole problem again—resulting in a zero. Let us save this life. Let us save this one moment in the present—that is life.

[*The lights get dimmer as he finishes. Behind him is a table with chairs near it and outside the door there is a bench. The Writer goes away. Amal, Vimal, Kamal and Indrajit come and sit on the bench. They are well-dressed and serious. A bell rings. Amal gets up and goes in. He greets the invisible interviewers on the chairs. Sits on the chair in front with their permission. Answers questions silently.*]

VIMAL. Do you know the names of all the Cabinet Ministers?

KAMAL. No. Couldn't look them up.

VIMAL. We should have brought the Year Book along.

KAMAL. It wouldn't have helped. There's a limit to what one can look up.

VIMAL. Indrajit, what's the time?

INDRAJIT. Twenty-past-twelve.

KAMAL. They asked us to come at eleven. And the *burra sahib* turned up at twelve to interview us.

VIMAL. This is all a show, after all. They have already chosen their man.

KAMAL. Who's it? The one they interviewed before Amal?

VIMAL. I don't know. It won't be us. I know that.

KAMAL. How long has Amal been there?

INDRAJIT. About five minutes.

VIMAL. What do they ask for such a long time?

[*Amal gets up inside. As he tries to walk out through the front door, he is rebuked by the chairman. He giggles sheepishly and stumbles out of the other door.*]

KAMAL. Do they ask very technical questions?

VIMAL. Not very. Actually it's not the answer that matters. It's the way you answer.

KAMAL. If you don't know the answer, you should say 'I don't know' smartly.

INDRAJIT. It's very difficult to say 'I don't know' smartly.

[*The bell rings. Vimal goes in.*]

KAMAL. I've a sore throat today. Do you have any peppermints on you?

INDRAJIT. No.

[*Kamal takes out a cigarette.*]

INDRAJIT. You have a sore throat and you smoke?

KAMAL. True. It won't help, will it?

[*Puts the cigarette back.*]

KAMAL. How many interviews have you had so far?

INDRAJIT. Five.

KAMAL. Good for you! This is my fourth. Have you heard from them?

INDRAJIT. Yes, a regret letter.

KAMAL. [*Pause.*] Father is retiring next month.

[*The Writer comes in and sits by Indrajit. Pause.*]

KAMAL. What time is it?

INDRAJIT. Half-past.

KAMAL. What time were you asked to come?

WRITER. Eleven. I had another interview at ten-thirty, so I had given up all hopes of coming here. I just took a chance, that's all.

KAMAL. Are you sure they haven't called you in yet?

WRITER. Yes. I'm very lucky.

KAMAL. You *are* lucky.

[*Exit Vimal. The bell again. Kamal goes in.*]·

WRITER. Cigarette?

INDRAJIT. No, thanks, I don't smoke.

WRITER. [*Lights a cigarette himself.*] Do you know what questions they are asking?

INDRAJIT. No. They send them out through the other door.

WRITER. That's what they do usually. After all they can't have an unlimited stock of questions.

INDRAJIT. What was your other interview like?

WRITER. Not very good. Probably won't click. But it was a good job.

INDRAJIT. I see—that's why you went there first.

WRITER. Yes. But do you know—I am sure that is a wrong policy. When you badly need a job, you must go to the interview for the worse job first. The chances are better there.

INDRAJIT. Now you have made both.

WRITER. I was lucky this time. But when two interviews clash like this, I can't sleep nights. You don't know how much I need a job.

INDRAJIT. [*Smiles.*] We all need one.

WRITER. That's true enough. Generally everyone needs a job. But I need it particularly badly. The fact is—I have hired a flat —borrowed some money for it. After all one doesn't get a flat with all conveniences easily. This one is not a beauty—but at least it has an independent water closet.

INDRAJIT. I'm sorry—I don't follow you.

WRITER. The point is—I have got married without my father's permission. If I don't get a job this month, I'll lose the flat. You understand, don't you? How long can one keep a flat on borrowed money?

[*Kamal goes out. Then Amal, Vimal and Kamal come in and act as the silent interviewers. Amal rings the bell and Indrajit goes in. The entire interview is mimed.*]

WRITER. [*Throwing away his cigarette.*] Amal retires. His son Amal takes up a job. Vimal is ill. His son Vimal takes up a job. Kamal is dead. His son Kamal takes up a job. And Indrajit. And Indrajit's son Indrajit. There on the pavement is a seven-year-old boy with a box in his hand and a baby in his arms. There—on the pavement near him is a woman. Her name is Leela. Her husband died of TB. Beyond there is an orange sky under which Manasi wants to love life. Life. So many loves. So many parts and bits and parcels and pieces and molecules and atoms and they mix and mingle and move and turn and go round and round till they become a giant ferris wheel. And I have to write about them. I have to put into language the drama of these atoms going round and round. But language is senile and words are battered and maimed. [*Indrajit finishes his interview. The bell is rung.*] The bell keeps ringing. One atom is lost and another is summoned by the bell. Three atoms are ringing the bell. More atoms, many more atoms, mix and mingle and make up the ferris wheel of this giant earth that goes round and round. And one by one, seconds, minutes, hours go round and round, round and round. [*The bell rings again. The interviewers are getting impatient.*] The bell is ringing. It will ring again. Still the earth goes on, the century goes on. Our earth—our century. The ferris wheel be damned. The question itself be damned. We are here—Amal, Vimal, Kamal. And Indrajit. And I. We are here, still here, here on earth.

[*Amal, Vimal, Kamal stand up. Ring the bell frantically. But the dark deepens, leaving only the Writer in light.*]

I am divided. I am broken into pieces, into atoms. I'm a symphony composed of atoms.

> The earth is crushed, but it's still alive
> The century's old, but it listens still
> All the lights go off
> A whisper in chorus in the dark
> The earth is crushed, but it's still alive
> The century's old, but it listens still
> The earth is crushed, but it's still alive
> The century's old, but it listens still.

ACT TWO

An office. Four chairs in a row. In another part of the stage, a big chair, a big table with a telephone on it. The Writer is dusting the furniture—barely touching it with the duster.

WRITER. [*Coming downstage.*] From home to school. From school to college. From college to the world. The world is an office. Like this one. A lot of business is transacted here—very important business. A lot of people work here—Amal, Vimal, Kamal and Indrajit.
[*Amal and Vimal come in.*]

AMAL. The 8.52 was ten minutes late today.

VIMAL. A tram broke down near Sealdah station and there was a huge traffic jam.
[*Kamal and Indrajit come in. Amal and Vimal sit down.*]

KAMAL. Today I missed the 9.13 again.

INDRAJIT. I had to let two buses go. There wasn't even enough space to hang on.
[*Kamal and Indrajit sit down.*]

AMAL. [*To Vimal.*] How is your son?

VIMAL. Better. [*To Kamal.*] Has your daughter secured admission?

KAMAL. No such luck. [*To Indrajit.*] Have you found your pen?

INDRAJIT. No. Must have been stolen.

AMAL. Hareesh...

VIMAL. Hareesh...

KAMAL. Hareesh...

INDRAJIT. Hareesh...

AMAL. [*A little more loudly.*] Hareesh...

WRITER. Yes, Sir.

AMAL. Bring me a glass of water.

VIMAL. [*Loudly.*] Hareesh...

WRITER. Yes, Sir.

VIMAL. Bring me a betel-leaf and *zarda*.

KAMAL. Two cigarettes—'Scissors'!

INDRAJIT. [*Loudly.*] Hareesh...

WRITER. Yes, Sir.

INDRAJIT. Post this letter.

[*The Writer doesn't move. Nor do they give him anything. They don't even look at him.*]

AMAL. The pick-pockets have become such a terrible nuisance. The other day when the Dharamtalla tram left the Mowlali stop...

VIMAL. If you want homoeopathic medicine see Kanai Bhatta-charya. My brother-in-law had chronic dysentery...

KAMAL. They are giving her an admission test for the third stan-dard. Can you imagine! English, Bengali and Arithmetic! On top of that they want the birth certificate.

[*The Writer becomes the boss and strides in. The three half rise and then sit down scratching their heads. The Writer takes his seat and the telephone rings.*]

WRITER. Hello—hello—yes—yes—order—invoice—delivery—fifteen per cent—yes—yes—bye.

[*Changes files from the 'In' tray to the 'Out' and back again. Amal goes in and gets a file signed. Comes out. Then Vimal. Then Kamal. Then Indrajit. Then the phone.*]

WRITER. Hello—hello—yes—yes—order—invoice—delivery—fifteen per cent—yes—yes—bye.

[*Changes files from 'In' to 'Out'.*]

AMAL. Hareesh...

VIMAL. Hareesh...

KAMAL Hareesh...

INDRAJIT. Hareesh...

[*The Writer moves to the peon's stool with the duster in his hand. Again the calls.*]

AMAL. Hareesh...

VIMAL. Hareesh...

KAMAL. Hareesh...

INDRAJIT. Hareesh...

WRITER. [*Gets up. To each of them.*] Yes, Sir—Yes, Sir—Yes, Sir—Yes, Sir...

AMAL. Vimal Babu.

[*The Writer takes Amal's file to Vimal. Vimal takes it and gives him another one.*]

VIMAL. Kamal Babu.

[*The Writer takes Vimal's file to Kamal. Kamal takes it and gives him another one.*]

KAMAL. Nirmal Babu.

WRITER. Nirmal Babu has already retired, Sir.

KAMAL. Oh! Indrajit Babu.

[*The Writer takes Kamal's file to Indrajit. Indrajit gives him another file.*]

INDRAJIT. Amal Babu.

AMAL. Vimal Babu.

VIMAL. Kamal Babu.

KAMAL. Indrajit Babu.

[*This happens thrice, getting faster each time, until the Writer is practically hurling himself from table to table. The bell rings. The Writer goes in to the Boss at the sound of the bell.*]

AMAL. Hareesh...

VIMAL. Hareesh...

INDRAJIT. Hareesh...

WRITER. [*Comes out.*] I've to bring tea for the sahib.

AMAL. O...

VIMAL. O...

KAMAL. O...

INDRAJIT. O...

[*The Writer takes a round instead of bringing tea and returns downstage.*]

WRITER. After the files, tea. Then files. Then snacks. Then files. Then tea. Then files. Then tram-bus-train. There are bigger offices where even more important business is transacted. There files—then tea—then files—then lunch—then files—then coffee—then files and then office transport, taxi, car.

AMAL. [*To Kamal.*] Hello Ghosh, old boy! Going to the club tonight?

VIMAL. I'm afraid not. My wife has invited a few old friends home.

KAMAL. Hello Ray, old boy! Have you got your car back from the garage yet?

INDRAJIT. No such luck. The clutch plate's burnt out, I'm told. Couldn't even get a taxi in time this morning. My servant took forty-five minutes to find one.

[*The Writer has become the boss again. The phone rings.*]

WRITER. Hello—hello—yes—yes—the Board of Directors— conference—budget—Annual Report—yes—yes—bye! Miss Malhotra. . .

MANASI. [*Enters with a steno-pad.*] Yes, Sir.

WRITER. [*Walking about as Manasi takes dictation.*] With reference to the above letter—in connexion with the above matter, I would request you—I shall be obliged if—forward us at your earliest convenience—let this office know immediately—fif- teenth ultimo—twenty-fifth instant—thanking you—assuring you of our best cooperation—yours sincerely, sincerely yours.

[*Telephone.*]

Hello—yes—yes—the Board of Directors—conference—budget —Annual Report—yes—yes—bye!

That's all, Miss Malhotra.

[*Manasi leaves. The Writer comes out front.*]

That's all, Miss Malhotra. That's all, ladies and gentlemen. That's all

AMAL. That's all.

VIMAL. That's all.

KAMAL. That's all.

ALL THREE. [*Together.*] That's all.

[*Indrajit is quiet. They look at him wondering, then burst out laughing.*]

AMAL. Buck up, old boy.

VIMAL. Cheerio, old boy.

KAMAL. All the best, old boy.

[*They slap him on the back and go out. The Writer takes a round and becomes the peon. Goes to Indrajit who is looking at a file absently.*]

WRITER. Looking for something, Sir?

INDRAJIT. What? Yes, I am.

WRITER. What?

INDRAJIT. Something besides all this.

WRITER. Like what?

3

INDRAJIT. Well—nothing—nothing really. Is there nothing except this?

WRITER. I can't understand what you are looking for, Sir.

INDRAJIT. I don't seem to find anything, Hareesh...Anyway, let that be. Now look. Just put this file on Amal Babu's table tomorrow morning, this one on Vimal Babu's and this one on Kamal Babu's. Get the sahib's signature on this letter. I may not come tomorrow.

WRITER. Aren't you feeling well, Sir?

INDRAJIT. Well? Probably I shall not feel well tomorrow. That's possible. Good night.

[*Goes out.*]

WRITER. Amal's left. Vimal's left. Kamal's also left. Only Indrajit sits there thinking...Now he's also left. And me? I am thinking. Yes, I am thinking. Am thinking. Only thinking.

   I sit with the part, and think of the whole. I sit in the dust and think of the earth. And I screen the dust that is the earth that is crushed. Why? Are the seeds of life mixed with the dust? But the earth is crushed, the sky is barren, and the century nods in senile stupor. But I still sit and think. I still think of Man, the whole Man, and the fragments of my consciousness are still searching—searching for something else.

[*Auntie comes in.*]

AUNTIE. So you are here! I have been searching for you everywhere. What are you doing?

WRITER. Thinking. I am sitting and thinking.

AUNTIE. I see. And what are you thinking about?

WRITER. I am wondering...Who are we?

AUNTIE. What's there to think so much about in that? You are you. Who else?

WRITER. That's true enough. We are us. I hadn't thought of that; I must admit. But what are we?

AUNTIE. Listen to him. What are we? You are all bright pieces of gems, that's what you are. You've got good degrees, good jobs!

WRITER. Right again. Pieces of gems. Pieces. Scraps. I had seen that part. But I had not seen the gems aspect of it.

AUNTIE. What are you babbling now?

WRITER. That answers two riddles. Now the third one—this is not that easy.

AUNTIE. Yes...

WRITER. *Why* are we?

AUNTIE. What do you mean?

WRITER. I mean, why are we here?

AUNTIE. Oh, shut up. Why shouldn't you be here? You haven't done any harm to anyone, have you?

WRITER. No, no, no. That's not a logical answer.

AUNTIE. Who wants your logic? Forever asking such stupid questions. This is what happens when one doesn't get married at the right age.

WRITER. But how does marriage come into this?

AUNTIE. Why won't it come? Who are we—why—how—where! Why do they come into this? Why don't you get married? Answer that first.

WRITER. That's no easy question to answer, when I don't even know why I should!

AUNTIE. Listen to him. Why? Why shouldn't you? Everyone gets married. Why shouldn't you?

WRITER. That's it. That's it. That's the answer....
Everyone does it.
Why should you sneeze? Why should you cough?
Why should you smile and why should you laugh?
Why should you sulk and why should you sigh?
Everybody does it, that's why, that's why.

AUNTIE. God! He's started on his poetry again. I'm going...
[*Tries to go out. Writer stops her.*]

WRITER. Why should you love? Why should you hate?
Why should you suffer and blame it on fate?
Why should you weep and why should you cry?
Everybody does it. That's why, that's why.

AUNTIE. When did I weep or cry?

WRITER. Why should you always sleep in the night?
Why should you always try to be right?

Why should you live? Why should you die?
Everybody does it! That's why, that's why.

AUNTIE. Silly boy! I'm not going to listen to you any more. You
would be all right if you got married.

[*Exit.*]

WRITER. Yes! Marriage! Birth, marriage and death! Birth, then
marriage and then death. A long time ago I read a beautiful
story. I don't know whether you've read it or not. I've forgotten
most of it, but...There was a prince. There was a princess.
After a lot of to-do they got married. Then comes the real point
of the story. Then they lived happily and ruled over their kingdom. Kingdom or home? I can't remember the details...But
I do remember that they lived happily ever after. They lived so
happily that there was no more story to tell.

[*Marriage music. Manasi comes in, in a ghoonghat, blushing like a
bride.*]

Marriage. A man and a woman.

Dampati, jampati, jaya-pati.

A couple. In other words, bridegroom and bride.

[*Amal enters looking like a recently married man.*]

MANASI. [*Happily.*] What! Are you back already?

AMAL. I told my boss that I didn't feel well.

MANASI. [*Concerned.*] Is that true?

AMAL. I didn't feel well without you.

MANASI. [*Laughing.*] You silly!

AMAL. Aren't you glad to see me?

MANASI. [*Smiling.*] No, why should I be?

[*They laugh. Manasi comes to Amal and they embrace.*]

WRITER. *Dampati, jampati, jaya-pati.*

A couple. In other words, husband and wife.

[*Manasi becomes a housewife. Vimal sits on a chair and reads the
newspaper.*]

MANASI. Has anything special happened today?

VIMAL. No. The same old stuff.

MANASI. I thought perhaps a calamity was about to strike the
world.

VIMAL. Why? What happened?

MANASI. You haven't taken your head out of the newspaper all morning.

VIMAL. I was just glancing through. [*Puts the paper down.*] What did you want?

MANASI. Nothing. Wanted to ask you what you were doing this evening.

VIMAL. Why? What's the matter?

MANASI. Nothing really. I thought we could go for a walk.

VIMAL. For a walk?...But I had to attend a farewell party in the office. One of our men is retiring. Anyway, where did you want to go?

MANASI. Nowhere. It's all right...It's nine o'clock and you haven't shaved yet!

VIMAL. Nine! Oh my God!

[*Exit Vimal.*]

WRITER. *Dampati, jampati, jaya-pati.*

A couple. In other words, father and mother.

[*Kamal enters.*]

MANASI. What's wrong with you? Your son's down with fever and you come back at ten o'clock.

KAMAL. Here. I've brought you some barley.

MANASI. So you've brought some barley! Now! At ten o'clock! There must be a limit to how irresponsible one can be. He hasn't eaten all day.

KAMAL. Hasn't he?

MANASI. I got hold of whatever I could and gave him something.

KAMAL. How's he now? Any temperature?

MANASI. Ninety-nine. Where is the *mosambi*?

KAMAL. Our fruit-vendor is a rascal. Asked me a rupee for four. I'll bring some from the market tomorrow.

MANASI. Go in and have a wash. I'll lay the food.

[*Manasi and Kamal go out in different directions.*]

WRITER. *Dampati, jampati, jaya-pati.*

Bride—bridegroom—husband—wife—father and mother.

Amal, Vimal, Kamal and Indrajit.

[*Enter Indrajit.*]

Hello—Indrajit!

INDRAJIT. You? What a delightful surprise! I never thought we would meet here like this.

[*They shake hands.*]

WRITER. Well, well. How many years is it since we met?

INDRAJIT. About seven—I think.

WRITER. Where were you all those years? In Bhopal?

INDRAJIT. No. The Bhopal job lasted only about a year. I've been around since then. Bombay, Jullunder, Meerut, Udaipur. It's a transferable job. I keep moving.

WRITER. That's what you wanted.

INDRAJIT. Is it? I don't know.

WRITER. Why, have you forgotten? Penguin, Kangaroo, Eskimo...

INDRAJIT. Oh. The Simple School Geography. You still remember it!

WRITER. Why, have you forgotten?

INDRAJIT. No, I haven't. But my views have changed. I wonder what it would have been like—if I had really started from Howrah that day with a rupee and twelve annas in my pocket. But now I feel that there is no world beyond our geography. At least not in this country.

WRITER. Is it there in other countries?

INDRAJIT. How should I know? I have never been abroad. I had an interview for a job in Malaya. Didn't get it.

WRITER. Would you have gone if you had got it?

INDRAJIT. Why not?

WRITER. So you are not married yet?

INDRAJIT. No. Never had the time for it. You?

WRITER. The same.

INDRAJIT. What about the others?

WRITER. The others?

INDRAJIT. You know. Amal—Vimal—and Kamal.

WRITER. They are well. They have got jobs. They are married. They own houses.

INDRAJIT. Your tone doesn't indicate that all's well.

WRITER. No. No. They really are doing very well. I don't envy them, though. Would you?

INDRAJIT. I don't know.

WRITER. How is Manasi?

INDRAJIT. Manasi? Oh, yes, her! You always called her Manasi! Yes, she is all right.

WRITER. Where is she?

INDRAJIT. [*Laughs.*] What you are actually asking is whether she is married or not. No—she isn't. She is teaching in a school at Hazaribagh.

WRITER. [*Pause.*] Is that all? Nothing more?

INDRAJIT. What more do you want to learn?

WRITER. Whatever you tell me.

INDRAJIT. [*Smiles.*] There isn't anything more. Nothing worth mentioning ever happens. I have a job. She has a job. I write. She replies. We meet about once a year. We arrange to meet in Calcutta. That's all.

WRITER. Aren't you two getting married?

INDRAJIT. Not that we won't. We haven't yet, that's all.

WRITER. Why don't you get married and be done with it?

INDRAJIT. I don't know why—can't give a reason. If we had got married immediately after my graduation without thinking about it, that would have been it. We didn't know then, didn't think. We talked of so many things, sitting there in that park. Planned so many projects. Argued about so many problems. One day it just happened that. . .

[*Manasi comes and sits on the grass. Indrajit sits by her side. The Writer walks into a dark corner.*]

MANASI. I can't, Indra, I can't.

INDRAJIT. Why not?

MANASI. Don't force me, please. Give me some more time.

INDRAJIT. Time—time—time! I have been waiting for six months now.

MANASI. What am I to do? I don't have courage.

INDRAJIT. It's not a question of courage. Do you want to say

'Yes'?

MANASI. Not everything is achieved by mere wanting...

INDRAJIT. I don't know about 'everything'. But marriage, yes.

MANASI. Men can do...

INDRAJIT. I know—I know—Men can do what they like—but not women. Women can think, accept and ask for more time.

MANASI. Why are you getting annoyed?

INDRAJIT. [*Pause.*] I am not getting annoyed. I'm leaving for Bhopal tomorrow. That's why I wanted to know today.

MANASI. But Bhopal isn't the end of the world.

INDRAJIT. [*Pause.*] I don't know.

MANASI. Indra...

INDRAJIT. Manasi, I don't know—I don't know anything.

MANASI. [*Pause.*] Then try and get to know. Go to Bhopal and see...

INDRAJIT. Now who's getting annoyed?

MANASI. I'm not annoyed, Indra. I've thought about it a lot. Life isn't a game of dolls.

[*Indrajit stares at her. Darkness. A beam of light falls on the Writer.*]

INDRAJIT. So the two of us couldn't have our doll's game either. We thought a lot. Measured a lot. Counted a lot. I do even now. And I wonder if life may just remain a game of dolls. All this priceless life. Do you read the newspapers?

WRITER. Sometimes.

INDRAJIT. I read a long time ago that all those atomic weapons are controlled by buttons. And there are interlocking systems so that nobody can spark off an atomic warfare by pushing the wrong button. Just imagine, a minor oversight could destroy the whole world!

WRITER. So?

INDRAJIT. Nothing. This priceless, invaluable life—about which we think so much, measure and count...

WRITER. You mean you want to get married now but Manasi won't decide...

INDRAJIT. No, not that—at least not now. One doesn't really think of the atom bomb all the time. You look at the starlit sky

and you think of what astronomy tells us—about the insigni-
ficance of this minute earth in the solar system. What's this
human life worth, sticking to it like germs to a speck? Still, if
one thought of all this all the time, one wouldn't live.

WRITER. Yet you do think of it!

INDRAJIT. Can't help it. But there are times when I think life is
vast, when I forget how ephemeral my life is in the total flow
of time—a mere second. I forget that my existence is a pointless
particle of dust. I start believing that nothing is more valuable
than my life in this world.

WRITER. That's nature's greatest gift to us—this ability to forget.
It helps us to live.

INDRAJIT. But it's not enough! It's the gift of the Tree of Knowledge. The starlit sky confuses everything. It confuses every little
thing. You—me—Manasi—Kamal—Vimal—Amal—all.

[*Music rises in the background. Song. Darkness on stage. The Writer
and Indrajit are lit up. In the background, Manasi, standing like a
statue. On the other side appear the silhouettes of Amal, Vimal, Kamal.
The music changes slowly into a chorus of voices.*]

To seek a break in the unchanging rhythm of death is perhaps
the most foolish and futile attempt of Man in this world.

[*Manasi becomes brighter as light is focussed on her.*]

MANASI. I may be a germ, but still I seek, seek without shame.
The audacious assertion of life claims immortality in its brief
spark.

[*Light goes off. When it comes back the Writer is alone, downstage.*]

WRITER. The audacious assertion of life. Whose life? Indrajit,
Manasi, me and who else? Amal, Vimal and Kamal?

[*Amal enters.*]

AMAL. How are you, Poet?

WRITER. Fine, thank you.

AMAL. Still writing?

WRITER. Yes, occasionally.

AMAL. Have you finished your play yet?

WRITER. No. How are you?

AMAL. Not well, not well, my dear fellow.

WRITER. Why? What happened?

AMAL. I'm working in this rotten A.B.C. Company. I've wasted my life there. Six years as the Senior Assistant. Yet they have taken a Madrassee Babu as the Assistant Manager.

WRITER. Is he good?

AMAL. What are you asking? This is the day of the Madrassees. We Bengalis will die at the hands of other Bengalis. Actually it's all my fault. I had an offer from P.Q.R. Company. Didn't take it. Thought I should get promotion in my office—so why go? What's the point? I'm fed up with life.

WRITER. How are things at home? All right?

AMAL. How can they be all right? How long can I continue to be in the same post? Senior Assistant for the last six years! All right, Brother. I must go. I have got some work.

[*Exit Amal. Enter Vimal.*]

VIMAL. How are you, Poet?

WRITER. Fine, thank you.

VIMAL. Still writing?

WRITER. Yes, occasionally.

VIMAL. Have you finished your play yet?

WRITER. No. How are you?

VIMAL. Oh! Well, carrying on. Our firm has got a good heavy engineering contract. So have been transferred to Ranchi. Am leaving tomorrow.

WRITER. Are you taking your family along with you?

VIMAL. Yes, yes, we have been given good quarters. As for 'family' there's only the Mrs. I've sent my son to La Martiniere School. I don't know what schooling is like in Ranchi, you see.

WRITER. In short, you are doing quite well.

VIMAL. Well. Muddling along, what? All right. I've to go now. Have to do some last-minute shopping in the New Market. Can I give you a lift?

WRITER. No thanks.

VIMAL. O.K. then. So long.

[*Exit Vimal. Enter Kamal.*]

KAMAL. How are you, Poet?

WRITER. Fine, thank you.

KAMAL. Still writing?

WRITER. No.

KAMAL. I know. I know. Problems of life kill all those hobbies. I too used to play the mouth-organ once. Couldn't develop that talent. When it got damaged, I couldn't even get it repaired. Inflation you know. Have you insured yourself?

WRITER. Not yet.

KAMAL. Tut, tut, tut. This is not proper—this carelessness. You need security in life, Brother. What other security is there in life? Get yourself insured—at once—for at least ten thousand.

WRITER. In whose name?

KAMAL. Aren't you married?

WRITER. No.

KAMAL. Oh—ho! But that can be mended easily. It doesn't take much time to get married. And children will start arriving soon. Later you will have to pay a higher rate of premium. Besides, you'll need some support in your old age. Come—tell me. Tell me—how much do you want to get insured for? I'll make all arrangements...

WRITER. Have you given up your job then?

KAMAL. Given my job up? In this day and age? You think I've gone mad? Still—I am involved in a business deal. If it clicks, I'll be able to kick my job, insurance, everything. Listen, do you know any financier who could lend about twenty-five thousand? It's a marvellous scheme. Forty per cent profit guaranteed. I can prove it to you...

WRITER. I'm afraid all that's beyond me rather.

KAMAL. Not to worry. I'll catch someone. It's such a gold mine, there'll be no shortage of financiers. I'll say bye then. Think about your insurance seriously.

[*Exit.*]

WRITER. The audacious assertion of life claims immortality of its brief spark. These are sparks. I have to write my play on the story of the claims of immortality of these brief sparks—Amal, Vimal, Kamal and Indrajit.

[*Indrajit enters.*]

WRITER. And what immortality does your life claim, Indrajit?

INDRAJIT. Immortality? What do you mean?

WRITER. Nothing. Have you met Manasi?

INDRAJIT. No. Not yet. But I've to meet her in that park, over there.

[*Goes upstage.*]

WRITER. That park over there. Under that shaggy tree. So many words, so many old hopes are mixed in the dust there. And in the green grass, life germinated, was nurtured, was reared up, by so many words weaving and entwining one another in so many glowing days. Indrajit and Manasi, they will sit in that park again. They'll sit on that green grass, and they'll talk. More words. But words grow old. The same words come back again and again. But still, let's go and sit on that grass sweet with the smell of earth. And sit together, for some time, in the rosy breeze of the twilight.

[*Manasi comes and sits near Indrajit. They begin to talk. The Writer goes to one corner.*]

INDRAJIT. We won't meet again for a long time.

MANASI. Why?

INDRAJIT. I want to go out.

MANASI. Out? But you are out of Calcutta already.

INDRAJIT. No. Further out. Abroad.

MANASI. Where exactly?

INDRAJIT. London.

MANASI. Have you found work there?

INDRAJIT. Not yet. But I've collected enough money to let myself go. I have enrolled in an engineering school. The passport is all ready. I'll look for some work when I get there.

MANASI. And if you don't find any?

INDRAJIT. I'll find something.

MANASI. But what if you don't?

INDRAJIT. I'm bound to find something. I'm alone after all. Won't need much.

MANASI. How long are you going to go on like this?

INDRAJIT. As long as I can.

MANASI. Do you like this sort of existence?

INDRAJIT. No.

MANASI. Then?

INDRAJIT. Then what?

MANASI. Why don't you settle down in one place?

INDRAJIT. Will that improve matters?

MANASI. I don't know.

INDRAJIT. I don't either. Actually words mean little. I don't know what 'improvement' means any more. There's no question of improvement.

MANASI. [*Pause.*] Indra...

INDRAJIT. Yes...

MANASI. Would you settle down if we got married?

INDRAJIT. I don't know. I can't decide anything now. I could once.

MANASI. Do you often feel angry with me?

INDRAJIT. Not any more. Who knows what marriage would do to us. Perhaps even our friendship would die.

MANASI. Perhaps there will be another type of friendship—something deeper, more meaningful...

INDRAJIT. I don't know, Manasi, I don't know anything. I've thought a lot. Argued a lot. But I can't find an answer. I'm tired now. Now arguments don't mean a thing. Nor can I do anything. I just feel tired—exhausted. I just do what I feel like doing at the moment.

[*Silence.*]

MANASI. Let's go for a walk.

INDRAJIT. Come.

[*They go. The Writer enters with heavy steps.*]

WRITER. I am tired—I am very tired
      Let all these rapid questions be.
      In the mute enveloping darkness let me just go to sleep.
      What's the use of all these words?
      Why fling arguments in the wild winds?
      I am sick of reasoning now.

Alone, in the depth of shadows, let me just go to sleep.
My quests are tired and still is unknown the last analysis
of the world.
My efforts limp while the heavy earth lies immobile
and numb.
Hope, waiting hope, waiting on the banks of death is
tired too.
Go, take your questions, logic, arguments with you.
Let me be...
In the dark womb of shadows let me sleep...
I am very tired.

ACT THREE

Amal, Vimal and Kamal are playing cards. Each line is followed by the throw of a card. After every third card, the cards are mixed and the game begins anew.

AMAL. On 15 August 1947 India became Independent.

VIMAL. We escaped from the clutches of the British Empire.

KAMAL. Now we have to build a self-sufficient, self-supporting society.

AMAL. We have to dismantle the capitalist system.

VIMAL. Fascism is leading the world to destruction.

KAMAL. Communism kills man's sense of himself and his freedom.

AMAL. The democratic process is agonizingly slow.

VIMAL. Dictatorship has always been proved an evil.

KAMAL. Most people have to suffer under any system.

AMAL. Our country has become the home of anarchy and corruption.

VIMAL. Our government can't be trusted to do anything.

KAMAL. Power corrupts...

AMAL. Politics is dirty...

VIMAL. Just concern yourself with your own work.

KAMAL. If I am alive, all is well.

AMAL. There has been no promotion.

VIMAL. The living quarters are terrible.

KAMAL. Business is bad.

AMAL. My family is ill.

VIMAL. My son failed again.

KAMAL. My father has died.

AMAL. Bloody shame.

VIMAL. Damned nuisance.

KAMAL. Ugh!

AMAL. Vimal...

VIMAL. Kamal...

KAMAL. Amal...

AMAL. Vimal...

VIMAL. Kamal...

KAMAL. Amal...

VOICE. [*Off-stage.*] And Indrajit.

[*Enter the Writer.*]

AMAL. How are you, Poet?

VIMAL. How are you, Poet?

KAMAL. How are you, Poet?

WRITER. Received a letter from Indrajit yesterday.

AMAL. What does he say?

VIMAL. Hasn't he gone abroad?

KAMAL. Hasn't he returned yet?

WRITER. He has finished his course successfully.

AMAL. That's good news.

VIMAL. He won't have any difficulty finding a job. Engineers are in great demand.

KAMAL. Foreign degrees have great value in our country.

WRITER. Do you want to hear what he says?

AMAL. Yes, indeed.

VIMAL. Is it a very long letter?

KAMAL. Let it be—let it be.

[*The Writer reads the letter. The three go on playing cards silently.*]

WRITER. Calcutta, Bhopal, Bombay, Jullunder, Meerut, Udaipur, Calcutta, London. Everything goes round and round like a wheel. Still it's not a proper wheel, it's a spiral. And that precisely is the tragedy—the tragedy of knowing. I catch something. And just when I understand it, it suddenly ends and I throw it away. Then again I grab at something else. Still the hope for a sudden, unexpected, wonderful happening doesn't die. One continues to feel that this isn't all. Some time something must happen to fill the world with a dazzling light, throwing the past into obscurity. What a silly dream. The sleep ends—but not the hangover of the dream.

[*Indrajit comes in and stands by the Writer.*]

INDRAJIT. Whatever I wished to have, I have got. But there is no sense of achievement in it—that is the bitter truth. It is stupid to hope that more will come and one will sprout more hands to seize it. It's pathetic. Just a dream. The past and the present are two ends of a single rope. They are apart because the dream is alive. Otherwise the future could easily be broken down and thrown into the arms of the past. The past instead of remaining a wait for the vague, smoky future could be turned into a well-defined point—Death!

MANASI. [*Enters.*] Death!

INDRAJIT. Yes, death. Dying! That is the greatest happiness. Who knows how many became happy by dying. They have caught all the future in the mould of the past—that's why they are happy. I shall have to die like that one day. Then why not now?

MANASI. Don't say that... Live! Live long!

INDRAJIT. One needs faith to live. Faith in God, faith in fortune, faith in man, faith in work, faith in revolution, faith in oneself —faith in love. Tell me—which of them is alive in me today?

MANASI. Not faith in life?

INDRAJIT. Life? Engaging oneself in petty trivialities when one can't answer the only question that matters. What meaningless poses and lies for which there is no real need. No real need. Still, one must do it. There's life. Man's life. And I am one among a million. The lie in my life is the lie in the lives of millions.

MANASI. What do you want to do?

INDRAJIT. What shall I do? Shall I go to sleep? Or shall I laugh it off? Perhaps that's better. Life is so farcical that it is no use hiding one's laughter away...

[*Indrajit bursts into laughter, suddenly. The Writer and Manasi walk off in different directions. Amal, Vimal, Kamal, suddenly start laughing. The Writer re-enters and walks downstage. Loud laughter which slowly dies away as...*]

WRITER. [*To the audience, as though they have been laughing.*] Don't laugh. For God's sake, don't laugh. I beg of you, be quiet, please. True, I am not succeeding with the play. But don't you see I'm trying my best. A Play—a play about Amal, Vimal, Kamal? And Indrajit?

[*Auntie enters.*]

4

AUNTIE. Aren't you eating?

WRITER. No.

[*Auntie departs. Manasi comes in.*]

MANASI. Aren't you eating?

WRITER. [*Hides his face in his hands.*] Not you too...

MANASI. Sorry—I forgot—Have you written anything?

WRITER. How can I? Indrajit isn't coming back. He has written three letters in three years. Every time, the same old thing.

MANASI. What?

WRITER. About going round and round and round and not dying. Those arrogant dreams going round in the head are not dying. Tell me—how can you write a play about someone who sees life realistically and dreams about it romantically?

MANASI. I can't think of a better protagonist for a play.

WRITER. No. It is not possible. The more I tie him up in a plot the more he escapes; says it isn't real. The more lines I write for him, the more he stands outside them. Says they are not real. Oh! He knows too much—altogether too much.

MANASI. Still he dreams.

WRITER. That dream will collapse one day.

MANASI. I know.

WRITER. And then?

MANASI. Let it.

WRITER. And then what?

MANASI. Then he won't try to clutch at a dream.

WRITER. What then? Won't he go under?

MANASI. Let him. Then he may find firm earth at the bottom. Then he may start living again.

WRITER. How do you know that?

MANASI. Me? What do I know? Nothing. I am stupid. I know nothing. I only believe...

[*Exit.*]

WRITER. Belief? Belief in the firm earth at the bottom?

INDRAJIT. [*Comes in reciting.*]
    Keeping afloat
    Cl utching at a piece of straw,

Life resting on a wretched faith
Of a believer.
The land is blurred
In a grey mist of sighs,
The bright realms beyond the clouds
Are lost in lies
In this love sojourn.
So take away the crutches
Of false consolations!
Take away the blindfold of faith
From the eyes!
Get drowned!
Go under and see
How far is the bottom
How deep!
Man moves;
Man is the strangest of creatures!
He builds his house on the rocks
In the depth of the seas.

WRITER. Indrajit...

INDRAJIT. Yes.

WRITER. You are back.

INDRAJIT. Yes.

WRITER. When did you come?

INDRAJIT. Some time ago.

WRITER. Where are you now?

INDRAJIT. In Calcutta.

WRITER. What are you doing?

INDRAJIT. Working.

WRITER. Married?

INDRAJIT. Yes.

WRITER. Ah! So Manasi agreed...

INDRAJIT. No.

WRITER. Then?

INDRAJIT. Married somebody else.

WRITER. Somebody else?

INDRAJIT. Yes.

WRITER. Whom?

INDRAJIT. A woman...

WRITER. Name?

INDRAJIT. Manasi.

WRITER. But how is that possible?

INDRAJIT. That's what usually happens. Manasis come and go. One can get married to only one of them. The others come and go. Manasi's sister Manasi. Manasi's friend Manasi. Manasi's daughter Manasi.

WRITER. Like Amal, Vimal and Kamal?

INDRAJIT. Yes, like Amal, Vimal, Kamal and Indrajit.

[*Enter Manasi as Indrajit's wife.*]

Ah! Meet my wife Manasi. A very old friend of mine—he's a Writer.

WRITER. *Namaskar.*

MANASI. *Namaskar.* What do you write?

WRITER. Whatever's possible.

MANASI. You are writing anything now?

WRITER. I'm trying to write a play.

MANASI. Could you read it out to me?

WRITER. Yes, indeed. When I finish it.

MANASI. Oh! But is there a lot left?

WRITER. Not much. I'll start in a day or two.

MANASI. You mean you haven't started yet?

WRITER. How could I?

MANASI. But you just said you would soon finish it.

WRITER. Well, you see, in this play there isn't much difference between the beginning and the end. It's a circular play.

MANASI. I'm afraid I don't quite understand...

INDRAJIT. Of course you don't, Manasi. It's not meant to be understood...

MANASI. But surely one says something to be understood.

INDRAJIT. One used to. But now it's a question of habit.

MANASI. Go on...Don't be silly...

INDRAJIT. It is silly. Look there...

[*Amal, Vimal, Kamal enter and stand chatting at the other end of the stage.*]

MANASI. Who is that?

WRITER. They are Amal, Vimal, and Kamal.

AMAL. Plutocracy—monarchy—democracy.

VIMAL. Imperialism, fascism, marxism.

KAMAL. Economics, politics, sociology.

AMAL. Quotations, tender, statement.

VIMAL. Report, minutes, budget.

KAMAL. Meeting, committee, conference.

AMAL. Civilization, education, culture.

VIMAL. Literature, philosophy, history.

KAMAL. *Brahma, nirvana, bhooma.*

AMAL. Raj Kapoor, Mala Sinha, Vishwajit.

VIMAL. Umrigar, Krishnan, Milka Singh.

KAMAL. Hemant Kumar, S. D. Burman, Lata Mangeshkar.

AMAL. Doctor, homoeopath, poet.

VIMAL. Tram, bus, train.

KAMAL. Heat, dirt, mosquitoes.

AMAL. Son, daughter, wife.

VIMAL. Master, driver, chief.

KAMAL. Uncle, niece, mother-in-law.

MANASI. What are they saying?

INDRAJIT. They are talking.

[*Amal, Vimal, Kamal go out, gesticulating silently.*]

MANASI. About what?

INDRAJIT. I don't know. Ask the Writer.

MANASI. [*To the Writer.*] Is there nothing besides that?

WRITER. There should be—there must be!

[*To the audience.*] Don't you think there is anything to talk about besides that? No? Then what should one write? A play with such stuff? Who will produce it? Who'll see it?

[*Indrajit and Manasi start to go out.*]

Indrajit, wait a bit.

[*Indrajit comes back. Exit Manasi.*]

Tell me one thing before you go.

INDRAJIT. What?

WRITER. Where is Manasi?

INDRAJIT. You saw her a moment ago.

WRITER. Not this Manasi. But the Manasi of Hazaribagh.

INDRAJIT. She is in Hazaribagh.

WRITER. Don't you write to her?

INDRAJIT. Sometimes.

WRITER. Do you meet her?

INDRAJIT. Occasionally.

WRITER. Where?

INDRAJIT. In that park. Under that tree.

WRITER. Do you talk?

INDRAJIT. Yes.

WRITER. About what?

INDRAJIT. The same things as usual. About me and her.

WRITER. As usual? The sort of things Amal, Vimal and Kamal
were saying?

[*No answer.*]

What Indrajit?

[*He enters the park. Manasi is sitting there under the same old tree.*]

MANASI. Say something.

INDRAJIT. What?

MANASI. Whatever you were going to say.

INDRAJIT. What was that?

MANASI. About yourself, about your family.

INDRAJIT. Oh yes! My wife looks after the house. I work in the
office. My wife goes to a film. I go with her. My wife goes to
her parents' house. I eat in a restaurant. She comes back. I go
marketing.

MANASI. What is all this, Indrajit?

INDRAJIT. Life at home. You wanted to hear about it.

MANASI. I don't want to hear all this.

INDRAJIT. Then what do you want to know?

MANASI. About you.

INDRAJIT. Me? I walk between the rails of the railway line. It's
a straight line. I look back—the iron rails meet in a point far

away. I look ahead—the same two iron rails meet in a point far away. The further I move the more the points move too. What is behind is ahead. There is no distance between the past and the future. What's there in the past is in the future as well.

MANASI. Then?

INDRAJIT. I used to hope for the arrival of the train.

MANASI. What would happen then?

INDRAJIT. I would jump off or run or at least fall under it. Do something. But nothing happens. Because no train runs on those rails. I have found that out. Sometimes I think...

[*Pause.*]

MANASI. Yes?

INDRAJIT. I think I must stop. Not walk any further. Sleep on the track.

MANASI. [*Pause.*] How is that possible, Indrajit?

INDRAJIT. And why not?

MANASI. You have to walk the road.

INDRAJIT. I have been walking all these years.

MANASI. You have to go on walking.

INDRAJIT. I'm tired.

MANASI. You will have to go on.

INDRAJIT. But why? Why? Why? The same old road...I walk and walk and walk. Keep on walking. And yet is there no escape?

MANASI. No. There is no escape.

WRITER. No, there's no 'scape
　　　　　And yet,
　　　　　There's no 'scape.
　　　　　Hungry mornings. Wakeful nights.
　　　　　Shattered days. Bitter hours.
　　　　　I am. Even today.
　　　　　Alive. Awake. And remembering.
　　　　　There's more left,
　　　　　More of this life.
　　　　　What I was, I still am,
　　　　　Will be, beyond,

Far, far away,
Being more and more and more
It's all me—it's all I am.
And yet,
There's no escape.
I fly on the wings of fatigue
In a stupor of winged rest
My childhood flies,
And rises and dips,
And floats...
Fragments of time past.
I whirl in the wheel of work
I blow up balloons
With empty words.
I fill the grottoes with heavy echoes
And yet,
There's no escape.
You know me well.
You know all of me,
All the words of music,
Of crashing cymbals
All the dazzling lights
Sick with drunkenness
You know the multicoloured shroud
That covers the rotting corpse,
You know all that's there before
Is only a garland
Of flowers that have been
You know I end here
I'm dead.
Within me.
And yet why do I insist
That I go on?
For there is—Oh! yet there is
No escape!

INDRAJIT. But why?

MANASI. One has to carry on.

INDRAJIT. Why does one have to carry on? What is there beyond the path? Why should I carry on?

MANASI. Why does everyone carry on?

INDRAJIT. Everyone?

[*Amal enters. Sees the Writer.*]

WRITER. Hello! Amal. Where are you off to?

AMAL. I've to take an exam.

WRITER. An exam? At your age?

AMAL. Well, it's an exam arranged by the Institute of Bettermanship! I tried last year—but failed. Let's see this time—one more chance. This time I've even taken a correspondence course!

WRITER. What use is the Diploma?

AMAL. Use? Brother, every use. If I get the Associate Membership of the Institute, no one can stop my promotion. I may even become the Manager. Well, I must be off. I'm getting late.

[*Goes. Vimal comes in.*]

WRITER. Hello! Vimal. Where are you off to?

VIMAL. I am trying to get a cement permit. You know, if one does not grease the palms, the files just don't move.

WRITER. What's the cement for?

VIMAL. I'm building a house. I have taken some land under the C.I.T. scheme. The reserve price is six and a half thousand. In the auction it went up to nine thousand, eight hundred and fifty. That's just for the land, mind you. After that how much would be for the house, do you think? Government loan, Insurance loan, Employment Credit loan—I took them all—but the house doesn't rise beyond its second floor.

WRITER. Then why do you have to build it right now?

VIMAL. What else would you do? No one cares for the rupee any more. If one builds a house now, one will have a roof over one's head in old age. Besides one has to think of one's children. But I'm getting late...Goodbye.

[*Vimal goes off. Kamal comes in.*]

WRITER. Hello! Kamal. Where are you off to?

KAMAL. I've to see Shyamal at his office. He has got hold of a financier. One must have a bash at persuading him...

WRITER. Persuade him to do what?

KAMAL. Well, you see. We've got hold of an excellent business scheme. Absolutely fool-proof. There will be no difficulty about the import licence. Assembling will be easy. The demand is expanding. The goods won't even reach the market—all booked in advance! The difficulty is about the capital, you see. Shyama! and I have collected a little, but it's nowhere near enough. Even at fifteen per cent interest no money is forthcoming.

WRITER. Then don't go in for it!

KAMAL. But, my dear fellow, what will I eat? This is my work. By God's grace, I have six children. I spent a thousand on my daughter's illness. The second boy failed in the exam—so that was a net loss of a year's fees. How long can one go on like this? Anyway I can't stay long here. Goodbye.

[*Kamal goes out, along with the Writer.*]

INDRAJIT. Everyone! This is everyone! Amal, Vimal and Kamal.

MANASI. Still they carry on...

INDRAJIT. Manasi, they are happy. They have something to look forward to. A hope—an ambition—a dream—

MANASI. You don't?

INDRAJIT. No.

MANASI. Didn't you ever have one?

INDRAJIT. Oh yes, I had. I was myself then. I had accepted that I had to do something. Didn't know what, but something unusual, important, unprecedented. I used to dream then of coming up like a shooting star shattering the sky into shivers— coming up filling the sky with light from one corner to another —coming up and up until the fire in one burnt down to ashes and only a momentary flame remained in the sky...

MANASI. Are you burnt to ashes now?

INDRAJIT. Oh no! The light never came. The sky didn't burn. I could not leave the solid earth.

MANASI. Why not?

INDRAJIT. I didn't have it in me to do that. Never did. I just dreamt that I could, that's all. So long as I couldn't accept my ordinariness I dreamt. Now I accept it.

MANASI. Indrajit...

INDRAJIT. No, Manasi, don't call me Indrajit, please don't. I am Nirmal. Amal, Vimal, Kamal and Nirmal. Amal, Vimal, Kamal and Nirmal...

[*Walks downstage repeating this line. The Writer comes and stands behind him. Manasi remains seated.*]

WRITER. Indrajit...

INDRAJIT. You must be mistaken. I am Nirmal Kumar Ray.

WRITER. Don't you recognize me, Indrajit?

INDRAJIT. Who are you?...The Writer?

WRITER. I can't finish the play, Indrajit...

INDRAJIT. What's the point of finishing it? It won't ever get completed. Its end is its beginning...

WRITER. Yet one has to write.

INDRAJIT. It's your job to write. So write away. What have I to do with it? I am Nirmal.

WRITER. But you are not looking for promotion—or building a house—or developing a business scheme. How can you be Nirmal?

INDRAJIT. But...but I'm just an ordinary man.

WRITER. That does not make you Nirmal. I am ordinary too—common! Yet I am not Nirmal. You and I can't be Nirmals.

INDRAJIT. Then how shall we live?

WRITER. Walk! Be on the road! For us there is only the road. We shall walk. I know nothing to write about—still I shall have to write. You have nothing to say—still you will have to talk. Manasi has nothing to live for—she will have to live. For us there is only the road—so walk on. We are the cursed spirits of Sisyphus. We have to push the rock to the top—even if it just rolls down.

INDRAJIT. Must we, even when we know?

WRITER. Yes, we must, even when we know. We have no hope because we know the future. Our past is one with our future. We know what's behind us will also be ahead of us.

INDRAJIT. Must we still live?

WRITER. We must, we must, we must. We must live. We must
walk. We know no sacred places. Yet we must go on with the
pilgrimage...There's no respite.

[*Manasi comes and stands between the two. They look out in the distance at the horizon. The stage gets dark—except for a single ray of
light which lights them up. They intone together.*]

> And hence
> There's no end.
> There's no hope
> Of fulfilment
> By the holy shrine
> At journey's end.
> Forget the questions
> Forget the grief,
> And have faith
> In the road—
> The endless road.
> No shrine for us
> No God for us
> But the road,
> The endless road.

Vijay Tendulkar

SILENCE!
THE COURT IS
IN SESSION

Translated by
Priya Adarkar

INTRODUCTION

SHANTATA! COURT CHALU AHE is in some respects typical of Tendulkar's writings. The experience of the play, as is usual with him, stems not from a concept but a real incident. In this particular case the stimulus came from an amateur group on its way to stage a mock trial in Vile Parle (the suburb where Tendulkar lives); the bits of conversation he heard as he guided the members to their destination suggested the outline of the play. Secondly, in the actual writing of a work, Tendulkar is invariably conditioned by pressures from directors, actors and friends. The play was written for *Rangayan* at the instance of Arvind and Sulabha Deshpande and even two days prior to the performance the final draft could not be said to have been completed.

But, in another sense, the play appears uncharacteristic of Tendulkar. In his earlier works he had dwelt on the woes of the middle class with a degree of sympathy, bordering on sentiment. With *Shantata* came a parting of ways. The transformation is difficult to explain. The change was possibly the result of a deep personal experience. For, on the one hand, it unleashed characters (Benare, Sakharam, Ghasiram) in a state of collision with accepted norms and, on the other, it revealed ineffectual middle class types with an ugly, vicious leer lurking under a smug surface.

All this might, of course, sound like hindsight today. When the play was staged, ten years ago to be precise, it was received no differently than the usual Tendulkar play entered for the Annual State Drama Competition. In fact, it never even made the finals. The Jury was probably influenced by one of its members who is reported to have declared, 'This cannot be described as a play.' But undeterred by this setback, *Rangayan* went on to do thirty-five performances, risking a loss of six thousand rupees in the bargain. But the play did have an impact. In the following year Satyadev Dubey (Theatre Unit) produced it in Hindi and this time it carried the day at the competition with Sulabha Deshpande winning the prizes for both direction and acting. In 1970, Tendulkar was awarded the Kamladevi

Chattopadhyay Award and *Shantata* was adjudged 'The Play of the Year.' In 1971, he won the Sangeet Natak Akademi's Award for Playwriting. *Shantata* was translated into several languages. Tripti Mitra, the eminent actress, appeared in the main role in the Bengali version. A little later the play was made into a film by Satyadev Dubey with support from the Film Finance Corporation. The BBC broadcast it in English. There were in all more than 150 performances in Marathi and, after the first thirty-five shows, *Rangayan* could always count on a good house and even some profit.

Shantata brought Tendulkar recognition on a national scale. He came to be regarded with Mohan Rakesh, Badal Sircar and Girish Karnad as a leading force in a national theatre movement.

Obviously audiences were in a mood to listen to a playwright ready to fix a remorseless gaze on the contradictions within a personality, even the most insignificant one, a playwright who refused to offer easy legal remedies to social problems or to pin his faith on a change of heart in men. Acutely conscious of the violent impulses behind a respectable facade and of the overwhelming compulsions of sex, he could place his discoveries within a recognizably Indian context, essentially middle class, and rooted. His long association with the theatre had yielded dividends. It had taught him to mould this familiar material into dramatic shape.

Today it is easy to detect the craft that went into the plotting of the play. It is conceived as a game and the idea that all that is happening on the stage is part-mock, part-earnest gives it a 'theatrical' edge. The mock-element is all-pervasive What we are witnessing is a mere enactment of what is a rehearsal of sorts of nothing more than a mock-trial to be staged later in the day. Nowadays the game-sequence appears frequently enough in a play. It lifts the performance somewhat since it offers so much scope for uninhibited physical movement, for horse-play. Even so, it is, for the most part, little more than an inset. But in

Shantata the play and its structure revolve wholly round the idea of a game and include the essential ingredient of 'reversal'. Benare, who is on the offensive in the beginning, finds herself trapped at the close of the play. The innocuous latch which has hurt her finger and drawn her blood (as she enters the place) later shuts the group in and, in fact, takes on the dimension of a barricade. The claustrophobic atmosphere inside becomes the kind of setting where social masks are shed.

When the members of the troupe entered the room, we half-expected banter and cordiality, as among friends. Banter there was, but alongside a strong streak of pettiness. Perhaps for them theatre activity had reduced itself to an escape from personal disappointments! Benare lets out that Sukhatme is, in real life, a lawyer without a brief; here he will be seen bursting to exhibit his knowledge of the legal process. Sukhatme, for his part, has a dig at Karnik's so called grasp of 'intimate' theatre. Supported by Balu Rokde, he riles at the unfortunate Ponkshe, who has, actually failed his Inter Science Exams but professes during the trial to be an expert on scientific affairs. Ponkshe, in turn, jeers at Rokde for his total dependence on the Kashikars. And the group unites to ridicule the absurd gestures of mutual devotion made by the couple and also their childlessness. The whole lot of them try to needle Benare but at least in the first half of the play she is able to out-smart them. The name of Prof. Damle, who has failed to turn up, hovers in the air, giving rise to some inexplicable uneasiness.

They have plenty of time to kill before the performance. So they pick on the expedient of initiating the local chap Samant into the intricacies of Court procedure and later using him as a replacement. Benare will be on trial; after all it is nothing more than a harmless game.

But before long the game begins to assume a grim aspect. The accusations against Benare are based partly on conjecture, partly on hearsay. But the darts strike home. She has tried to seduce almost every male present, lure him into marriage. Ironically enough, it is the local 'innocent' who delivers the final blow. In his excitement, he reads out a passage from a novel. The details seem to fit Benare's case. (Here is a typical instance of someone, poor in experience, feeding his own imagination with popular reading fare. It is a subject to which Tendulkar returns in *Baby*, but from a different angle.)

The door latch has long since fallen into place. The group has by now safely insulated itself. What began as a game has evolved into a hunt. Benare is the quarry and the group, accuser and judge rolled into one. The sentence meted out to her is savage : the infant in her womb must be destroyed ; she must lose her teaching job, her only source of livelihood. There is no mention of the 'intellectual' who abandoned her, the absent Damle.

Having created this situation, the playwright seems to have had no other option except to allow Benare her say. Her inert frame stirs a little to communicate to us what she knows about men who profess love but, in fact, only hunger for the flesh. Perhaps a realization such as this (which also embodies an awareness of the cravings of her own body) needed a better dramatic equivalent. As it stands, the soliloquy sounds more like self-justification than knowledge of self. Paradoxically, spectators find this final declaration quite the most absorbing part of the play. One would like to believe that this is not what the playwright intended !

KUMUD MEHTA

SILENCE ! THE COURT IS IN SESSION was first presented in English by the Madras players at the Museum Theatre, Madras in March 1971. It was directed by Ammu Mathew. The cast was as follows:

SAMANT	Viraf Kanga
BENARE	Vishalam Ekambaram
SUKHATME	S. Ramchander
SERVANT	V. Narayanam
BALU ROKDE	Nickoo
PONKSHE	P. C. Ramakrishna
KARNIK	Matthew Huntley
MRS KASHIKAR	Lakshmi Krishnamurty
MR KASHIKAR	S. V. Krishnamurty
LOCAL RESIDENT	Pradeep Singh Mehta

NOTE

I must express my thanks to Amol Palekar and Professor D. N. Govilkar for their help in checking respectively the language of the first and final drafts of the translation.

P. A.

ACT ONE

The lights go up on a completely empty hall. It has two doors. One to enter by, and one to go to an adjoining room. One side of the hall seems to go leftwards into the wings. Within the hall are a built-in platform, one or two old wooden chairs, an old box, a stool—and sundry other things lie jumbled together as if in a lumber-room. A clock, out of order, on the wall. Some worn-out portraits of national leaders. A wooden board with the names of donors. A picture of the god Ganesha, hung on the door. The door is closed.

There are footsteps outside. Someone unlocks the door. A man sidles in, and stands looking around as if seeing the hall for the first time. This is Samant. In his hands, a lock and key, a toy parrot made of green cloth, a book.

SAMANT [*looking around*]. This is it. Come in. This is the hall. They seem to have cleaned it up a bit this morning —because of the show. [*Miss Benare has entered after him, and is standing in the doorway. One fingertip is between her lips. She holds a basket of equipment, and a purse.*] What's the matter ? Did you catch your finger in the bolt ? These old bolts are all the same. They just won't slide straight. And if the bolt stays out just a little bit, and you don't pull it clean to one side, then what happens ? Shut the door—and you've had it ! Locked yourself in ! Suck it a little. You'll feel better. This finger of my right hand once got caught in the lock. For five days it was so swollen, I couldn't tell the difference between my finger and my thumb. I had to do *everything* with four fingers !

BENARE. Goodness ! [*to him*]. It's nothing. Nothing at all. It's just a habit with me. But I *am* feeling marvellous. I got down at the station with all the others, and suddenly, after many days, I felt wonderful !

SAMANT. Why's that ?

BENARE. Who knows ? And I felt even more wonderful coming here with you. I'm so glad the others fell behind !

We rushed ahead, didn't we ?

SAMANT. Yes, indeed. I mean to say, I'm not in the habit of walking so fast. You do set a very lively pace, very lively.

BENARE. Not always. But today, how I walked ! Let's leave everyone behind, I thought, and go somewhere far, far away—with you !

SAMANT [*in confusion*]. With me ?

BENARE. Yes, I like you very much.

SAMANT [*terribly shy and embarrassed*]. Tut-tut. Ha ha ! I'm hardly . . .

BENARE. You're very nice indeed. And shall I tell you something ? You are a very pure and good person. I like you.

SAMANT [*incredulously*]. Me ?

BENARE. Yes, and I like this hall very much, too. [*She walks round it.*]

SAMANT. The hall too ? It's just an old one. Whenever there are functions in the village, they take place here. You could say this hall just exists for the sake of functions. Speeches, receptions, weddings . . . to say nothing of the women's *bhajan* group. They practise here in the afternoons. Tonight there's this programme, you see. So the *bhajan* practice must be off. They give *bhajans* a holiday when there's a show at night ! How else would the women finish their chores by nightfall ? Eh ?

BENARE [*cautious but inquisitive*]. Your wife is in the *bhajan* group, I suppose ?

SAMANT. Uh huh. Wrong. Not wife, sister-in-law. I don't have a wife at all.

BENARE [*pointing a finger at the green cloth parrot in his hand*]. Then who is *that* for ?

SAMANT. This, you mean ? For my nephew. A lovely child ! Do you like this toy ?

BENARE. Yes.

SAMANT. I'm not married yet. No particular reason. I earn enough to keep body and soul together. But I never got married. Do you know—there were magic shows here some time ago ? Sleight of hand, hypnotism and all that. . .

BENARE. Did you see them ?

SAMANT. What do you think! I'm here for every show.

BENARE. Is that so ?

SAMANT. Yes. I don't miss a single one. What other amuse-ment is there in the village ?

BENARE. That's true. [*She goes very close to him, and says in confiding tones.*]Did you see the magic—from very near ?

SAMANT. Yes. That is, I wasn't *very* close. But still, close enough. Why ?

BENARE [*as close as ever*]. How do they do that—cutting a tongue, and putting it together again ?

SAMANT [*backing away a little*]. A tongue ? Tongue... well, it's hard to describe...

BENARE. But tell me ?

SAMANT. Eh ? But ...

[*She comes as close as before. Embarrassed, he backs away once more.*]

It's like this ... I'll try ... I mean, I won't be able ... look, this is my tongue ...

[*He stretches the first joint cf his finger towards her.*]

BENARE. Let me see.

[*She makes it an excuse to get even closer to him. For a moment or two, she is keenly aware of his nearness to her. But he is not.*]

SAMANT [*with concentration*]. This is my tongue. Look, it's cut ! Now what ? It'll bleed ! But it doesn't ? Why doesn't it bleed ? There must be something for it in hypnotism— that is, some trick. That's why it doesn't bleed. Nothing happens, nothing at all ... it doesn't even hurt—so ...

[*Perhaps as a response to his complete innocence, she moves away from him.*]

BENARE. Why haven't they reached here yet ? They always amble along. People should be brisk !

SAMANT. Yes. I was telling you about the tongue ... hypno-tism—

BENARE. In school, when the first bell rings, my foot's al-ready on the threshold. I haven't heard a single reproach for not being on time these past eight years. Nor about my teaching. I'm *never* behindhand with my lessons! Exercises corrected on time, too !   Not a bit of room for disapproval—I don't give an inch of it to any one !

SAMANT.   You're a schoolmarm, it seems ?

BENARE.   No, a teacher ! Do I seem the complete schoolmarm to you ?

SAMANT.   No, no ... I didn't mean it like that ...

BENARE.   Say it if you like ...

SAMANT.   But I didn't say it at all ! A schoolmarm just means ... someone who—teaches—instructs !—children—that's what I meant to say ...

BENARE.   They're so much better than adults.   At least they don't have that blind pride of thinking they know everything. There's no nonsense stuffed in their heads. They don't scratch you till you bleed, then run away like cowards. Please open that window. It's become too hot for me. [*He opens the window eagerly. Benare takes a deep breath.*] Ah ! Now I feel better. No, no, I feel wonderful ! [*She starts walking freely round the hall once more.*]

SAMANT.   Shall we finish that tongue trick now ? The hypnotism ? [*putting his finger out again.*] See that now. That's my tongue. Now it's cut.

BENARE.   No! Not now.

SAMANT [*obediently*]. All right. [*He lowers his hand. Then suddenly comes forward, picking up a chair, and puts it down near her.*] Why are you wandering about ? Do sit down. Your feet will hurt.

BENARE.   I'm used to standing while teaching. In class, I never sit when teaching. That's how I keep my eye on the whole class. No one has a chance to play up. My class is scared stiff of me ! And they adore me, too. My children will do anything for me. For I'd give the last drop of my blood to teach them. [*In a different tone*]. That's why people are jealous. Specially the other teachers and the management. But what can they do to me ? What can they do ? However hard they try, what *can* they do ? They're holding an enquiry, if you please ! But my teach-

ing's perfect. I've put my whole life into it—I've worn myself to a shadow in this job ! Just because of one bit of
slander, what can they do to me ? Throw me out ? Let
them ! I haven't hurt anyone. Anyone at all ! If I've
hurt anybody, it's been myself. But is that any kind of
reason for throwing me out ? Who are these people to say
what I can or can't do ? My life is my own—I haven't sold
it to anyone for a job ! My will is my own. My wishes are
my own. No one can kill those—no one ! I'll do what
I like with myself and my life ! I'll decide...
[*Unconsciously, her hand is on her stomach. She suddenly
stops. Seeing Samant, she falls silent. Gradually she regains
her poise. Samant is embarrassed.*]
SAMANT [*awkwardly*]. Shall I go and see why the others
haven't arrived yet ?
BENARE [*hastily*]. No. [*then coming back slowly to normal.*] I feel scared when I am alone, you know.
SAMANT. Then I won't go. Are you not feeling well ?
BENARE [*with a sudden access of energy*]. Nonsense ! Nothing's the matter with me. I'm fine. Just fine ! [*Clapping
her hands she starts crooning an English song to herself.*]

> Oh, I've got a sweetheart
> Who carries all my books,
> He plays in my doll house,
> And says he likes my looks.
> I'll tell you a secret—
> He wants to marry me.
> But Mummy says, I'm too little
> To have such thoughts as these.

[*She leaves off singing.*] Do you know what we are going
to do today. Mr—er—
SAMANT. Samant.
BENARE. Just so.
SAMANT. Yes. There's a notice by the temple. The Sonar
Moti Tenement (Bombay) Progressive Association's Mock
Law... law ... what was it ? Yes, Lawcourt ! At eight

sharp tonight.

BENARE. But what does that mean, do you think ?

SAMANT. That I don't know. Something to do with the court . . .

BENARE. Quite right. Not a real court; a fake one, a make-believe one !

SAMANT. In other words, some fun to do with a court.

BENARE. Exactly. Fun. But Samant, 'spreading enlighten-ment is also one of the Prime Objectives behind our pro-gramme'. So our chairman Kashikar will tell you. Kashi-kar can't take a step without a Prime Objective ! Besides him, there's Mrs Hand-that-Rocks-the-Cradle. I mean Mrs Kashikar. What an excellent housewife the poor woman is ! A real Hand-that-Rocks-the-Cradle type! But what's the use? Mr Prime Objective is tied up with uplifting the masses. And poor Hand-that-Rocks-the-Cradle has no cradle to rock !

SAMANT. You mean they have no—[*He rocks an imaginary baby in his arms.*]

BENARE. Right. You seem to be very bright, too ! Mr Kashikar and the Hand-that-Rocks-the-Cradle, in order that nothing should happen to either of them in their bare, bare house—and that they shouldn't die of boredom !—gave shelter to a young boy. They educated him. Made him toil away. Made a slave out of him. His name's Balu—Balu Rokde. Who else ? . . . Well, we have an Expert on the Law. He's such an authority on the subject, even a desperate client won't go anywhere near him ! He just sits alone in the barristers' room at court, swatting flies with legal precedents! And in his tenement, he sits alone kil-ling houseflies ! But for today's mock trial, he's a very great barrister. You'll see the wonders he performs! And there's a 'Hmm !' with us ! (*Puts an imaginary pipe in her mouth.*) Hmm ! Sci-en-tist ! Inter-failed !

SAMANT. Oh, it does sound good fun!

BENARE. And we have an Intellectual too. That means someone who prides himself on his booklearning. But when there's a real-life problem, away he runs ! Hides his head.

He's not here today. Won't be coming, either. He wouldn't
dare !

SAMANT. But what's today's trial about ?

BENARE. A case against President Johnson for producing
atomic weapons.

SAMANT. Good heavens !

BENARE. Ssh ! I think they're here. [*She has an idea.*]
Come here. Come on, hide like this. I'll stay here, too.
Hide properly. Now ask them to come in.

[*Samant and Benare hiding behind the door that leads outside. Their bodies touch. Voices are heard saying, 'Here it
is !' 'Found it at last !' as lawyer Sukhatme, science student
Ponkshe and Balu Rokde, the Mock Lawcourt's general
factotum, carrying between them two or three suitcases, two
bags, a battery-operated microphone set, and the like, come
in through the door. A lighted* beedi *in Sukhatme's mouth.
A pipe between Ponkshe's lips. After them, a servant carrying two wooden enclosures—the dock and the witness-box.
As they come in, Benare and Samant leap out from behind
the door. She shouts 'Boo' in a tremendous voice. They
all start for just a moment. Then one by one they recover
their poise. Benare laughs to her heart's content. Samant
stands looking around at all this, eagerly and wonderingly.*]

ROKDE [*going and setting down all his luggage at one spot*].
How loudly, Miss Benare ! All this might have fallen
down ! I would have been scolded by Mrs Kashikar. And
all for nothing. Whatever happens, it's me she blames. I
got a free education of them, didn't I ? So I'm paying for
my sins !

[*The servant goes and puts the enclosures into the wings at
left, and returns. Ponkshe pays him his porter's fees. Exit
the servant.*]

PONKSHE [*weightily, removing his thick-framed spectacles*].
Oh, gosh ! Where is it ? ... [*He goes muttering into the
inner room, to hunt for the lavatory.*]

SUKHATME [*inhaling deeply, and blowing out smoke*]. There
is a little lassie, deep in my heart. Miss Benare, whatever
happens, you don't want to grow up, do you ? Eh ?

BENARE. Why, in the class room, I'm the soul of seriousness!

But I don't see why one should go around all the time with
a long face. Or a square face ! Like that Ponkshe ! We
should laugh, we should play, we should sing ! If we can
and if they'll let us, we should dance too. Shouldn't have
any false modesty or dignity. Or care for anyone! I mean it.
When your life's over, do you think anyone will give you
a bit of theirs ? What do you say, Samant ? Do you think
they will ?

SAMANT. You're quite right. The great sage Tukaram said
. . . at least I *think* it was him—

BENARE. Forget about the sage Tukaram. I say it—I, Leela
Benare, a living woman, I say it from my own experience.
Life is not meant for anyone else. It's your own life. It
must be. It's a very, very important thing. Every moment,
every bit of it is precious—

SUKHATME [*clapping*]. Hear ! Hear !
[*Ponkshe comes out.*]

BENARE. Not here. [*She points to Ponkshe.*] There ! [*Tries
hard to control her laughter, but can't.*]

PONKSHE [*puzzled*]. What's the matter ?

BENARE. Ponkshe, tell the honest truth. Did you or did
you not go in looking for the 'arrangements' ? To deal
with your usual nervousness before a show ?

SUKHATME. Say what you will, Miss Benare. Our Ponkshe
looks most impressive during the trial. The scientist in the
witness-box ! A pipe and all that ! No one would believe
he has just taken his Inter-Science for the *second* time. Or
works as a clerk in the Central Telegraph Office !

[*Here Rokde, unable to control himself, laughs a little.*]

PONKSHE [*irritated*]. Don't you laugh, Rokde ! I didn't get
my education on Mrs Kashikar's charity ! I may have
failed my Inter-Science. But at least I did it on my own
father's money. Nonsense !

BENARE. Nonsense ! [*She catches his exact intonation, and
laughs*]. Shall I, tell you people something amusing ?
When I was small, I was very, very quiet. I just used to sit
and make plans—all by myself. I wouldn't tell anyone.
And at the slightest excuse, I used to cry loudly !

PONKSHE. In other words, the exact opposite of what you are now.

BENARE. Yes ! Yes! Do you know, Samant—

SAMANT. [*promptly*]. Yes ! That is, perhaps I don't... probably not, in fact...

BENARE. On the first day of school, I used to put nice fresh covers on every book I had. On the first page I used to write, in beautiful tiny letters, with pictures of flowers and things :

> The grass is green,
> The rose is red.
> This book is mine
> Till I am dead !

Till I am dead ! And do you know what happened ?

SAMANT. What happened ?

BENARE. Every single book got torn one by one and went I don't know where—but I am still here. I am not dead ! Not dead ! The grass is still green, the rose is still red, but I am not dead ! [*She starts laughing once more.*]

ROKDE. [*Quickly takes a notebook out of his bag and starts writing down the verse.*].

That's lovely ! The grass is—green. The—rose—is—red ... What was the rest of it, Miss Benare ?

BENARE [*the smile off her face*]. Rokde, this is a bad habit! I always tell the girls in class, don't be in a hurry to write down what you've hardly heard ! First listen... say it to yourself slowly...send it deep inside you. Then it'll stay with you. It must mingle with your blood. It'll only stay once it's in your blood. No one can take it from you then—or make you forget it !

SAMANT. Our dear teacher used to say the same thing. He taught us verses by heart in just this way. This is, he didn't say all that about blood...

SUKHATME. Go on, Miss Benare.

BENARE [*suddenly expansive*]. Shall I tell you a story ? Children, be seated. There was once a wolf...

ROKDE [*suddenly sitting down cross-legged*]. Do tell it, miss.
Sit down, Mr Sukhatme. Ponkshe, sit down.
[*Ponkshe goes out with a look of annoyance on his face.*]
BENARE.   No. I'll recite a poem...

> Our feet tread on upon unknown
> And dangerous pathways evermore.
> Wave after blinded wave is shattered
> Stormily upon the shore.
> Light glows alive again.   Again
> It mingles with the dark of night.
> Our earthen hands burn out, and then
> Again in flames they are alight.
> Everything is fully known,
> And everything is clear to see.
> And the wound that's born to bleed
> Bleeds on for ever, faithfully.
> There is a battle sometimes, where
> Defeat is destined as the end.
> Some experiences are meant
> To taste, then just to waste and spend...*

[*leaving the poem in the middle*]. No—I'll sing a song.
'An old man from Malad came up to the fireside...An old
man from Malad, the old man's wife, the wife's little baby,
nurse, the nurse's visitor ...'
[*Sukhatme seated. Samant curious. As Benare sings, for a
moment they all start beating the rhythm. Sukhatme claps
hands as if at a religious ceremony. Enter the experimental
theatre actor, Karnik. He is chewing* pan.]
KARNIK [*entering*]. Here we are. I thought I had lost my
way. [*He notices the others.*] What's happened ?

---

* from a Marathi poem by Mrs Shirish Pai.
   Vijay Tendulkar, in the preface to the Marathi original of this
play, writes, 'The central character of Miss Benare came to me
through a poem. This beautiful poem by Mrs Shirish Pai has
been put into the first Act, in the lips of Miss Benare herself.'

ROKDE. Oh no ! That's spoilt everything !

SUKHATME. Benare was singing. [*In affected tones*]. Very nice. Very sweet, Miss Benare.

[*Benare sticks out her tongue at him to signify, 'I know what you mean!' and goes on laughing. Karnik is gazing round the hall. Rokde stands up.*].

SUKHATME [*in a flamboyant lawyer's voice*]. One minute, Mr Karnik! shall I tell you what's going through your mind right now ? This hall, you are thinking, is ideal for Intimate Theatre—in other words, for those plays of yours for a tiny audience. Which go over their heads in any case! Yes or not ? Answer me.

KARNIK [*on purpose, calmly chewing his* pan]. No. I was saying to myself, this hall would put even a real court to shame.

BENARE. *Goodness!* That's wonderful! Our mock court tonight should go over well! Just like a real one!

ROKDE [*anxiously*]. But where's Mrs. Kashikar got to ?

KARNIK [*chewing his* pan]. She's on her way here. They stopped because Mr Kashikar wanted to buy a garland for her hair. So I bought my *pan*, and came ahead. Rokde, I hope the mike's batteries are all right. Test them now if you like. Or else you'll make a mess of it tonight! We must avoid last-minute disasters. But somehow they always happen. Last month, right in the middle of our show, a fuse blew ! I myself was on stage. So what if the role was a small one ? Somehow or other I managed to carry it off.

ROKDE. It was just an ordinary amateur play for the Ganapati Puja.

KARNIK. But the *mood* was destroyed!

BENARE [*yawns ; then mischievously*]. Oh, it's not at what you were saying, Karnik. You see, I have to get up so early every day. There's the Morning Session, then the Afternoon Session. And on top of that, private tuition in the evening! I say, who's noticed something about Mr and Mrs Kashikar ?

ROKDE [*with instinctive, unconscious interest*]. What ?

PONKSHE [*re-entering*]. Yes, what ?

SUKHATME. I'll tell you. But no, I won't. You tell us
yourself first, Miss Benare...eh ? Let me see...come on—
out with it—

BENARE. You haven't understood a thing, Sukhatme. Don't
give yourself those meaningless legal airs ! Well, although
our Kashikar is a social worker and Mrs Kashikar is quite
—er—quite uneducated and so on—of course, *I* don't think
that education has any connection with a person's intelligence—well, although Mrs. Kashikar is not so educated,
they are both so full of life ! I mean, Mr Kashikar buys
garlands for Mrs Kashikar. Mrs Kashikar buys readymade
bush-shirts for Mr Kashikar...It really makes one feel nice
to see it !

[*Karnik opens a window backstage, spits* pan *juice through
it, and comes downstage again.*]

KARNIK. When I for one see such public formalities between
husband and wife, I suspect something quite different in
private.

ROKDE [*rather angrily*]. That's the effect of modern theatre !

KARNIK. Don't meddle in what you don't understand, Rokde.
You're still a child. Just stick to your college work. For
my part, I never buy garlands for my wife. Even if I feel
like it, I suppress the idea.

[*Benare tut-tuts audibly.*]
What's the matter ?

BENARE. If I were in your place, I would buy one for her
daily!

SUKHATME. Then hurry up and start buying bush-shirts for
your husband, Miss Benare ! I wonder what that most
fortunate man will be like ! If he's half as mischievous as
you are, you've both had it !

BENARE. Never mind about that. [*suddenly looking around,
to Samant*] Couldn't we please have some chairs here, Mr—
What's-your-name—

SAMANT. Chairs ? Oh, my name's Samant, I mean ! [*Gets
up and looks here and there*]. I'll have a look. How
should I know...[*Exits, hunting.*]

PONKSHE. They're inside. Folding chairs. I could do with

some tea.

SUKHATME.   When we had some at the station, you said no. ['*So now do without,*' *says his tone.*]

PONKSHE.   Gosh, I didn't want it then.   I don't agree with the way you people plan everything in advance.   Call that living ?   In this scientific age, it's fun to get everything at the last minute, without effort. [*Snaps his fingers.*] Like that!

[*Just then, Samant enters from the inner room, and stands in the doorway, both arms full of as many folding chairs as he can carry.*]

SAMANT [*putting them down in the hall*].   There are more if you want. Inside. [*All of them snappily open the chairs and sit down wherever they can. Conversation. Ponkshe still standing showing off his pipe*].

SAMANT [*to Ponkshe, awed by his sahib-like appearance*]. Do sit down, sahib.

PONKSHE [*pleased at the 'sahib'*]. No, thank you. I was sitting in the train Er—what's your name ?

SAMANT. Samant. I'm from this village, sir.

PONKSHE. Good ! Can we have some tea here ?

SAMANT. Tea ? Yes, sir. But sugar will be the problem. You can't get sugar these days. If *gur* will do—

PONKSHE. No. You probably don't know, Mr. Samant. *Gur* in tea is poisonous.

SAMANT. But at our house, that's what we grown-ups usually take.   Normally the sugar ration isn't even enough for my brother's children.   They just can't drink tea without sugar. So what can we do ?

PONKSHE [*pipe in mouth, most scientist-like*]. Hmm !

BENARE [*unable to resist teasing him, mimics him from where she is sitting*]. Hmm. Once there was a Hmm ! And he knew a girl called Erhmm !

PONKSHE. Stop it, Benare ! Don't be childish. [*Samant still standing. Mr and Mrs Kashikar enter.*]

MRS KASHIKAR [*unconsciously stroking the garland in her hair*]. Look, here they all are, after all !

SUKHATME. Come in, Kashikar ! How did the garland-buying go ?

[*Benare is pointing them out to Samant with gestures.*]

ROKDE [*coming forward*]. Yes, how did it ?

MRS KASHIKAR. Balu, have you brought all the luggage ?

ROKDE. Absolutely.

KASHIKAR. Each time you say you've brought it all, Rokde, and each time you forget something. Have you got the usher's staff ? Don't just nod your head. Show it if you have it. Let me see.

ROKDE [*producing it*]. Here it is. (*Pathetically*) I've got the uniform too. I only forget things sometimes. Not all the time.

KASHIKAR. I don't care if you always forget. At least today I hope everything's in order. Or you'll make a mess of things. My judge's wig ? Did you bring it ?

ROKDE. Yes. I brought that first. [*Rokde grows increasingly miserable and irritated.*]

KASHIKAR. You, Sukhatme ? Did you bring your lawyer's gown ?

SUKHATME [*bowing as if in court*]. Yes, milord ! I don't forget that even in my dreams ! What about you, Ponkshe ?

PONKSHE. Well, I come fully dressed, so I won't forget a thing. I have this nervous temperament a bit, you know. If I don't have my pipe, I can't remember a thing in the witness-box.

MRS KASHIKAR. I'll rehearse your lines with you a little, before today's show.

PONKSHE. No need for that.

MRS KASHIKAR. I say, Benare—(*stroking the garland in her hair*) I did mean to buy a garland for you too—

BENARE [*in Ponkshe's tones*]. Hmm !

[*Ponkshe bites his lips angrily.*]

MRS KASHIKAR [*to Mr Kashikar*]. Didn't I, dear ? But what happened was that—

BENARE [*laughing heartily*].—The garland flew away—pouf ! Or did the dicky-bird take it ? I never want garlands. If I did, couldn't I afford to buy them ? I earn my own living, you know. That's why I never feel like buying garlands and things.

[*Benare hands out the snacks Mrs Kashikar has brought.*]

MRS KASHIKAR. Well, what does your school have to say for itself ?

BENARE [*carefully*]. My school says nothing.

KASHIKAR. I wonder, should we have the judge's chair this side or that ?

KARNIK. Here, of course. The entrance is over there. That room next door can be used for the judge. You can enter from there. President Johnson will stand over here like this—

SAMANT [*amazed*]. President Johnson !

KASHIKAR. No, no. Johnson's dock should be left over there. So when I speak as the judge—

KARNIK. I don't agree. If you look at it from the audience's point of view, it should be right here—

SUKHATME. Mr Karnik, I shall prosecute you for seeing things from the audience's point of view ! And you a man of the modern theatre ! [*A lawyer's laugh.*]

KARNIK. Yet again ! Will someone please tell me what this Modern Theatre is supposed to be ? People just play with words without knowing what they mean. I do what seems right to me. Whether it's modern or old-fashioned doesn't matter. [*They begin to argue.*]

SAMANT [*stopping Rokde*]. What's this business about President Johnson ?

ROKDE [*Deep in his own thoughts, starts*]. Who ?

SAMANT. They said 'President Johnson' or something just now.

ROKDE. Oh, that !

SAMANT. Do you mean President Johnson will really—probably he won't, however—I mean, what's it all about ?

ROKDE. Not the real one ! This fellow Karnik here plays him ! [*He is getting his revenge on Karnik for putting him in his place earlier.*]

SAMANT. President Johnson !

ROKDE [*Suddenly remembering, comes and stops Mrs Kashikar*]. Madam, Professor Damle hasn't arrived yet !

[*Benare, who had been talking to Mrs Kashikar, suddenly falls silent and motionless. Then she goes by mistake to Ponkshe, and stands talking to him, with an artificial air. He is silent.*]

MRS KASHIKAR. Well, he'll come late as usual. He told me on the phone that he wouldn't be able to catch our train. He was doing a symposium—or something—in the university. I've told him about this twice. Benare, did you meet him ?

BENARE [*who is talking to Ponkshe*]. Whom ?

MRS KASHIKAR. Professor Damle.

BENARE. No, I didn't.

[*Starts talking to Ponkshe again. He is silent. No response at all.*]

ROKDE [*after consulting Samant, to Mrs Kashikar*]. But madam, Samant here says that the next train doesn't reach here till nine p.m. How will that do? It'll be too late!

PONKSHE [*in the gap in the conversation*]. What happened afterwards to that friend of yours, Miss Benare ? That girl—the one in trouble—whom you found for me to marry . . .

[*Benare confused. In her confusion she goes to Samant.*]

MRS KASHIKAR. There was a train in between, wasn't there? [*to Kashikar*] Dear, Balu here says there's no train in between—

KASHIKAR [*interrupting his argument with Karnik.*] In between what ?

ROKDE [*to him*]. Samant here says there's no train now before the show !

SUKHATME. There's one afterwards, isn't there ? That's good enough !

KASHIKAR. But my dear Sukhatme, how will Professor Damle get here ? He'll arrive late. If he comes at all ! There's no train in between.

KARNIK. Then he won't come at all, I'm telling you. Professor Damle is quite calculating, that way. When you talk of being late, he just cancels the programme, and sits comfortably at home.

ROKDE [*tense*]. Madam, I did drop a postcard to him as usual—when I sent one to all the others—I mean, it's no fault of mine—I even wrote the address right—

KASHIKAR. Here's a hitch !

SUKHATME. What's so serious about it ? Don't worry in the least !

KASHIKAR. How can I not worry ? We owe something to the people, Sukhatme. A performance is no laughing matter.

PONKSHE [*coming up*]. What's happened ?

MRS KASHIKAR [*to Sukhatme*]. But now who'll play the counsel for the accused ?

SUKHATME. Don't you worry. For today, I'll do that role along with that of the prosecuting counsel. What's so serious about that ? I'm a lawyer to the marrow ! I tell you, Kashikar, just leave it to me.

KARNIK. Yes, I think that will be much more dramatic !

PONKSHE. Definitely ! [*A pompous puff at his pipe.*]

BENARE. Definitely !

[*Ponkshe looks at her angrily.*]

ROKDE [*consulting a paper he is holding*]. And the fourth witness. Mr Sukhatme, he's missing, too. Rawte is sick with flu. We'd decided to take a local man. [*He catches sight of Mrs Kashikar, and corrects himself.*] That is, *you* had decided . . .

SUKHATME. True. A local man—that means . . .

ROKDE [*gathering up his courage*]. Can I please do that part today ? It's just a small one—anyone can do mine— I know the fourth witness's lines off by heart . . .

KARNIK. I oppose it ! Even if you're just an usher, your character isn't an easy one to play. So what if he has no lines ? It can't be managed by putting up someone else at the last minute. Stick to your part, Rokde.

ROKDE. But how does it matter if just one day I play another role ?

KASHIKAR. No.

MRS KASHIKAR. Balu, if he says no, then don't do it !

2

[*Rokde falls back.*] But then, who will be the fourth witness ?

SUKHATME [*staring at Samant*]. I—know ! [*suddenly*] Here's your fourth witness—[*points to him*] Samant !

SAMANT [*starting*]. What's the matter ?

PONKSHE [*puffing at his pipe*]. Not bad !

KASHIKAR [*to Samant*]. Have you ever acted in a play ?

SAMANT. Good heavens, no ! Never at all. What's the matter ?

MRS KASHIKAR. Will you be the fourth witness ? Look here, Benare. [*She comes over.*] What do you think of this gentleman as the fourth witness ?

BENARE. This gentleman ? Not bad—I think he's lovely !
[*Samant embarrassed. Benare smiling.*]
As a witness, I mean. The fourth witness.

SUKHATME. Mrs Kashikar, Karnik, Ponkshe, don't worry ! I'll take the responsibility. Nothing to it ! I'll prepare him. Mister—what's your name ?—

SAMANT. Raghu Samant.

SUKHATME. Mr Samant, you have been called as fourth witness for today's Living Lawcourt.

SAMANT [*flabbergasted and trembling*]. But I honestly don't know anything about it !

MRS KASHIKAR. You've seen a court, haven't you ?

SAMANT. Never in my life !

KARNIK. In a play, at least ?

SAMANT. No. Not at all ! No play like that has ever been seen here.

SUKHATME [*taunting Karnik*]. It's a good thing, he hasn't seen a courtroom in a play. At least he won't have all kinds of wrong notions about it !

KARNIK. Confine your remarks to *certain* plays !

SUKHATME. Mr Samant, I'll have you word-perfect before the show. After all, you don't have to teach a lawyer how to coach witnesses ! [*He gives a lawyer's laugh.*]

SAMANT. But I'm not used to it at all ! The very thought that it's a court will terrify me !

MRS KASHIKAR. I suggest we have a rehearsal with him. [*to

Mr Kashikar] What do you think, dear ? [*He pays no attention, so*] What do you think, Benare ?

BENARE. Yes. I've no objection at all. I was wondering what
to do till the show. I forgot to bring a book to read.

SAMANT. Oh. Would you like the new novel by Suryakant
Phatarphekar ? I've just got it. [*Fishes it out and proffers
it.*] His novels are so thrilling ! This is the 105th.

BENARE. Then I certainly don't want it !

SUKHATME. Well, we have the Bible and the Bhagavad-
Geeta for the oath-taking—I mention it because you want
something to read. By the way, Rokde, you did bring
along the Bible and the Geeta, didn't you ? Or have you
forgotten ?

ROKDE [*in an agonized voice*]. No, they're here. I'll show
them to you if you want.

[*Goes towards the bags. But doesn't show the Geeta.*]

BENARE. Learned Counsel, I'm not yet so old as to be reading
those books !

KASHIKAR. Then you must be reading *True Stories* or maga-
zines like that. That's what my wife reads. Quite amusing,
they are. Because of my social work, I can't manage to
do more than look at the pictures.

MRS KASHIKAR [*protesting*]. Really !

KASHIKAR [*annoyed*]. What do you mean, 'Really' ! Wasn't
I speaking the truth ?

[*Mrs Kashikar's face falls.*]

KARNIK. I think the idea of a rehearsal is excellent. If only
someone would fetch four or five packets of cigarettes.
That's all we need, so we won't have to go out in the
middle.

PONKSHE. I don't mind. [*Puffing at his pipe.*]

SAMANT [*to Rokde*]. Then it doesn't matter. If I see it all
once, there's no question about it. That'll reassure me. Eh ?

[*Rokde doesn't answer.*]

BENARE. Shall I tell you something ? We've done tonight's
atomic weapons trial seven times in the past three months.
Tonight's the eighth time. I've no objection to doing it
once more before that. But I do think tonight's proper

show will fall flat.

SUKHATME. I agree with Miss Benare. I have an idea. See if you like it. When we lawyers are at ease in the barristers' room, we sometimes play rummy. Or patience. Or a certain other game. Just to pass the time, that's all. You bring a new and imaginary case against someone. Eh? Shall we do that? Let's have an imaginary case. So Samant here will understand how a court works. And we'll pass the time more pleasantly. What do you say, Mr Kashikar? Do we have your sanction?

KASHIKAR. That's all right. It doesn't do for a man in public life to show too much hesitation. One must act according to the majority's wishes.

KARNIK [*excited*]. Three cheers for this new idea! In Drama Theory we call this a Visual Enactment. I heard of it at the Government Drama Camp last year.

SUKHATME. Why give such a hard name to a simple thing? This is just a game. Eh, Miss Benare?

BENARE. I'm even willing to play hopscotch, if you're talking of games. Games are very good for you. I often play quite happily with the children at school. It's fun.

PONKSHE. All right, we'll play. Mr Samant, could you please fetch some packets of cigarettes from the corner? Capstans for me. Here you are. [*Gives him money.*]

MRS KASHIKAR. Why are you paying, Ponkshe? Samant, give it back. What I say is, let's call it Performance Expenses—that'll be all right. In any case, we have to demonstrate our lawcourt to Samant because of the performance, don't we? That settles it. Samant, [*opening her purse, and taking out a banknote*] take this. Bring half a dozen packets of the kind everyone wants. And bring some *pan*, three or four. Sweet ones.

SAMANT. Yes. [*Goes out with the money. Coming back*] Don't start, will you? I'll be back in a minute. [*Exit.*]

BENARE. Poor thing! I'll be back.

[*Takes a face towel and a cake of soap out of her basket. Goes inside humming to herself.*]

MRS KASHIKAR. Balu, start arranging the court.

[*He sets to work.*]

KARNIK. Ponkshe, come here a minute. [*To Sukhatme and the others*] The same cast as tonight ? In other words, the same judge, counsel etc. ?

SUKHATME. Oh yes. By all means. Why change it ? I'll play the lawyers.

MRS KASHIKAR. But what I say is, let the accused at least be different. What do you think, Karnik ?

KARNIK. No. It's not necessary. [*Aside to Ponkshe, who has reached him*] Do you know something, Ponkshe ?

PONKSHE. What ?

KARNIK [*indicating the inner room*]. About her ? About Miss Benare. Rokde told me.

PONKSHE. What ?

KARNIK. Not now. Remind me tonight. After the show.

PONKSHE. I've got something to tell you, too. About Miss Benare. [*To the others*] If you ask me, it's a good idea. A different prisoner.

KASHIKAR. It'll add that bit of variety, I would say.

MRS KASHIKAR. Exactly.

KASHIKAR. What do you mean, exactly ? Hold your tongue. Can't say a word ! . . .

[*Mrs Kashikar is silenced.*]

SUKHATME. I don't mind. The accused—I feel—why not Rokde ? [*Rokde is delighted.*]

ROKDE. Yes, indeed. I'm ready to—

PONKSHE. No! (*To Karnik*) I also have something to tell you—about her !

KARNIK. I'll be the accused.

KASHIKAR. I suggest that if we are going through with it, it should not be a frivolous, facetious affair ! I'll be the accused, Sukhatme. Make me the accused.

KARNIK. What importance for him ! He'll be the judge, he'll be the accused !

PONKSHE [*puffing at his pipe*]. Consider me, then ! I'm not keen, as such, you know. But if I'll do, I'm game.

ROKDE [*to Mrs Kashikar*]. But what's wrong with me, madam ?

MRS KASHIKAR. Shall I do it ? I will if you like.

KASHIKAR. No !

[*Mrs Kashikar falls silent.*]

She can't get among a few people without wanting to show off ! Shows off all the time !

MRS KASHIKAR [*quite put out.*] Enough. I won't do it ! Satisfied ? [*She is thoroughly disheartened.*]

SUKHATME. We don't need to take any of you. Kashikar, let's have a really different kind of accused. Eh ? Let's have our Miss Benare ! Eh, Ponkshe ? What d'you think of my choice ?

PONKSHE. It's good.

SUKHATME. Then where's the need for argument ? Well, Mrs Kashikar ?

MRS KASHIKAR. If you say so, it's all right. In any case, we'll be able to see what the trial of a woman is like. [*Out of sheer habit, to Mr Kashikar*] Isn't that so, dear ? One should have that experience—

KASHIKAR [*sarcastically*]. Of course ! I suppose they're just about to make you a judge of the Supreme Court !—

MRS KASHIKAR. That's not how I meant it . . .

SUKHATME. There's not much difference between one trial and another. But when there's a woman in the dock, the case does have a different complexion, that's true. That is my experience. Well, Mr Karnik ?

KARNIK. It's all right. I won't stay outside the team. I believe in team spirit.

MRS KASHIKAR. Then it's settled. Our accused for now is Benare. But what's the charge ?

KASHIKAR. It should be a charge with social significance.

PONKSHE. All right. [*Gets up.*] Sh ! Shall we do something ? Come to me, all of you. Come on. Come here.

[*Whispers some plan to them, gesticulating. Every now and then, he points to the room where Benare is.*]

KASHIKAR. Rokde, haven't you finished arranging the court yet ?

ROKDE. I've finished. [*Bustles about, showing haste.*]

KARNIK. That's why I drew you a ground plan, Rokde. To

show which properties go where.
ROKDE [*angrily*]. I don't understand your theatrical matters.
I'm not used to them.
[*All of them arrange the furniture as in court, Ponkshe taking the lead. Kashikar supervises. On Ponkshe's instruc-
tions Rokde picks up Benare's purse from the luggage on
the dais, and places it on a stool at left. The furniture ar
rangement is completed. Ponkshe and Kashikar go and
stand by the door of the inner room. All the others go into the wings at the left.*]
KASHIKAR [*to the people going into the wings*]. I'll give
you a signal.
[*Now Benare comes out singing, wiping her face on the
towel. She looks very fresh.*]
BENARE [*singing while she puts away the napkin, soap etc.
in the basket on the dais at right.*]

> The parrot to the sparrow said,
> 'Why, oh why are your eyes so red ?'
> 'Oh, my dear friend, what shall I say ?
> Someone has stolen my nest away.'
> Sparrow, sparrow, poor little sparrow !

PONKSHE [*coming from the doorway of the inner room
and standing before Miss Benare on the dais*]. Miss Leela
Benare, you have been arrested on suspicion of a crime of
an extremely grave nature, and brought as a prisoner before the bar of this court.
[*She stiffens where she is. She looks around her numbly. He
is gazing at her. She goes towards the wings at left, looking for her purse, to put the comb in her hands away.
Picks up the purse from the stool. Meanwhile, Kashikar
comes and seats himself on the judge's chair on the dais.
He signals to the people in the wings. Karnik and Rokde
silently bring the wooden dock and arrange it around Benare. Sukhatme comes from the wings putting on his black
lawyer's gown, and sits in a chair next to the broken-
down lawyer's table. The others go to their places. Samant
enters and stands in the doorway.*]
KASHIKAR [*clearing his throat*]. Prisoner Miss Benare, under

Section No. 302 of the Indian Penal Code you are accused of the crime of infanticide. Are you guilty of the afore-mentioned crime ?

[*Benare looks stunned. All are silent for the moment. The atmosphere is extraordinarily sombre.*]

CURTAIN

ACT TWO

The same hall. The situation is the same as at the end of Act One.

KASHIKAR [*sitting at the table with the dignity of a judge*]. Prisoner Miss Benare, under Section No. 302 of the Indian Penal Code, you have been accused of the crime of infanticide. Are you guilty or not guilty of the aforementioned crime?

[*The atmosphere is extraordinarily sombre. Miss Benare stands numbly with a chair for support.*]

SAMANT [*still standing in the doorway, says softly to Karnik.*] Here they are. *Masala pan* and cigarettes.

[*At this, the atmosphere at once lightens.*]

MRS KASHIKAR. A sweet one for me.

KARNIK. A packet of Wills for me.

PONKSHE. Samant, one special *pan* here.

SUKHATME. One *pan*, one packet of *beedis*. What about you, Kashikar?

KASHIKAR. A *masala pan*.

[*Rokde takes the* pan *from Samant and brings it over to Kashikar.*]

ROKDE [*with great politeness, to Kashikar*]. I've taken the astringent out of it.

SUKHATME [*offering a* pan *to Benare*]. Here, have one, Miss Benare.

BENARE [*who is sitting on the chair*]. What? Yes—I mean no. Thank you.

SUKHATME. Why are you so grave all of a sudden? After all, it's a game. Just a game, that's all. Why are you so serious?

BENARE [*trying to laugh*]. Who's serious? I'm absolutely —lighthearted. I just got a bit serious to create the right atmosphere. For the court, that's all. Why should I be afraid of a trial like this?

SAMANT [*lighting a cigarette Karnik has given him, to Karnik*]. It seems there was some joke just now?

KARNIK [*inhaling*]. What joke?

SAMANT. No, he made some accusation—Mr Kashikar...
but I didn't quite catch it.

KARNIK. The charge ? Infanticide.

SAMANT. That's right. But what's that ? I just don't understand, that's why I ask...I'm just an ignorant person.

SUKHATME. The crime of killing a new-born child.

SAMANT. Good heavens ! A terrible charge ! That's exactly
what happened in our village—it must be one or two years
ago now—the poor woman was a widow.

SUKHATME. Is that so ? Who was the lawyer on the case ?
Kashikar, you've really picked some charge ! A first-class
charge ! There's no fun in a case unless there's a really
thundering charge !

KASHIKAR. Did you notice, also, Sukhatme, that this charge
is important from the social point of view ? The question
of infanticide is one of great social significance. That's
why I deliberately picked it. We consider society's best
interests in all we do. Come on, Miss Benare. Rokde, my
gavel.

[*Rokde brings over the gavel fussily.*]

It wouldn't have mattered, if I didn't have it just now. I
was checking whether you'd brought it. [*Banging the gavel*] Now to business. Come on, come on, Sukhatme.
Make a start. *Adhikasya adhikam phalam.* 'Best efforts
bring best results.' First my earpick... [*Searches for it in
his pocket, and places it by him.*]

SUKHATME [*moving his lawyer's gown about with an important air, and chewing* pan]. Milord, in the interests of the
smooth functioning of the matter before this court, I be-
seech the court for an adjournment of a quarter minute
at the beginning, so that all present may spit out the *pan*
in their mouths.

KASHIKAR [*spitting out bits of* pan *with all the dignity of a
judge*]. Counsel for the accused should present his plea
in the matter.

SUKHATME [*immediately rising, and becoming the counsel
for the accused*]. Milord, I strictly oppose the suggestion
of my learned friend, the counsel for the prosecution. Whe-

reas ten seconds are enough to spit out *pan*, my learned friend is asking for a quarter minute. It is clear that my learned friend has an aim of wasting time, which is injurious and troublesome to my client. Therefore we move that an adjournment of ten seconds only be granted.

BENARE [*unable to restrain herself*]. Yes. Or else no—only nine-and-a-half seconds.

KASHIKAR. Miss Benare, the accused is not supposed to interrupt the court. It's one thing for Samant. But should I have to explain the court's etiquette to you afresh ? [*Gravely summoning Karnik*] Clerk of the court, please bring to the attention of this court the legal precedent concerning the matter which has been moved before us.

KARNIK [*removing the cigarette from his mouth, and blowing out a great deal of smoke*]. Considering that it has not been the normal practice in court to conduct a case while chewing *pan*, I do not think any precedent has been established in this matter. Moreover, this instance of a judge's chewing *pan* in court is the first one, and so somewhat unprecedented, Milord.

KASHIKAR. Counsel for the defence, are you able to establish before the court that it is possible to spit out *pan* in ten seconds ?

SUKHATME. By all means. [*Goes outside, spits, and shutting the door*] Exactly ten seconds, Milord.

KASHIKAR. We must see for ourselves. [*Rising, goes inside to do just that.*]

BENARE [*sighing*]. Is this a court of law, Karnik, or a spitting contest ?

[*Karnik pays no attention.*]

SAMANT [*after a moment, to Karnik*]. Sir, does a real court truly work like this ? It's very interesting.

KARNIK [*blowing out cigarette smoke, with mock seriousness*]. Ssh. You'll commit contempt of court. Just listen. [*Winks at Ponkshe.*]

KASHIKAR [*coming back and sitting down*]. Clerk of the court, how long did that take ?

KARNIK [*looking at his watch*]. Who knows ?

MRS KASHIKAR. I'll tell you. It was fifteen seconds.

SUKHATME [*As the counsel for the prosecution, with a triumphant laugh*]. There ! Not ten, but a full fifteen seconds—that is, a quarter minute. A quarter minute ! Exactly the time I told you, Milord.

KASHIKAR [*maintaining his grave manner throughout*]. Yes. Now, seeing that more than half a minute of the court's time has been wasted in this research and experimentation on the subject of spitting *pan*, it is this court's serious decision that the matter before it should proceed without further delay. So long as it is done individually by you, and is inoffensive to the court, everyone may of course spit *pan*.

PONKSHE [*rising*]. Hear, hear !

KASHIKAR [*banging his gavel*]. Silence ! Silence must be observed.

MRS KASHIKAR [*to Samant*]. Samant, all this about *pan* and and so on is just in fun, you know. Just notice the practice in court. The important thing is, you need the court's permission for everything. Or you'll make a mistake tonight.

SAMANT [*excitedly*]. No. Of course, I'm watching. But—

KASHIKAR [*banging the gavel*]. Silence must be observed while the court is in session. Can't shut up at home, can't shut up here !

MRS KASHIKAR. But I was just telling Samant here—

SUKHATME. Let it pass, Mrs Kashikar. He's just joking.

MRS KASHIKAR. So what ? Scolding me at every step !

BENARE [*a little worried, to Rokde, who is playing the usher*]. I say, Balu . . .

ROKDE [*angry but controlling his voice*]. Don't call me Balu !

KASHIKAR [*clearing his throat, and banging the gavel*]. Now, back to infanticide. Prisoner Miss Leela Benare, are you guilty or not guilty of the charge that has been brought against you ?

BENARE. Would *you* admit yourself guilty of it ?

KASHIKAR [*banging the gavel*]. Order, order ! The dignity of the court must be preserved at all costs. Or Samant will not grasp how a court really works.

BENARE. Or how infanticide really works ? Really, I don't like your word at all ! Infanticide. . .infanticide ! Why don't you accuse me instead of—um—snatching public property ! That has a nice sound about it, don't you think ? Scunds like 'snatching' !

MRS KASHIKAR. I don't think so at all. There's nothing wrong with the present charge.

BENARE [*banging her hand on the chair*]. Order, order ! The dignity of the court must be preserved at all costs. Can't shut up at home, can't shut up here ! [*Imitating a lawyer*] Milord, let the court's family be given a suitable reprimand. She has never committed the crime of infanticide. Or stolen any public property except for Milord himself !

MRS KASHIKAR. That's enough, Benare !

BENARE [*softly, to the usher Rokde*]. I say, Balu—[*He bites his lips angrily.*]

SAMANT [*enthusiastically, to Mrs Kashikar*]. Ha ha ! Miss Benare is really amazing !

PONKSHE [*seriously*] In many respects.

KASHIKAR. Prisoner Miss Benare, for abrogating the authority of counsel, and for obstructing the due process of the law, a reprimand is hereby issued to you.

BENARE [*getting up from her seat, and coming up to him. and offering him the* pan *near him*]. Thanks ! For that. a *masala pan* is hereby issued to you.

KAFNIK. This is it ! This is what I meant ! If nothing is going to be taken seriously at all, there's the end of the matter. Miss Benare, at least so that Samant can understand something, please obey the rules of the court. Be serious !

SUKHATME. Otherwise, this game becomes really childish. We need seriousness.

BENARE [*coming back to her place*]. Now, back to infanticide. I was wrong, Milord. But there's no reason for the prisoner to show such respect for the judge. I plead not

guilty. I couldn't even kill a common cockroach. I'm scared to do it. How could I kill a newborn child ? I know
I got annoyed this morning in my class at school. And
gave a naughty pupil a good whack ! So what ? What
can one do ? The brats won't listen to you.

KASHIKAR. Rokde, the book for the oath-taking ?

[*Rokde hurriedly takes out a fat volume, places it on the
stool nearby.*]

The witness-box ?

[*Rokde goes to fetch it.*]

MRS KASHIKAR [*to Samant*]. After this, there's the prosecution's speech.

SUKHATME [*who is sitting with his feet stretched across
another chair, and his hands clasped behind his head, gets
up lazily. Mechanically, he says*]. Milord, the nature of
the charge brought against the accused (*lights up his
beedi from Karnik's cigarette, and breathes out smoke*)
is a most terrible one. Motherhood is a sacred thing—

BENARE. How do *you* know ? [*seeing everyone's expres-
sions*] Order, order !

[*Ponkshe, fed up, goes into the inner room.*]

KASHIKAR. Prisoner Miss Benare, for obstructing the work
of the court, a second reprimand is hereby issued to you.
Counsel for the prosecution, continue.

SUKHATME. Motherhood is pure. Moreover, there is a great
—er—a great nobility in our concept of motherhood. We
have acknowledged woman as the mother of mankind.
Our culture enjoins us to perpetual worship of her. 'Be
thy mother as a god' is what we teach our children from
infancy. There is great responsibility devolving upon a
mother. She weaves a magic circle with her whole existence
in order to protect and preserve her little one—

KASHIKAR. You've forgotten one thing. There's a Sanskrit
proverb, *Janani janmabhumishcha svargadapi gariyasi.*

'Mother and
The Motherland,
Both are even
Higher than heaven.'

MRS KASHIKAR [*with enthusiasm*]. And of course, 'Great are thy favours, O mother' is quite famous.

BENARE. Order, order ! This is all straight out of a school composition-book. [*Bites her tongue ironically.*] Prisoner Miss Benare, for abrogating the authority of the court, a reprimand is *once more* issued to you ! [*Pretends to bang a gavel.*]

SUKHATME. I am deeply grateful, Milord, for your addition. In short, 'Woman is a wife for a moment, but a mother for ever.'

[*Samant claps.*]

MRS KASHIKAR. It's all right now, but you mustn't do that tonight, you know.

SAMANT. All right. I just couldn't help it. What a sentence, eh ?

SUKHATME. It is true. Considering this, what would we respectable citizens say if any woman were to take the life of the delicate bundle of joy she has borne ? We would say, there could be no baser or more devilish thing on earth. I intend to establish by means of evidence that the prisoner has done this same vile deed.

[*Rokde brings the witness-box.*]

BENARE [*softly and mischievously, to Rokde*]. I say, Balu— [*He is thoroughly annoyed. Ponkshe comes out of the inner room.*]

SUKHATME. My first witness is the world-famous scientist, Mr Gopal Ponkshe. Well, Ponkshe ? Are you happy ? I've suddenly promoted you to world fame, eh ?

KASHIKAR. Call the witness to the witness-box. [*He is picking his ear.*]

[*Ponkshe enters the witness-box. Rokde holds the big volume in front of him.*]

PONKSHE [*glancing at the first page of the volume, and placing his hand on it, says gravely*]. I, G. N. Ponkshe, placing my hand upon the Oxford English Dictionary, do hereby solemnly swear that I shall tell the truth, the whole truth, and nothing but the truth.

[*Benare laughs and laughs.*]

MRS KASHIKAR [*in intimidating tones*]. Balu, where is the Geeta ?

ROKDE. [*miserably*]. I forgot it. I brought the Dictionary by mistake. [*grumbling*] How much can I possibly remember ?

BENARE. Poor Balu !

ROKDE. Don't pity me, I'm warning you !

KASHIKAR [*banging his gavel*]. Begin the examination !

MRS KASHIKAR [*to Samant, in a conspiratorial whisper*]. Just observe this examination. All right ?

[*Samant nods his head.*]

SUKHATME [*approaching Ponkshe*]. Your name ?

PONKSHE. G. N. Ponkshe. Go further on. We can have all the details tonight.

SUKHATME. Mr Ponkshe, are you acquainted with the accused ?

BENARE [*suddenly, in Ponkshe's manner*]. Hmm !

PONKSHE [*looking carefully at Benare*]. Yes. Very well indeed.

SUKHATME. How would you describe her social status ?

PONKSHE. A teacher. In other words, a schoolmarm.

BENARE [*sticking her tongue out at him*]. But I'm still quite young !

SUKHATME. Mr Ponkshe, is the accused married or unmarried ?

PONKSHE. Why don't you ask the accused ?

SUKHATME. But if you were asked, what would you say ?

PONKSHE. To the public eye, she is unmarried.

BENARE [*interrupting*]. And to the private eye ?

KASHIKAR. Order ! Miss Benare, self-control. Don't forget the value of self-control. [*to Sukhatme*] You may continue. I'll just be back. [*Rises and goes to the inner room, where the toilet is.*]

MRS KASHIKAR. All this is all right for now, you know. It won't be like this at night. That'll have to be done properly.

SUKHATME [*to himself*]. The wrong things always seem to happen to Mr Kashikar at the wrong time...(*aloud*) Mr Ponkshe, how would you describe your view of the moral conduct of the accused ? On the whole like that of a normal unmarried woman ? You at least should take this trial seriously.

BENARE. But how should he know what the moral conduct of a normal unmarried woman is like ?

PONKSHE [*paying no attention to her*]. It is different.

SUKHATME. For example ?

PONKSHE. The accused is a bit too much.

SUKHATME. A bit too much—what does that mean ?

PONKSHE. It means—it means that, on the whole, she runs after men too much.

BENARE [*provoking him*]. Tut! tut! tut! Poor man!

SUKHATME. Miss Benare, you are committing contempt of court.

BENARE. The court has gone into that room. So how can contempt of it be committed in this one ? There's not much point in that remark, Sukhatme !

[*Samant laughs heartily.*]

SUKHATME [*to Benare*]. There's no point in coming to grips with you ! Mr Ponkshe . . .

[*Ponkshe has slid out of the witness-box and is talking to Karnik.*]

Nobody at all is serious!

[*Ponkshe returns to the witness-box.*]

Mr Ponkshe, can you tell me—does the accused have a particularly close relationship with any man—married or unmarried ? [*Stressing the words*] Any married or unmarried man ?

BENARE [*interrupting*]. Yes, with the counsel for the prosecution himself ! And with the judge. To say nothing of Ponkshe, Balu here or Karnik.

ROKDE. Miss Benare, I'm warning you, there'll be trouble !

PONKSHE. In these circumstances, Sukhatme, is there any point in continuing this farce of a trial ? Nobody is serious! Kashikar's gone inside. Benare's acting like this. No one lets me speak—

KARNIK. Even the rehearsals for our plays are more serious than this!

3

MRS KASHIKAR. Don't make trouble, Benare. It won't do if tonight's show's a flop because of you.

BENARE. I'm just helping the trial along.

KASHIKAR [*returning*]. What's happened ? Sukhatme, continue. Where's my earpick ?

BENARE. I think I'll go out for a stroll through the village. You can carry on your trial. Infanticide ! Ha! At least I'll get some fresh air.

KARNIK. If that's so, let's call it a day.

MRS KASHIKAR. No. At least let's finish the trial. Let's at least complete the job in hand.

SAMANT [*courteously, to Mrs Kashikar*]. Does that mean it all ends here ?

KASHIKAR [*finding his earpick*]. Found it ! Come on now. The hearing is to continue. [*Gestures 'Patience !' to Benare*] Sukhatme, what are you waiting for ?

SUKHATME. For your earpick to be located, milord. [*Then, striking the alert attitude of a barrister*] Mr Ponkshe—

[*Ponkshe, who has come out of the witness-box, once more enters it hurriedly.*]

Has anything ever struck you about the prisoner's behaviour?

PONKSHE. Yes, a lot.

SUKHATME. What ? [*Breathes out smoke.*]

PONKSHE. The prisoner sometimes acts as if she were off her head. That is, there's sometimes no sense at all in her actions.

SUKHATME. For example ?

PONKSHE. For example, once she tried to arrange a marriage for me, and—why go further ? Right now she's sticking out her tongue like a lunatic ! [*Benare hurriedly retracts her tongue.*]

SUKHATME [*as if he has discovered an important clue*]. Good! You can sit down now, Mr Ponkshe—the great scientist. Our next witness is Mr Karnik—the great actor.

[*Ponkshe comes out and, looking steadily at Benare, goes and leans against the wall at one side. Karnik enters the witness-box dramatically, and strikes an attitude.*]

KARNIK. Ask !

SUKHATME. Oath—name—occupation—all over ? Now, Mr Karnik, you are an actor ?

KARNIK [*like a witness in a melodrama*]. Yes, and I am proud of it.

SUKHATME. Be proud ! But Mr Karnik, do you know this lady ? [*Points to Benare.*]

KARNIK [*going through the stage motions of seeing her*]. Yes, sir, I—think—I—know—this—lady.

SUKHATME. What do you mean by 'think', Mr Karnik ?

KARNIK. 'Think' means to consider or feel. There's a dictionary here if you want it.

SUKHATME [*who has moved unconsciously towards the dictionary, checks himself, and turns.*] I don't need that Mr Karnik, please state definitely whether or not you know this lady.

KARNIK [*shrugging his shoulders*]. It's strange ! Sometimes we feel we know someone. But in fact we don't. Truth is stranger than fiction.

SUKHATME. How did you get to know each other ?

KARNIK. Through this group, you see. We do performances cf the Living Lawcourt. She's a member. Yes, I remember it clearly. [*Theatrical throughout.*]

SUKHATME. What kind of performances are those, Mr Karnik ?

KARNIK Smash hits !

SUKHATME [*to Kashikar in a lawyer's tone*]. Milord, I submit that this important statement be noted in the official record.

KASHIKAR [*picking his ear*]. It shall be arranged. Proceed.

SUKHATME. Mr Karnik, tell me truthfully. In the plays you perform, what is the description of a mother ?

KARNIK. The new plays don't mention them at all. They're all about the futility of life. On the whole, that's all man's life is.

KASHIKAR. That's it ! That's what I disagree with ! Men should have some purpose in life. 'Endless is our zeal for striving' should be one's motto. A purpose in life, that's what one needs.

SUKHATME. Let that pass. If you had to give a definition of a mother, how would you do it ?

KARNIK [*after he has thought it over*]. A mother is one who gives birth.

SUKHATME. Mr Karnik, who is the mother—the woman who protects the infant she has borne—or the one who cruelly strangles it to death ? Which definition do you prefer ?

KARNIK. Both are mothers. Because both have given birth.

SUKHATME. What would you call motherhood ?

KARNIK. Giving birth to a child.

SUKHATME. But even a bitch gives birth to pups !

KARNIK. Then she's a mother, of course. Who denied it ? Who says only humans can be mothers, and not dogs ?

BENARE [*stretching lazily*]. Bully for you, Karnik !

[*Karnik ignores her.*]

SUKHATME. Karnik's in form today.

KASHIKAR. Show us the form tonight, Karnik. Just now let's have straight answers.

SUKHATME. Mr Karnik, think carefully before you answer my next question. What is your opinion of the prisoner's conduct ?

KARNIK [*after striking two or three tremendous 'thinking' poses*]. Do you mean, in this mock trial, or in real life ?

SUKHATME. In real life, of course.

KASHIKAR [*picking his ear*]. I think it's better if these little questions refer to the trial, Sukhatme.

KARNIK. That's right, is it ? Then it doesn't matter. I don't know anything about the moral conduct of the accused.

SUKHATME. Nothing ? Are you sure ?

KARNIK. Nothing at all. Nothing where the trial is concerned.

[*Benare's expression is tense.*]

SUKHATME. Mr Karnik—[*with sudden fervour*] Have you, in any circumstances, on any occasion, seen the accused in a compromising situation ? Answer yes or no. Yes, or no ?

KARNIK. Not me. But Rokde has.

ROKDE [*confused*]. Me ? I don't know a thing!

SUKHATME [*his chest swelling in great lawyerlike style*]. Mr Karnik, thank you very much. You may take your seat now.

[*Karnik leaves the witness-box.*]
Now, Mr Rokde, please enter the witness-box. Please enter it.
MRS KASHIKAR [*to Samant*]. You're grasping it all, aren't you?
SAMANT. Yes.
ROKDE [*staying where he is, in total confusion*]. Not me!
SUKHATME. Milord, the usher Rokde's evidence is extremely necessary to the trial. He should be summoned to the witness-box without delay.
ROKDE [*wretchedly*]. I won't come! You'll see! I'll go away—
[*Benare is laughing silently.*]
KASHIKAR. Rokde!—
[*Rokde obediently goes and stands in the witness-box. His body is trembling. He is visibly disturbed.*]
PONKSHE [*to Karnik*]. I say, what did he see?
KARNIK. Who says he did? I was just joking, that's all. You passed the buck to me, I passed it to him. The game's got to go on, hasn't it? Sukhatme's, I mean.
SUKHATME. Oath—name—occupation—to continue, Mr Rokde—
[*Rokde is close to tears.*]
Mr Rokde, you heard Mr Karnik refer to you while giving his evidence. Can you throw any further light on that subject?
MRS KASHIKAR. Balu, now give a marvellous, unbroken bit of evidence! If you can manage this, you'll get a chance later on in the show. You'll never get such a big chance again. Watch it all, Samant, watch it carefully.
[*Kashikar glares at her. Mrs Kashikar is silent.*]
SUKHATME. Speak on, Mr Rokde. What did you see?
[*Rokde is genuinely disturbed. He swallows convulsively.*]
Mr Rokde, take God as your witness, and tell me what you saw there.
[*Rokde is speechless.*]
[*Like a lawyer in a film*] Mr Rokde, what did you see in certain important circumstances, on a certain occasion?

Answer me, please.

ROKDE [*with difficulty*]. I saw—hell!

[*This is what he is experiencing at the moment. He is all in a sweat. Benare is laughing unrestrainedly. Karnik winks at Ponkshe.*]

KASHIKAR [*picking his teeth*]. He's been a buffoon like this from the start.

MRS KASHIKAR. Balu, you won't have another chance. Answer him at once! How dare you be so scared! Shouldn t a man have *some* guts about speaking up in public? What do you think, Samant?

SAMANT. But it's difficult...

KASHIKAR. Speak quickly, Balu.

BENARE. Speak, Balu, speak. A—B—C—

ROKDE [*to Benare, furious in spite of his state*]. That's enough! [*Wipes away sweat repeatedly.*]

SUKHATME [*abandoning his legal voice*]. Mr Rokde—

ROKDE [*stopping him*]. No. Wait a minute. [*He summons up his courage and looks once or twice towards Benare, who is still laughing at him.*] I'll tell you. I went to his house some time ago—

SUKHATME [*in a lawyer's voice*]. Whose house? Mr Rokde, to whose house did you go?

ROKDE. Don't keep interrupting me! I went to—to Damle's house!

[*Benare tense.*]

PONKSHE. Our Professor Damle?

KARNIK. You must have been to his room in the college hostel, you mean?

ROKDE. Yes. I went there in the evening. As night was falling. And there—*she* was! Miss Benare.

ALL. Who?

ROKDE [*looking at Benare*]. Now laugh! Make fun of me! This lady was there. Damle and this—Miss Benare!

[*Benare has stiffened. Karnik signals to Ponkshe.*]

SAMANT [*to Mrs Kashikar*]. Is this true, or just for the trial?

SUKHATME [*with peculiar care*]. Mr Rokde, you went to Professor Damle's house, as night was falling. What did you see there ? [*in a deep, cruel voice*] What did you see ?

KASHIKAR [*although he is enjoying it all greatly*]. Sukhatme.
I feel this is getting on to too personal a level—

SUKHATME. No, no, no, not at all, milord. It's just for the
trial ; so, Mr Rokde—

BENARE. I don't agree. I'm telling you ! what's all this got
to do with the trial ?

MRS KASHIKAR. But why are you getting into such a state,
Benare ? [*to Kashikar*] Go on.

BENARE. There's no need at all to drag my private life into
this. I can visit whom I like. Damle wasn't eating me up.

SUKHATME. What did you see there, Rokde ? Yes, tell us.
Tell us ! Miss Benare, listen to me. Don't spoil the mood
of the trial. This game's great fun. Just be patient. Now,
Rokde, don't be shy—tell everything you saw.

ROKDE [*looking straight ahead, after a pause*]. They were
sitting there.

SUKHATME. And ?—

ROKDE. What do you mean—and ? They were both sitting
there—in that room.

SUKHATME. What else did you see ?

ROKDE. That's all.

[*Sukhatme is disappointed.*]
But I got such a shock ! Sitting there in Damle's room—the
night falling...

BENARE. What a baby the poor thing is !

ROKDE. Then why did your face fall when you saw me ?
Just explain that ! Damle got rid of me. Without letting me
come in. Usually he always asks me in—into the room !

BENARE [*laughing*] Damle alone knows why he got rid of
you. And do you know why you imagine that my face fell ?
Because Damle snubbed you in front of me. Why should
my face fall ? It stayed right where it should be!

SUKHATME [*to Kashikar*]. Milord, I submit that what the
witness Mr Rokde saw—and he alone knows why he stop-
ed at that—I submit that what he saw be noted in record.
Even to an impartial observer, it reveals that Miss Benare's
behaviour is certainly suspicious.

BENARE. It reveals nothing of the sort! Tomorrow I may be seen in our Principal's office. Does that mean my behaviour is suspicious? Ha! Our principal is sixty-five!

SUKHATME. Milord, I request that this statement made by the accused may also be noted, as we wish to introduce it in evidence.

BENARE. If you like, I'll give you the names and addresses of twenty-five more people with whom I am alone at times. Holding a trial, are you? Suspicious, indeed. You don't even understand the meaning of simple words!

[*Karnik signals to Ponkshe.*]

SUKHATME. Milord, since I consider that statement, too, to be valuable, the prosecution requests that it be noted in evidence.

KASHIKAR [*picking his teeth*]. Which statement? 'You don't even understand the meaning of words'?

SUKHATME. No—'the names and addresses of 25 people'—with whom she sometimes—

BENARE. A little while ago, Mr... Mr...Samant and I were quite alone together. Go on, write his name down, too. Why don't you?

SAMANT [*rising suddenly, in confusion*]. No, no, this lady behaved in a most exemplary manner. We just talked of magic shows—hypnotism and the like—that's all—

SUKHATME. Milord, I request that the reference to hypnotism, being most important, should be noted in evidence.

KASHIKAR [*picking his teeth*]. But, Sukhatme, to what extent is all this within the jurisdiction of the court?

KARNIK. This is just a rehearsal, in any case. Just a rehearsal.

PONKSHE. This is just a game. A game, that's all! Which of us is serious about the trial? It's fun, Sukhatme! Do go on. [*To Karnik*] I say, this chap seems to be a good enough lawyer. How's it that his practice is so small?

SAMANT [*to Mrs Kashikar*]. But by hypnotism I only meant—that is—it was nothing—you know—only ordinary hypnotism—

PONKSHE [*making him sit*]. Do sit down! It's all just a joke.

KARNIK. Sukhatme, don't stop. Let the case go on. Well,

Mrs Kashikar, what do you think, eh ?

MRS KASHIKAR. The whole affair's warming up nicely. I wouldn't have imagined... Sukhatme, don't stop ; carry on.

SUKHATME [*encouraged by all this*]. Mr Rokde, you may leave the witness-box.

[*Rokde heaves a sigh of relief at this and comes out of the witness-box, to go straight into the inner room*].

Now, Mr Samant.

SAMANT [*standing up, distrustful and confused*]. Me ? Did you say me ?

SUKHATME. Come.

[*He indicates the witness-box. Samant comes and stands in it.*]

Don't be scared. You just have to answer—

SAMANT.—the questions I'm asked.

SUKHATME. How very clever you are !

MRS KASHIKAR. There are no odds and ends to remember. Besides, this is just a practice trial. The real one is tonight.

SAMANT. Yes, indeed. It's at night. I'm not at all scared. I just get a bit confused, that's all. [*To Sukhatme*] I'll take the oath, just for practice.

SUKHATME. All right. Usher Rokde !

[*Rokde is absent.*]

SAMANT. I think he's gone there, inside. I'll do it myself. [*At a bound, goes and fetches the dictionary. Placing his hand on it*] I, Raghunath Bhikaji Samant, do hereby swear to tell the truth, the whole truth, and nothing but the truth. True enough for the trial, I mean. Of course, what's true for the trial is quite false really. But I'm just taking the oath for practice. [*His hand is still on the dictionary.*] You see, I don't want the sin of falsehood. [*In apologetic tones*] I'm quite religious ... The oath's over. Now. [*Enters the witness-box again.*] Go on. [*This is to Sukhatme ; then, to Mrs Kashikar*] You see ? I'm not frightened. I just get confused because I'm new to all this. [*To Sukhatme*] Well, you may go on.

SUKHATME. Name—occupation—that's all dealt with.

SAMANT. No. Do you want to ask all that ? Then go ahead.

SUKHATME. No. Now, Mr—

SAMANT [*proudly*]. Samant. Sometimes people forget my sur-
name. That's why I have to tell it.

SUKHATME. It's all right. Mr Samant, do you know the prisoner, Miss Benare ?

SAMANT [*proudly*]. Of course ! But not all that well. After
all, how well can you get to know a person in two hours
or so ? But I am acquainted with her. She's a very nice
lady.

SUKHATME. But your opinion, or the favourable impression
you have formed of her, cannot be regarded as reliable in
court, can it ?

SAMANT. Yes—No, no, why not ? Of course it can. My
mother used to be able to sum up a person's worth in just
one minute. From his face ! Now the poor thing can't see
at all. She's grown too old.

[*Rokde enters and takes up his position. Benare is sitting in
the dock, her eyes closed, her chin propped up in one
hand.*]

She seems to have fallen asleep, Miss Benare. I mean.

BENARE [*her eyes shut*]. I'm awake. I can never, never sleep
just when I want to. Never.

SAMANT. I don't have that problem. I can sleep any time
I want. [*To Sukhatme*] What about you ?

SUKHATME. My sleeping habits are quite different. When I
am going to fall asleep it happens in a flash. Otherwise, I
lie awake for hours at a stretch.

KASHIKAR [*still picking his teeth and ears*]. Put some
corn oil on your head, Sukhatme, and rub it well in. That's
what I do. Whatever important social problem there may
be, corn oil gives me peaceful sleep. Basically, if your sleep's
calm, your brain's bound to be so too. But if your brain's
not calm, how on earth will social problems be solved ?
Most important things, your brain and your digestion. Both
of them !

SAMANT. Yes. [*To Sukhatme*] Let's get those questions over
with.

SUKHATME. [*picking up the thread with fresh energy*]. Mr—

SAMANT. Samant.

SUKHATME. Mr Rokde saw the accused—Miss Benare—in Professor Damle's room in the evening when it was quite dark.

SAMANT. That's right ...

SUKHATME. On that occasion, there was no third person there with Professor Damle and the accused.

SAMANT. Correct. But now, do ask me something.

SUKHATME. That's just what I am going to do. Half an hour after that, you reached there.

SAMANT. Where ? No, no ! Why, that room's in Bombay ! And I was in this village. Hardly ! It's silly—I don't know your Professor Damle from Adam. How could I get to his room ? Isn't that right ? What are you up to ?

SUKHATME. You reached there.

SAMANT. You've got it all mixed up, counsel ...

SUKHATME. Mr Samant, for the sake of the trial, we're taking some things for granted.

KARNIK. The crime itself is imaginary. What more do you want ? It's all imaginary ... that's what it is.

PONKSHE. Only the accused is real !

SAMANT [*to Mrs Kashikar*]. There ! Now I'm in a mess ! [*To Sukhatme*] All right. After half an hour, I reached Professor Damle's room. What next ?

SUKHATME. You tell us that.

SAMANT. How can I tell you ?

SUKHATME. Then who will ?

SAMANT. That's true. I'll have to. But it's hard. The prisoner and Professor Damle. Room ... evening ...

PONKSHE. It was quite dark.

KARNIK. Half an hour after that. In other words, when it was very dark. Throughout the college grounds, complete silence...

SAMANT [*suddenly*]. Go on, ask me—so I reached there, eh ? I reached there and—and what happened was—the door was locked !

SUKHATME. The door was locked !

SAMANT. Yes. The door was locked. Not from outside. From

inside. And I banged on the door. No, that's wrong. I rang
the bell. The door opened. An unknown man stood before
me. Guess who it was. Professor Damle! I was seeing him
for the first time. So he'd be unknown to me, wouldn't he?

PONKSHE. Bravo, Samant!

MRS KASHIKAR [*to Karnik*]. Oh, he's giving his evidence
beautifully!

SAMANT [*gaining confidence*]. Damle was before me. When
he saw me, he said with an annoyed expression, 'Yes?
Whom do you want?'

PONKSHE [*to Karnik*]. He's describing Damle to the life!

SAMANT. I answered. 'Professor Damle.' He said, 'He's not
at home.' And he slammed the door shut. For a second, I
stood there stunned. I began to think, should I go home
or press the bell once more. Because I had an important
errand.

SUKHATME. What?

SAMANT. What?—Well, let's say—something. Let's suppose
that I wanted to arrange a lecture by Professor Damle. He
does lecture, doesn't he? I only ask, because he is a Professor—so he must lecture at times. So I stood there, wondering how I could go back without arranging the lecture.
At that moment I heard a vague sound from the room. Of
someone crying.

MRS KASHIKAR. Crying?

SAMANT. Yes. An indistinct sound of crying. It was a woman.

SUKHATME [*excitedly*]. Yes?

SAMANT. For a moment he stood where he was. 'He' means
me. He—I mean I—couldn't understand who was crying.
You will ask me why I didn't think it was some female
member of Professor Damle's family. Well, from the way
the woman was crying, she didn't seem to be a member of
his family. Why? Because the crying was soft. That is, it
was secretive. Now, why would anyone cry secretively in
her own house? Thinking over all this, I stood where I
was. Just then, I heard some words.

MRS KASHIKAR. Some words?

KARNIK & PONKSHE. Who spoke?

SAMANT. Tut, tut, tut! You're not supposed to ask. This gentleman—the counsel—will ask me.

SUKHATME. Who spoke ?

SAMANT. The woman, of course. The one inside.

MRS KASHIKAR. Good heavens ! Tell us, do tell us, who was she ? [*Looking unconsciously at Benare.*]

SAMANT. No. He will ask me—the counsel will. Not you.

SUKHATME. I'm asking. Tell us, quick, Mr Samant. What were the words you heard ? Don't waste time. Tell us quick—Mr Samant—be quick!

SAMANT. The words were—shall I tell it all ?

SUKHATME. Whatever you can remember—but *tell* us !

SAMANT [*hurriedly looking at a book in his hand*]. 'If you abandon me in this condition, where shall I go ?'

[*Benare is tense.*]

MRS KASHIKAR. Is that really what she said ?

SAMANT. 'How can I tell you ?'

SUKHATME [*snapping at him*]. Then who else on earth can ?

SAMANT. No, no ! I'm telling you the Professor's answer. His answer. Professor Damle's.

SUKHATME. Oh, I see,

SAMANT. 'Where you should go is entirely your problem. I feel great sympathy for you. But I can do nothing. I must protect my reputation.' At that, she said, 'that's all you can talk about, your reputation ? How heartless you are !' He replied, 'Nature is heartless.'

KASHIKAR [*picking his ear fast and furiously*]. I see, I see.

SUKHATME [*staggered*]. Amazing—amazing !—

SAMANTA. 'If you abandon me, I shall have no choice but to take my life.' 'Then do that. I also have no choice. If you kill yourself, I shall be in torment.'

SUKHATME. Simply thrilling !

SAMANT. 'But this threat will not make me budge an inch from my considered course of action,' he said. She replied, 'Bear it in mind that you will not escape the guilt of murdering two'—two ?—I'm wrong—no, I'm right ... 'Two living beings.' And then there came a terrifying laugh.

BENARE [*with sudden passion*]. That's enough!

KASHIKAR [*banging his gavel*]. Order, order!

BENARE. It's all a lie! A complete lie!

PONKSHE. Of course it is. So?

KARNIK. Even if it is a lie, it's an effective one!

MRS KASHIKAR. Do go on, Samant.

BENARE. No! Stop all this! Stop it!

SAMANT [*in confusion*]. But what's the matter?

BENARE. This has got to stop! Not a word of it is true!

SAMANT. Of course not.

BENARE. It's all made up! It's a lie!

SAMANT. That's quite right!

BENARE. You're telling barefaced lies!

SAMANTA. What else? [*Brings out the book hidden behind him, and shows it.*] You see, everything I'm saying is out of this!

SUKHATME. Mr Samant, a terrifying laugh…What happened after that?

BENARE. If anyone says one word after this, I—I'll go away!

SUKHATME. Mr Samant…

BENARE. I'll smash up all this! I'll smash it all to bits—into little bits!

MRS KASHIKAR. But my dear Benare, as your conscience is clear, why are you flying into such a violent rage?

BENARE. You've all deliberately ganged up on me! You've plotted against me!

SAMANT. No, no, dear madam, really it's nothing like that!

SUKHATME. Mr Samant, answer. Professor Damle gave a terrifying laugh. Then what did the unknown woman inside the room say?

SAMANT. [*hurriedly consulting his book*]. Wait, I'll find the page and let you know.

BENARE. Samant, if you say one word more—I'll—just you wait.

SUKHATME [*in the right soft and threatening tone*]. Mr Samant…

SAMANT. It's quite a problem. I just can't find the page—

SUKHATME [*to Kashikar*]. Milord, the occurrence as it has been related speaks so vividly for itself that there is hardly any need to add anything over and above it. This entire statement should be noted down as part of our evidence against the accused.

KASHIKAR. Request granted.

BENARE Note it down. Note everything down! Just take down note after note! [*Her eyes are suddenly full of tears. Her voice is choked. She is agitated. Then, with tearful defiance*]. What can you do to me? Just try! [*Tears flow freely from her eyes. Exit into the wings.*]

[*Deeper silence. Except for Samant, everyone's expression changes. A peculiar and cautious excitement breaks out on each face.*]

SAMANT. [*sympathetically*]. Dear, oh dear! Whatever's happened so suddenly to the lady?

KASHIKAR [*picking his ear*]. It's all become quite unexpectedly enjoyable—the whole fabric of society is being soiled these days, Sukhatme. Nothing is undefiled any more.

SUKHATME. That's why thoughtful people like us, Mr Kashikar, should consider these matters seriously and responsibly. This should not be taken lightly.

MRS KASHIKAR. You're absolutely right!

SUKHATME. And if thoughts alone are not enough, we must use deeds. Action! Eh, Karnik?

KARNIK. Yes. Action!

PONKSHE. Right!

SUKHATME. Here, feelings are not enough. We must all get together. We must act.

MRS KASHIKAR. But whatever's happened, really?

KASHIKAR. Keep quiet! What could have happened, Sukhatme? What's your guess?

SUKHATME [*as if he has a fair idea*]. That is the mystery! [*Samant stands there, dismayed.*]

And I think we know the answer to this mystery!

KARNIK
PONKSHE
ROKDE } —What?
KASHIKAR
MRS KASHIKAR

[*Benare comes out of the inner room and stands in the door-way.*]

SUKHATME [*unconscious of this*]. Well, children, the conclusion's obvious. There's some substance in what Mr Samant said. Even though it came from a book. It holds water!

MRS KASHIKAR. Do you mean that Miss Benare and Professor Da—

SUKHATME. Yes. Beyond a shadow of doubt! There's no question about it.

MRS KASHIKAR. Good gracious!

ROKDE [*now very daring*]. I knew it all along!

SUKHATME. Ssh!

[*Seeing Benare in the doorway, all fall silent. They all look at her. She comes in purposefully and picks up her bag and purse. She goes towards the other door, and unbolts it. All are watching The door does not open. She pulls at it. It will not open. She starts tugging at it hard. It is locked from outside. She bangs on it with vehemence. And louder. But it is locked. A peculiar joy begins to show on everyone's face but Samant's.*]

SAMANT. There! It's happened! The bolt's slipped shut outside. That's always the trouble with this door. [*Gets up and goes forward. Struggles with the door.*] If you don't pull the bolt properly to one side when you come in, and then you close the door from inside, you've had it! The door's locked from outside. It's always the case. Try as you will, it just won't open. And what's more, the offices are closed. So there won't be anyone outside just now. [*He bangs on the door again and again.*] It's no use. [*To Miss Benare, who is by him.*] Madam, when you pulled the bolt you did it the wrong way. You should have pulled it back fully. [*He tries giving the door another thump. It's no use. Then coming and standing at one side.*] It's locked!

[*Benare is still standing by the door with her back to the others.*]

KASHIKAR [*cleaning his ears with concentration*]. I think that in the circumstances, Mr Sukhatme, the case should continue.

SUKHATME. [*bowing in legal fashion, with a completely per-verse excitement*]. Yes, milord. [*His eyes gleaming.*] Milord, let the accused herself be summoned to the witness-box.

CURTAIN

ACT THREE

[*The same scene. Evening. The cast in the positions they were in at the end of the second act.*]

SUKHATME [*Bowing in the manner of a professional lawyer with a completely perverse excitement*]. Yes, milord, [*His eyes are gleaming.*] Milord, first let the accused herself be summoned to the witness-box.

KASHIKAR. [*Picking his ear*]. Prisoner Miss Benare, enter the witness-box. Enter it, Miss Benare.

[*Benare stands where she is.*]

Incredible ! Such insolence in court ! Usher Rokde, conduct the accused to the witness-box.

ROKDE [*Frightened, trembling a little*]. Me ?

[*Benare stands still.*]

MRS KASHIKAR. Wait, I'll take her. Why do you need him ?

[*She starts pulling Benare along forcibly.*]

Come on, now, Benare.

[*She puts Benare into the witness-box. Benare's face reveals the terror of a trapped animal.*]

SUKHATME [*Looking at Benare as he puts on his gown ceremoniously.*]. Milord, in consideration of the grave aspect which the case before us has assumed, it is my humble submission that if your lordship himself were to wear your gown henceforth, it would appear more decorous.

KASHIKAR. Exactly. Rokde, give me my gown.

[*He puts on the black gown that Rokde unpacks and hands to him. After that, his gravity and dignity increase.*]

SUKHATME. Mr Samant, Mrs Kashikar, Ponkshe, Karnik, seat yourselves there exactly as you should. [*He straightens up, closes his eyes, and meditates for a while. Then, slapping himself piously on the face, he raises his hands to his forehead in prayer twice or thrice.*]

My father taught me the habit, Kashikar, of praying to our family god at the beginning of any new enterprise. How pure it makes one feel ! The mind takes on new strength.

[*He takes one or two steps in the manner of a wrestler who has gained new strength.*] Good ! Now to business. Let the accused take the oath.

[*Rokde comes and stands in front of Benare with the dictionary. Benare is silent. Like a statue.*]

KASHIKAR [*Adjusting his cap*]. Prisoner Miss Benare, take the oath !

[*Benare is silent.*]

SAMANT [*Softly*]. Why not get it over with, Miss Benare ? It's all a game.

[*Benare is silent.*]

MRS KASHIKAR [*Coming forward*]. Give it to me, I'll make her take the oath ; just wait. [*Taking the dictionary from Rokde.*] Benare, say, 'I hereby swear to tell the truth, the whole truth and nothing but the truth.'

[*Benare is silent.*]

KASHIKAR. This is the limit.

MRS KASHIKAR [*Giving the dictionary to Rokde*]. Let's say she's taken the oath. Her hand was on the dictionary. Go on, ask her what you want, Sukhatme.

KASHIKAR. Prisoner Benare, the court hereby warns you. Henceforth there must on no account be any conduct that constitutes contempt of court. Go ahead, Sukhatme !

KARNIK. Fire away !

SUKHATME [*Walking around in front of Benare a while, and suddenly, pointing a finger*]. Your name is Leela Damle.

SAMANT. (*At once*) No—no—Be-na-re. Damle is the Professor.

MRS KASHIKAR. Do listen, Samant. Let her answer.

SUKHATME. Miss Leela Benare—

[*She tries not to listen to or look at him.*]

SUKHATME. Please tell the court your age.

[*He has struck an attitude, confident that she will not tell it. Benare is silent.*]

KASHIKAR. Prisoner Benare, it is your responsibility to answer any questions put to you as a witness. [*Pausing a little*] Prisoner Benare, what are you waiting for ? Answer the question !

MRS KASHIKAR. Why should *she* have to tell her age ? I can guess it. Say...it's over thirty-two. A year or so more perhaps, but not less. Just look at her face !

SUKHATME. Thank you, Mrs Kashikar.

KASHIKAR. Wait. What do you mean, 'Thank you, Mrs Kashikar?' The accused has not yet told you her age. I was listening carefully. Prisoner Benare, your age!

MRS KASHIKAR. But I—

KASHIKAR. It is not the custom of any court to accept someone else's answer when the accused is questioned. Don't interrupt! Prisoner at the bar! Answer! Your answer please!

[*Benare is silent.*]

SAMANT. The fact is—it isn't thought—courteous—to ask a lady her age...

KASHIKAR. This is intolerable rudeness! No answer to any question! Is this a court of law, or what is it? [*Bangs the table for effect.*]

PONKSHE. Exactly. This is contempt of court!

KASHIKAR. We will have to take steps to deal with the prisoner's refusal to answer. This is a matter of the court's dignity. The accused will be granted ten seconds to answer. [*Holding his watch in front of him.*] No nonsense, please.

SUKHATME [*In a melodramatic manner, at the end of the tenth second*]. Milord, I withdraw the question. The accused, by her silence, has as good as answered me.

KASHIKAR. All right. She's not less than thirty-four. I'll give it to you in writing! What I say is, our society should revive the old custom of child marriage. Marry off the girls before puberty. All this promiscuity will come to a full stop. If anyone has ruined our society it's Agarkar and Dhondo Keshav Karve. That's my frank opinion, Sukhatme, my frank opinion.

SUKHATME. [*With a lawyerlike bow*]. Yes, milord.

[*Rokde has meanwhile hastily written down Kashikar's sentence in his notebook. Benare is silent in the witness-box.*]

[*Going behind Benare, suddenly*]. Miss Benare.

[*She starts, jerking away from him.*]

Can you tell the court how you came to stay unmarried to such a mature—such an advanced—age? [*Waits; then*] Let me frame my question somewhat differently. How many

chances of marriage have you had so far in your life ? And
how did you miss them ? Tell the court.

KASHIKAR. Answer him ! [*Takes out his watch and holds it
in front of him. She is silent.*] This is really too much !

MRS KASHIKAR. It seems she's decided not to behave herself
and answer properly !

[*Benare is silent.*]

SUKHATME. Milord, I close the examination of the accused
for the time being. It could be resumed at the appropriate
time.

[*Benare leaves the witness-box and goes to the door. It is
locked. Ponkshe blocks the way, so she turns aside. By
then, Mrs Kashikar has caught hold of her, and leads her
to the dock.*]

KASHIKAR. Next witness.

SUKHATME. Mrs Kashikar.

[*At once, Mrs Kashikar eagerly enters the witness-box, tuck-
ing her sari round her fussily as she goes.*]

KASHIKAR. (*To Sukhatme*) Look. That's eagerness for you !
You've hardly called her, and there she is !

MRS. KASHIKAR. You needn't be like *that* ! [*Then, talking
like a stage witness*] I have already taken the oath. Benare
and I—let's say we took it together. And of course I'll
tell the truth Who's scared ?

SUKHATME. Very well. Mrs Kashikar, can you give me some
information, please ? How did Miss Benare remain unmarried till such a late age ?

MRS KASHIKAR. That's easy ! Because she didn't get married,
of course.

SUKHATME. That's it. But, Mrs Kashikar, at the age of
thirty-two—

KASHIKAR [*Interrupting*]. Thirty-four—count it as thirty-
four !

SUKHATME. How is it that, till the age of thirty-four, an educated, well-brought-up girl—

MRS KASHIKAR. Girl ? You mean 'woman' ! If you call her
a girl—you'd better call me young lady

SUKHATME. All right. Let's call her a woman then. But, why

isn't she married ? Can you explain that ?

MRS KASHIKAR. Damn the explanation ! Anyone who really wants to can get married in a flash !

SUKHATME. You mean that Miss Benare didn't want to—

MRS KASHIKAR. What else ? That's what happens these days. when you get everything without marrying. They just want comfort. They couldn't care less about responsibility ! Let me tell you—in my time, even if a girl was snub-nosed, sallow, hunchbacked, or anything whatever, she—could—still—get—married ! It's the sly new fashion of women earning that makes everything go wrong. That's how pro- miscuity has spread throughout our society. [*Rokde is jotting it down. To Rokde.*] Finished writing ? [*To Sukhatme.*] Go on. Ask me more.

SUKHATME. You said that this is what happens if you get everything without marrying.

MRS KASHIKAR. Yes, I did.

SUKHATME. What do you mean by 'everything' ? Give me an instance.

MRS KASHIKAR. Well, really ! [*She looks embarrassed.*]

KASHIKAR. [*Picking his ear*]. Come on, don't pretend to be shy, at your age. Just answer his question. You've grown old, but you haven't grown any wiser !

MRS KASHIKAR. My age has nothing to do with it !

KASHIKAR. Answer him !

MRS KASHIKAR. 'Everything' means—everything in this life.

SUKHATME. Don't you feel that to say this about the accu- sed might be unjust ?

MRS KASHIKAR. I Don't think so. We see too many such examples.

SUKHATME. Forget about the others. Have you any proof where Miss Benare is concerned ? Any proof ? Tell me if you have.

MRS KASHIKAR. What better proof ? Just look at the way she behaves. I don't like to say anything since she's one of us. Should there be no limit to how freely a woman can behave with a man ? An unmarried woman ? No matter how well she knows him ? Look how loudly she

laughs ! How she sings, dances, cracks jokes ! And wandering alone with how many men, day in and day out !

SUKHATME [*Disappointed at the 'proof'*]. Mrs Kashikar,
at the most one can say all this shows how free she is.

MRS KASHIKAR. Free ! Free ! she's free allright—in every-
thing ! I shouldn't say it. But since it's come up in court,
I will. Just hold this a minute. [*She puts her knitting into
Sukhatme's hands.*] Why must she have Professor Damle,
and Damle alone, to see her home after a performance ?
Tell me that !

[*Benare is deliberately silent.*]

SUKHATME. [*Brightening up*]. I see—so Miss Benare needs
Professor Damle to see her home after a performance ?

[*Ponkshe and Karnik are signalling to each other.*]

MRS KASHIKAR. What else ? Once we—my husband and I—
it was just last September—September, wasn't it dear ?

KASHIKAR. No prompting the witness ! You say what you
want !

MRS KASHIKAR. Yes, it was September. We both said, 'Come,
we'll drop you,' since she was to go home alone. But she
very slyly went off with Damle. We looked for her, but
she'd vanished !

SUKHATME [*In a lawyer's voice, sounding pleased*]. Peculiar !

MRS KASHIKAR. Just a while back, she was protesting, 'It's a
lie ! It's persecution !' Now how's she struck dumb ? That
shows you can't suppress the truth. Give me that wool.

SUKHATME. [*Handing over the wool and needles to Mrs
Kashikar*]. Mrs Kashikar, Professor Damle is a family
man.

MRS KASHIKAR. Yes. He has five children.

SUKHATME. Then how do you know Miss Benare doesn't
seek his company innocently, as a responsible elder person ?

MRS KASHIKAR. Then do you mean to say that we—my
husband and I—are just vagabonds ? And Damle may be
an older man—but what about Balu ?

[*Rokde gives a great start.*]

SUKHATME. [*Growing alert*]. What about him, Mrs Kashikar ?
What about Rokde ?

[*Benare's expression is tense.*]

MRS KASHIKAR. That's what I'm telling you. After another performance, Benare made overtures to him, too. In the dark. It was he who told me. Didn't you, Balu ?

[*Karnik excepted, commotion all round. Sukhatme is radiant.*]

ROKDE [*Weakly*]. Yes...no...

SAMANT [*To Karnik*]. No, no, she was alone with me a little while ago, and,...

[*Karnik silences him.*]

SUKHATME. Mrs Kashikar, you may step down. Your evidence is complete. Milord, I submit that Rokde be called once more to give evidence.

[*Rokde cringes where he is. Sukhatme strolls over to stand near Benare. In confidential tones.*] Miss Benare, the game's really warmed up, hasn't it ?

KASHIKAR. Rokde, come and give evidence.

[*Rokde hesitantly goes to the witness-box without looking at Benare.*]

MRS KASHIKAR. [*As he passes*]. Balu, speak the truth ! Don't be afraid.

SUKHATME [*Going towards the witness-box*]. Mr Rokde— you've already taken the oath. Well, Mr Rokde, in the course of her evidence, Mrs Kashikar has made a most disturbing statement about you and the accused.

[*Rokde begins to shake his head.*]

MRS KASHIKAR. Balu ! Didn't you tell me so ?

SUKHATME. Mr Rokde, whatever happened after the performance that night, good or bad, pleasant or unpleasant, tell it all to the court. That is your duty. The performance ended. What happened then ?

ROKDE. [*Feebly*]. I—I—

SUKHATME. After the performance all of us left the hall. Then— ?

KARNIK. And only these two remained behind.

MRS KASHIKAR. Then it seems, she took his hand—Balu's, I mean.

PONKSHE. Gosh !

SUKHATME. And then ? What did she do then, Rokde ?

What more did she do ? What next ?

MRS KASHIKAR. I'll tell you !

KASHIKAR. No, you won't. Let him tell it. Don't interrupt all the time !

SUKHATME. Yes, Mr Rokde—tell it bravely—don't be afraid.

KASHIKAR. Afraid ? Why should he be ? There's some law and order here, isn't there ?

[*Rokde takes stock of the situation. Then, realizing he has enough protection against Benare, he plucks up courage.*]

ROKDE. [*Bravely*]. She held my—my hand.

SUKHATME. Yes ?

ROKDE. So, then—So then I said—'This isn't proper. It's not proper ! —I —I don't like this at all— it doesn't become you'—That's—that's what I said !

SUKHATME. And then ?

ROKDE. I freed my hand. She moved away. She said, Don't tell anyone what happened.

BENARE. That's a lie !

KASHIKAR [*Banging the gavel*]. Order ! The accused is sternly reprimanded for disturbing the proceedings of the court. Continue, Rokde, continue.

ROKDE. If you tell anyone, I'll do something to you. That's what she said to me, Anna.

SUKHATME. When did this happen, Mr Rokde ?

ROKDE. Eight days ago, when we had our show at Dombivli.

SUKHATME. Milord, this means that the accused committed an outrage in a lonely spot, on a boy like Rokde, much younger than her—almost like her younger brother. Not only that, but she threatened him with consequences if the matter came to light. She tried to cover up her sinful deed !

MRS KASHIKAR. But the truth will out.

SUKHATME. So, Rokde, the accused threatened to harm you somehow. What next ? What happened then ?

ROKDE [*Unconsciously raising one hand to his cheek*]. I— I slapped her !

PONKSHE. What ?

KARNIK. How melodramatic !

ROKDE. Yes—I said, 'What do you take me for ? Do what-

ever you like ! I won't stay quiet about this.' That's why
I told Mrs Kashikar. Yes, that's why.

KASHIKAR. Go on, tell her everything, Rokde ; don't tell anything to *me* !

ROKDE [*Indistinctly*]. I'm sorry, Anna. I was wrong. I thought
—I thought, in any case you'd find out—from Mrs Kashikar
here, I mean—so I—

SUKHATME. What happened next, Rokde ? What next ?

ROKDE. Then ?—then nothing. That's all. Can I go ?

SUKHATME. Yes, Mr Rokde.

[*Takes a scrap of paper out of his pocket, and writes on
it, muttering loudly, 'Eight days ago, the performance at
Dombivli.' Rokde hastily leaves the witness-box, and stands
at a distance, wiping the sweat from his face. His expression
is calm and satisfied.*]

MRS KASHIKAR. But you hadn't told me this last bit, Balu—
about slapping her !

SAMANT [*To Ponkshe*]. Impossible ! I can't believe it!

[*A pronounced excitement is in the air.*]

PONKSHE [*From his seat, puffing hard at his pipe*]. Sukhatme, my evidence now—call me as a witness ! Call me
now !

[*His gaze is on the hapless Benare. ...His tone is impatient.*]
Just call me !

KASHIKAR. Sukhatme, call Ponkshe. Let's hear him...call
him now. Let's hear him once and for all !

SUKHATME. Mr Ponkshe be called to the witness-box!

ROKDE. Next witness, Mr Ponkshe !

[*Ponkshe enters the witness-box.*]

PONKSHE. Shall I take the oath again ? I hereby place my
hand upon the Oxford English Dictionary, and swear that
I—

KASHIKAR. It's understood. Sukhatme, proceed.

SUKHATME. Mr Ponkshe, the accused, Miss Benare—

PONKSHE [*Gazing at Benare*].—is what I have something
important to tell you about.

[*Benare stiffens where she is.*]
Just ask her this. Why does she keep a bottle of TIK-20 in

her purse ?

[*Benare flinches.*]

MRS KASHIKAR. What more now !

PONKSHE. That is a powerful bedbug poison. It's famous.

SAMANT [*To Karnik*]. Perhaps she was taking it home—

SUKHATME. Can you tell us, Mr Ponkshe, how and when you first found out that the accused was carrying such a terrible poison as TIK-20 in her purse ?

[*Benare has tensed completely.*]

PONKSHE. Yes. One of her little pupils stays in my tenement. About ten days ago, she came to me and said, our teacher's sent you this.

KASHIKAR. TIK-20 ?

PONKSHE. No, a note in a sealed envelope. I opened it. Inside there was another envelope. That, too, was sealed. There was a slip of paper in it, which said, 'Will you meet me, please ? I have something to discuss with you. Come at a quarter past one. Wait in the Udipi restaurant just beyond the school.' Of course, I didn't like it at all. But I said to myself, let's see what her game is. So I went along. Just for the heck of it.

Five minutes later, Miss Benare came there hurriedly, look-ing quite guilty.

[*Benare has tensed still more.*]

SUKHATME. I see—

KASHIKAR Then ? What happened then, Ponkshe ?

PONKSHE. She said, 'Not here—in public—someone'll see us—let's go into a family room.'

MRS KASHIKAR [*Sarcastically*]. Magnificent!

PONKSHE. So we sat in a 'family room.' We ordered tea. When Miss Benare's problem had been discussed, she opened her purse to take out her handkerchief. And out of it there rolled a small bottle—

[*For a moment, there is silence.*]

SUKHATME. A bottle of TIK-20 ! Good ! But Mr Ponkshe, what had happened between you and Miss Benare before that ? I mean, what was the thing she wanted to discuss with you ? You haven't told us that.

[*Benare is shaking her head with silent vehemence, telling him not to do so.*]

PONKSHE. She made known her desire to marry me.

KARNIK. What ?

KASHIKAR. What ?

[*Rokde and the others are astounded.*]

KASHIKAR. This appears terribly interesting, Sukhatme.

SUKHATME. True, milord, it is and it will be. [*His famished lawyer's gaze is on Benare.*] Did she tell you she was in love with you, etc. ?

PONKSHE. No But she told me she was pregnant.

[*Sensation. Benare is sitting like a block of stone, drained of colour and totally desolate.*]

KARNIK. Are you telling the truth, Ponkshe ?

PONKSHE. What do you think ? That I'm lying ?

KASHIKAR. Who was the father—continue, Ponkshe, continue —don't stop there !

SUKHATME. Mr Ponkshe—

PONKSHE. Miss Benare made me promise never to tell anyone the name of the man who—so she said—had made her pregnant. So far I've kept my word.

MRS KASHIKAR. But who *was* it ?

KASHIKAR. What'll you take to shut up ? The cat'll be out of the bag soon, anyway. Don't be so impatient ! But what I don't understand, Ponkshe, is why, if Miss Benare was pregnant by one man, she expressed a desire to marry another—I mean, to marry you !

PONKSHE. Exactly.

SUKHATME. What was your answer, Mr. Ponkshe ? Were you prepared to take a broad view of things for the sake of humanity, and accept the child along with the mother ?

PONKSHE. The answer is quite clear.

SUKHATME. You weren't prepared, of course.

PONKSHE. No, I wasn't.

SUKHATME. And it was after this, Mr Ponkshe, that the bottle of TIK-20 rolled out of Miss Benare's purse !

PONKSHE. Of course! I myself picked it up and returned it to her. Shall I give you the whole conversation ? If you want I'll tell that too.

BENARE. [*Shooting up on to her feet*]. No! No!

KASHIKAR [*Banging his gavel*]. Silence! Mr Ponkshe, give us the conversation. [*To Sukhatme.*] Now we'll hear the name—

BENARE. No! You promised, Ponkshe!

SUKHATME. Mr Ponkshe, what indeed could the conversation have been, for Miss Benare to be so agonized?

KASHIKAR. Tell us, Ponkshe—don't wait—tell it quick—this is a matter of social importance.

PONKSHE. But she won't like it.

KASHIKAR [*Banging the gavel*]. Who is the judge here, Ponkshe? Since when has the question of the accused's likes and dislikes being admitted in court? When? I say to you—continue!

BENARE. [*Coming in front of Ponkshe*]. Ponkshe—

KASHIKAR [*Banging the gavel*]. Order! The accused to the dock! To the dock! Rokde, conduct the accused to the dock!

[*Rokde moves forward a little and halts.*]

BENARE. Just you tell it and you'll see, Ponkshe—

KASHIKAR. Prisoner at the bar, go to the dock—Rokde, take her to the dock...

MRS KASHIKAR [*Coming forward and grasping Benare's hand*]. First stand over there. Come on, Rokde, hold her hand.

[*Rokde lingers behind them.*]

Come, Benare; come on.

[*She drags her to the dock. Mrs Kashikar and Rokde stand guard.*]

Discipline means discipline.

KASHIKAR. Speak, Mr. Ponkshe, What was your conversation about? Where's my earpick? [*He finds it.*] Go on. Mr Ponkshe, what was it about?

PONKSHE. First, we chatted aimlessly. 'Sukhatme's a good man, but he's smothered by ill luck, poor chap. His practice is poor; —he just sits in the barristers' room playing patience—they say it's well known that if you take your case to him, it's jail for certain! —he just goes dumb before the judge...'

SUKHATME [*Swallowing his rage and sense of insult*]. I see ...yes, go on—

PONKSHE. '...Kashikar torments poor Rokde. Because he constantly suspects an entanglement between him and his wife. Because they have no children, you see ...'

MRS KASHIKAR. Is that what she said?
[*Highly offended, she looks daggers at Benare.*]

MR KASHIKAR [*Picking his ear vigorously*]. Go on, tell us more, Ponkshe—

PONKSHE. After some talk of this nature, we came to the real issue.

KARNIK. Wait. What did she say about me, Ponkshe?

PONKSHE. Nothing.

KARNIK. She must have said something—that I'm a rotten actor, or something. I know what she thinks of me. I know it well.

PONKSHE. She asked jokingly; 'Well, are you fixed up somewhere?' So I said, 'Unless I find someone just to my taste, I'm not interested in marrying.' So she asked, 'What exactly do you mean by "to your taste"? What do you look for?' I replied, 'On the whole, girls are silly and frivolous—that's my opinion. I want a mature partner.' Then she asked, 'Don't you think that maturity—that is, a fully developed understanding—comes to a person only with experience?' 'I don't know,' I replied. She then said, 'And experience comes with age, with a slightly unusual way of life. And this sort of experience is never happy or pleasing. It gives pain to the person who gains it. And it's usually intolerable to others. But will you bear with it? I mean, supposing it is a really mature person. Older than you and more educated?' 'I haven't yet thought seriously about it.' 'Then you should,' she replied. So I asked whether she had some promising bride in mind, She said, 'Yes. I feel she's the kind you want. You just have to understand her unusualness.' I couldn't see why she was making this great effort to get me married. I asked casually,

'What sort of unusualness do you mean?' She replied,
'The girl's just gone through a shattering heartbreak, and'
—wait, I'll think of the exact words—yes—'the fruit of
that love'—here she stumbled a little—'is in her womb.
Actually it is no fault of hers. But her situation's very
serious indeed. She wants to bring up the child. In fact it's
only for the child she wants to go on living and get
married.' She spoke some more in the same vein. I grew
suspicious. So in order to get the truth out of her, I said,
'Oh! poor girl! Her luck seems really bad. Who is the
scoundrel responsible?'

SUKHATME. Thereupon she said it was Professor Damle!

PONKSHE. No. First she said, 'Please don't call him a scoundrel. He may be a good man. He may be very great and
wise. She may have fallen short. She may not have been
able to convince him how deeply she feels for him. The
woman is not the crucial factor. It's the baby that comes
first.'

SUKHATME. And then?

PONKSHE. Then she said, 'She worshipped that man's
intellect. But all he understood was her body.' She added
other things. On the same lines. How she couldn't find a
place in Damle's life. His—

SAMANT. ⎫
KARNIK. ⎬ Damle's?
SUKHATME. ⎭

KASHIKAR [*Banging on the table*]. The cat's out of the bag!

PONKSHE. To tell you the truth, I was bound by oath not to
tell the name, but—

SUKHATME. Doesn't matter, Mr Ponkshe, it doesn't matter
at all. It's no sin to break your oath inadvertently—at least,
not in court. So the child she's carrying is Professor
Damle's? Go on, go on—

PONKSHE. Then she fell at my feet.

KASHIKAR. I see—I see—

PONKSHE. Yes, she fell at my feet. And I said, 'This doesn't
become you, Miss Benare. It's an insult to have asked me

this at all. Do you think I'm so worthless ?' When she saw
my face, she got up at once, and said, laughing, 'Did you
really think I was telling the truth ? It was just a joke !
That's all !' Then she burst out laughing.

MRS KASHIKAR. A joke, did she say !

PONKSHE. But she had tears in her eyes. That made everything
quite clear. Then she went off in a hurry saying she was
late.

SUKHATME. Thank you, Mr Ponkshe, for your valuable
evidence.

[*Ponkshe comes out of the witness-box. Sukhatme takes out
the piece of paper, and muttering loudly, notes down, 'Ten
days before the incident of holding Rokde's hand.'*]

That's fine. Milord, this evidence needs no comment. It's
so clear—and. I may add, so self-evident. The accused
first accosted Mr Ponkshe. When she realized there was
nothing doing in that quarter, she committed the outrage
on Rokde. The next witness will be the accused, milord.

[*He points to Benare. She looks half-dead.*]

KARNIK [*Raising his hand in a stagey gesture*]. Wait! Wait!
I have something important to disclose regarding the case.

SUKHATME. Mr. Karnik, into the box.

[*He walks theatrically into it. Mr Kashikar is picking his
ear vigorously.*]

SUKHATME. Speak, Mr Karnik. What do you wish to tell
the court ?

KARNIK [*Stagily*]. The evidence given to the court by Rokde
concerning the accused, Miss Benare, and himself, is
incorrect.

ROKDE [*In a whining tone*]. What business is it of yours ?

KARNIK. [*Stagily*]. Because, by chance, I happened to be a
witness of what was said and done on that occasion.

KASHIKAR. [*Cleaning his earpick*]. Which one ? Tell us what
you have to, without complicating the issue...

KARNIK. [*Dramatically*]. Life itself is a complication these
days. The Western playwright Ionesco—

KASHIKAR [*Banging his gavel*]. To the point ! Don't digress !
Stick to the point !

KARNIK. I only mentioned him because the subject of complications cropped up—

SUKHATME. What amendment would you suggest, Mr. Karnik, to what has been stated before the court, regarding the accused and Rokde ?

KARNIK. As God is my witness, I must state that Rokde did not slap the accused.

ROKDE [*Whining*]. It's a lie !

KARNIK. What happened was roughly like this. The accused accosted Rokde. I saw that. So I stood aside in the darkness to see how it would develop. The accused asked, 'Then what have you decided ?' Rokde's answer came over, 'I can't do anything without Mrs Kashikar's permission. Don't press me.' The accused then said, 'How much more of your life will you spend under Mrs Kashikar's thumb ?' Rokde replied, 'I can't help it. That's one's luck. I can't think of marriage.' The accused said to him, 'Think again. I'll support you. You won't lack for anything then. You won't have to fear Mr and Mrs Kashikar. You'll be independent.' Rokde replied, 'I'm scared. And if I marry you when you're in this condition, the whole world'll sling mud at me. No one in my family's done a thing like that. Don't depend on me. Or else I'll have to tell Mrs Kashikar.' Upon this, the accused, in a rage—

ROKDE It's a lie !

KARNIK. —struck Rokde in the face.

[*Rokde's hand has unconsciously gone to his cheek.*]

ROKDE. It's a lie—a barefaced lie !

[*Mrs Kashikar is glaring at him.*]

SUKHATME. Thank you, Mr Karnik. This means that it is true the accused was pressing Rokde to marry her. The only difference in what you say is about who slapped whom.

KARNIK. Not just what I say—but what I saw.

SUKHATME. That's so, Mr Karnik [*Showing him the way out of the witness-box*]—

KARNIK. I have something more to say.

KASHIKAR. If it isn't anything useless and irrelevant, let's
5

hear it. No complications.

KARNIK. Milord—

KASHIKAR [*Banging the gavel*]. Order! what do you think you are? A lawyer? Just say 'Your lordship' like any other witness!

KARNIK. Your lordship—

KASHIKAR. That's it. That's the way. Speak. But no complications! We want everything straight and simple.

ROKDE. [*Piteously, to Mrs Kashikar, in a soft voice*]. Mrs Kashikar—

MRS KASHIKAR. Don't speak to me at all!

ROKDE. But Mrs Kashikar!...

[*She turns her head away. Rokde is still more miserable.*]

KARNIK. Your lordship, I happen to know a cousin of the accused's. I mean, I just got to know him by chance, at a cricket match at the Dadar Gymkhana. A common friend of ours was playing in the Bachelors' Eleven. My friend's friend turned out to be the cousin of the accused —so my friend told me. My friend knows the accused. I mean, not personally, but a lot of people know the accused, and like them, so did he. I mean, he knew *about* the accused.

KASHIKAR. I see. And with whom are you chatting like this? Show respect to the court.

KARNIK [*Striking the attitude of respecting the court*]. Yes. Well then, the cousin of the accused and I—we had just met—the subject casually came up. He gave me some important information.

SUKHATME. For instance?

KARNIK. For instance, the accused had attempted suicide once before.

SUKHATME [*Radiant*]. That's the point! There is a precedent for the bottle of TIK-20.

KARNIK. I can't say that exactly. I can only tell you what happened. My information is that the accused attempted suicide because of a disappointment in love. She fell in love at the age of fifteen, with her own maternal uncle! That's what ended in disappointment.

MRS KASHIKAR [*Totally floored*]. Her uncle !

SUKHATME. Milord—her maternal uncle—her mother's brother. What an immoral relationship !

KASHIKAR. In other words, just one step away from total depravity. Fine, Sukhatme, very fine!

SUKHATME. Milord, why do you say 'fine' ? The present conduct of the accused is totally licentious. We know that. But it now seems that her past, too, is smeared in sin. This shows it as clear as daylight.

[*Benare struggles to her feet and tries to reach the door. Mrs Kashikar grasps her and forces her back to the dock.*]

MRS KASHIKAR. Where d'you think you're going ? The door's locked ! Sit down !

KARNIK. I've finished.

[*Bowing dramatically to Kashikar, he leaves the witness-box and returns to his place.*]

KASHIKAR [*Banging his hand suddenly on the table as if he has all of a sudden remembered something.*] There's no doubt at all, Sukhatme ! No doubt.

SUKHATME. About what, milord ?

KASHIKAR. I'll tell you ! Sukhatme, I wish to set aside the tradition of the court, and give an important piece of evidence.

SUKHATME. Milord ?

KASHIKAR. This case has great social significance, Sukhatme. No joking ! I must put aside the practice of court, and give evidence. Sukhatme, ask my permission. Ask me. Ask!

SUKHATME. Milord, considering the importance of the case, I humbly submit that tradition should be broken, to allow the judge's worshipful self to enter the witness-box.

KASHIKAR. Permission granted. [*He comes and stands in the witness-box.*] Examine me. Come on. [*He is bursting to speak. His eyes are on Benare.*] Not a doubt of it !

SUKHATME [*Striking a lawyer's attitude*]. Mr Kashikar, your occupation ?

KASHIKAR. Social worker.

SUKHATME. Do you know the accused ?

KASHIKAR. Only too well ! A sinful canker on the body of

society—that's my honest opinion of these grown-up unmarried girls.

SUKHATME [*Taking an even more typical lawyer's pose*]. Do
not give your opinion unless you are asked, Mr Kashikar!

KASHIKAR. An opinion's an opinion. I don't wait for anyone's permission to give it.

PONKSHE. Bravo !

SUKHATME. Don't wait for it, then. Mr Kashikar, can you
place before the court any important evidence about the
charge that has been made here against the accused ?

KASHIKAR. Well, that's why I'm standing here !

SUKHATME. Then speak.

KASHIKAR [*Looking at Benare*]. I often have cause to visit
the famous leader Nanasaheb Shinde of Bombay. Of course,
the bond between us is that of a common love for social
work. Besides, he is the Chairman of the Education Society.
Well, his greatness is different from mine. That's not the
question here. But recently at his house, say at about nine
o'clock at night—when I was sitting there to discuss some
work, I heard conversation in the next room. [*Benare starts.*]
One of the voices was Nanasaheb's. But the other voice,
too, seemed familiar.

MRS KASHIKAR. Whose was it ?

KASHIKAR. Sukhatme, give her a reprimand, go on. You
mustn't interrupt a witness ! Before I could tell whose the
other voice was, the conversation was over. In a little
while Nanasaheb came out. In the course of our conversation I asked about it. He replied, 'A school-mistress from
our Education Society's High School had come here. She
comes here continually. She wants us to drop an enquiry
against her. She's a young woman. So I couldn't say no
straight away. I have called her again, for a quiet talk.'
Of course, I was still curious who this woman could be.
Though Nanasaheb did not tell me, I have just realized
that the woman, far from being some stranger, was this
one—I mean, she was Miss Benare ! I am 101 per cent
certain ! The same voice exactly. Not a doubt of it !

MRS KASHIKAR. Good gracious !

MR KASHIKAR Ask me, Sukhatme, how I'm so certain. This very morning I took over a garland of flowers to Nanasaheb's house, as it's his birthday. There Nanasaheb was talking angrily to someone on the phone, 'It is a sin to be pregnant before marriage. It would be still more immoral to let such a woman teach, in such a condition! There is no alternative—this woman must be dismissed,' he was saying. Finally, he instructed, 'Send the order for my signature this very day!'
[*A shock for Benare.*]
Now who else comes to your mind? Tell me! I *say* it was Miss Benare!

SAMANT. Dear, oh dear! Is she going to lose her job?

SUKHATME. It can't be helped. Tit for tat! As you sow, so shall you reap ... that's the rule of life. [*Rokde opens his notebook and writes it down.*] But Mr Kashikar, what made you think *that* woman was this one—was positively our Miss Benare?

KASHIKAR. My dear man, do you take me for a child, that I shoudn't understand such a simple thing? I've been studying society for the last forty years. I'll have you know! A word to the wise is enough! There is not the slightest doubt in my mind that I've guessed right. It was definitely Miss Benare. Just see whether or not she gets that order tomorrow, that's all! Order for dismissal! that's all I wanted to record here. [*He leaves the witness-box and seats himself on the judge's chair.*] The prosecution may continue.

[*A small bottle is in Benare's hand. Just as she is about to put it to her mouth, Karnik dashes forward and strikes it away. The bottle rolls towards Ponkshe's feet.*]

PONKSHE. [*Picking it up and looking at it, then putting it on the judge's table*]. TIK-20.

[*Samant is shocked. Kashikar looks at the bottle and takes charge of it.*]

KASHIKAR. The prosecution may continue.

SUKHATME. With this last and most important piece of evidence, the testimony for the prosecution is complete.

Milord, the case for the prosecution rests. [*He goes and sits down in his chair, as if exhausted.*]

KASHIKAR [*With all the gravity of a judge*]. Counsel for the accused!

[*Sukhatme goes and sits with lowered head on the stool reserved for the counsel for the accused.*]

Call the witnesses for your side!

SUKHATME [*Getting up with the gesture of a tired man, makes a lawyer-like bow and in equally exhausted tones. says*]. Yes, milord. Our first witness is Professor Damle.

ROKDE. [*Acting the usher*]. Damle! Professor Damle! [*To Kashikar*] Professor Damle is absent.

KASHIKAR. [*To Sukhatme*]. Next witness, please.

SUKHATME. Our next witness is Nanasaheb Shinde.

KASHIKAR. [*Picking his teeth*]. Absent! How could *he* come here? Next—

SUKHATME. The other member of this group, Mr Rawte—

KASHIKAR. He is absent, too. Are those all the witnesses for the defence?

SUKHATME. I wish to cross-examine the witness for the prosecution, milord.

KASHIKAR. Permission refused. Take your seat.

SUKHATME. [*Sighing*]. The case for the accused rests. [*Goes and seats himself on the stool kept for the counsel for the accused.*]

KASHIKAR [*Spitting out something*]. Good! Now counsel for the prosecution, plead your case. Don't waste time, now.

[*Sukhatme changes his place. Sits down energetically on his previous chair. Then springs to his feet like a wrestler and comes forward.*]

KASHIKAR. Be brief.

SUKHATME [*Now the counsel for the prosecution*]. Milord, the nature of the charge against the accused, Miss Leela Benare. is truly dreadful. The woman who is an accused has made a heinous blot on the sacred brow of motherhood—which is purer than heaven itself. For that, any punishment, however great, that the law may give her, will be too mild by far. The character of the accused is appalling. It is bankrupt of morality. Not only that. Her conduct has blackened all social and moral values. The accused is public enemy number one. If such socially destructive tendencies are encouraged to flourish, this country and its culture will be totally destroyed. Therefore, I say the court must take a very stern, inexorable view of the prisoner's crime, without being trapped in any sentiment. The charge against the accused is one of infanticide. But the accused has committed a far more serious crime. I mean unmarried motherhood. Motherhood without marriage has always been considered a very great sin by our religion and our traditions. Moreover, if the accused's intention of bringing up the offspring of this unlawful maternity is carried to completion, I have a dreadful fear that the very existence of society will be in danger. There will be no such thing as moral values left. Milord, infanticide is a dreadful act. But bringing up the child of an illegal union is certainly more horrifying. If it is encouraged, there will be no such thing as the institution of marriage left. Immorality will flourish. Before our eyes, our beautiful dream of a society governed by tradition will crumble into dust. The accused has plotted to dynamite the very roots of our tradition, our pride in ourselves, our culture and our religion. It is the sacred and imperative duty of your Lordship and every wise and thoughtful citizen amongst us to destroy that plot at once. No allowance must be made because the accused is a woman. Woman bears the grave responsibility of building up the high values of society. *'Na stri swatantryamarhati.'* 'Woman is not fit for independence.' …That is the rule laid down for us by tradition. Abiding by this rule, I make a powerful plea. *'Na Miss Benare swatantryamarhati.'* 'Miss Benare is not fit for independence.' With the urgent plea that the court should show no mercy to the accused, but give her the greatest and severest punishment for her terrible crime, I close the argument for the prosecution.

KASHIKAR. Good ! Counsel for the accused ! The accused's lawyer !

[*Sukhatme assumes that character and changes his place,*

rising once more with a downcast face.]

SUKHATME [*Walking forward with heavy steps, and in a tone full of false emotion*]. Milord, that the crime is very serious, I do not dispute. But consider this. Man is, in the last analysis, prone to error. Youth leads a person astray. Let the terrible crime that the accused has committed and is committing, be regarded with mercy. Mercy, milord— for humanity's sake, mercy.

[*He has come to the judge's table. Benare is motionless.*]

KASHIKAR. Good. Now, prisoner Benare—

[*She is quite still.*]

Prisoner Benare, before the sentence is pronounced, have you anything to say about the charge that has been made against you ? [*Putting forward his watch*]. The accused will be given ten seconds.

[*She is as motionless as before. From somewhere in the background, music can be heard. The light changes. The whole court 'freezes' in the positions they are in at the moment. And the motionless Benare stands up erect.*]

BENARE. Yes, I have a lot to say. [*Stretches to loosen her arms.*] For so many years, I haven't said a word. Chances came, and chances went. Storms raged one after another about my throat. And there was a wail like death in my heart. But each time I shut my lips tight. I thought, no one will understand. No one *can* understand ! When great waves of words came and beat against my lips, how stupid everyone around me, how childish, how silly they all seemed. Even the man I call my own. I thought, I should just laugh and laugh till I burst. At all of the them...that's all—just laugh and laugh ! And I used to cry my guts out. I used to wish my heart would break ! My life was a burden to me. [*Heaving a great sigh*] But when you can't lose it, you realize the value of it. You realize the value of living. You see what happiness means. How new, how wonderful every moment is ! Even *you* seem new to your-self. The sky, birds, clouds, the branch of a dried-up tree that gently bends in, the curtain moving at the window, the silence all around—all sorts of distant, little noises,

even the strong smell of medicines in a hospital, even that
seems full to bursting with life. Life seems to sing for you !
There's great joy in a suicide that's failed. It's greater even
than the pain of living. [*Heaves a deep sigh.*] Throw your
life away—and you realize the luck of having it. Guard it
dearer than life—and it only seems fit to throw away.
Funny, isn't it ? Look after it. And you feel like throwing
it away. Throw it away—and you're blissfully happy it's
saved ! Nothing satisfies. The same thing, again and again.
[*In a classroom manner.*] Life is like this. Life is so and
so. Life is such and such. Life is a book that goes ripping
into pieces. Life is a poisonous snake that bites itself. Life
is a betrayal. Life is a fraud. Life is a drug. Life is drud-
gery. Life is a something that's nothing—or a nothing
that's something. [*Suddenly striking a courtroom attitude.*]
Milord, life is a very dreadful thing. Life must be hanged.
Na jeevan jeevanamarhati. 'Life is not worthy of life'. Hold
an enquiry against life. Sack it from its job ! But why ?
Why ? Was I slack in my work ? I just put my whole
life into working with the children...I loved it ! I taught
them well ! I knew that life is no straightforward thing.
People can be so cruel. Even your own flesh and blood
don't want to understand you. Only one thing in life is
all-important—the body ! You may deny it, but it is true.
Emotion is something people talk about with sentiment.
It was obvious to me. I was living through it. It was burning through me. But—do you know ? —I did not teach
any of this to those tender, young souls. I swallowed that
poison, but didn't even let a drop of it touch them ! I
taught them beauty. I taught them purity. I cried inside,
and I made them laugh. I was cracking up with despair,
and I taught them hope. For what sin are they robbing me
of my job, my only comfort ? My private life is my own
business. I'll decide what to do with myself ; everyone
should be able to ! That can't be anyone else's business ;
understand ? Everyone has a bent, a manner, an aim in
life. What's anyone else to do with these ? [*At once, in
the light, playful mood she has at school.*] Hush ! Quiet

there! Silence! What a noise! [*Comes out of the witness-box and wanders as if in class.*] Sit still as statue! [*She is looking at each figure frozen still.*] Poor things! Children, who are all these? [*Light illuminates each face one by one. They all look fearsome, silent, ghostlike.*] These are the mortal remains of some cultured men of the twentieth century. See their faces—how ferocious they look! Their lips are full of lovely worn-out phrases! And their bellies are full of unsatisfied desires.

[*Sound of the hourly bell at school. A distant noise of children chattering. For a moment, she is silent and concentrates on the sound. She loses herself in it. The sound then recedes and is heard no more. Silence. Looking around her as if she is walking up, she is suddenly terrified of the silence.*] No, no! Don't leave me alone! I'm scared of them. [*Terrified, she hides her face and trembles.*] It's true, I did commit a sin. I was in love with my mother's brother. But in our strict house, in the prime of my unfolding youth, he was the one who came close to me. He praised my bloom every day. He gave me love.... How was I to know that if you felt like breaking yourself into bits and melting into one with someone—if you felt that just being with him gave a whole meaning to life—and if he was your uncle, it was a sin! Why, I was hardly fourteen! I didn't even know what sin was—I swear by my mother, I didn't! [*She sobs loudly like a little girl.*] I insisted on marriage. So I could live my beautiful lovely dream openly. Like everyone else! But all of them—my mother too—were against it. And my brave man turned tail and ran. Such a rage—I felt such a rage against him them—I felt like smashing his face in public and spitting on it! But I was ignorant. Instead, I threw myself off a parapet of our house—to embrace death. But I didn't die. My body didn't die! I felt as if feelings were dead—but they hadn't died either then. Again, I fell in love. As a grown woman. I threw all my heart into it; I thought, this will be different. This love is intelligent. It is love for an unusual intellect. It isn't love at all—it's worship! But it was the same mistake.

I offered up my body on the altar of my worship. And my intellectual god took the offering—and went his way. He didn't want my mind, or my devotion—he didn't care about them! [*Feebly.*] He wasn't a god. He was a man. For whom everything was of the body, for the body ! That's all ! Again, the body ! [*Screaming.*] This body is a traitor ! [*She is writhing with pain.*] I despise this body—and I love it ! I hate it—but—it's all you have, in the end, isn't it ? It will be there. It will be yours. Where will it go without you ? And where will you go if you reject it ? Don't be ungrateful. It was your body that once burnt and gave you a moment so beautiful, so blissful, so near to heaven ! Have you forgotten ? It took you high, high, high above yourself into a place like paradise. Will you deny it ? And now it carries within it the witness of that time— a tender little bud—of what will be a lisping, laughing, dancing little life—my son—my whole existence ! I want my body now for him—for him alone. [*Shuts her eyes and mutters in mortal pain.*] He must have a mother... a father to call his own—a house—to be looked after—he must have a good name !

[*Darkness. Then light. The loud ticking of a watch. Benare is motionless in the dock as before. The others are all in their places.*]

KASHIKAR [*Lowering the hand which holds the watch in front of him*]. The time is up. The accused has no state-ment to make. In any case, it would be of no use. The cup of her crime is now full. Now—the judgement. Rokde, my wig, please.

[*Rokde hurriedly unpacks it and hands it to him. Kashikar puts it on and with all the grandeur of a solemn ritual, says*] Prisoner Miss Benare, pay the closest attention. The crimes you have committed are most terrible. There is no forgive-ness for them. Your sin must be expiated. Irresponsibility must be chained down. Social customs, after all, are of supreme importance. Marriage is the very foundation of our society's stability. Motherhood must be sacred and pure. This court takes a serious view of your attempt to

dynamite all this. It is the firm opinion of this court that
your behaviour puts you beyond mercy. And, what is more,
the arrogance with which you conducted yourself in
society, having done all these things, that arrogance is the
most unforgivable thing of all. Criminals and sinners
should know their place. You have conducted yourself
above your station. The court expresses its indignation at
your presumptuousness. Moreover, the future of posterity
was entrusted to you. This is a very dreadful thing. The
morality which you have shown through your conduct was
the morality you were planning to impart to the youth of
tomorrow. This court has not an iota of doubt about it.
Hence not only today's, but tomorrow's society would have
been endangered by your misconduct. It must be said that
the school officials have done a work of merit in deciding
to remove you from your job. By the grace of God, it has
all been stopped in time. Neither you nor anyone else should
ever do anything like this again. No memento of your sin
should remain for future generations. Therefore this court
hereby sentences that you shall live. But the child in your
womb shall be destroyed.

BENARE. [*Writhing*]. No! No! No!—I won't let you do it—
I won't let it happen—I won't let it happen!

[*All are as still as statues. Benare comes sobbing to the
stool for the defence counsel. There she sits down, half
fainting. Then in paroxysms of torment, she collapses with
her head on the table, motionless. Stifled sobs come from
her.*

*Silence. By now it is quite dark in the hall. There is a noise
of someone opening the door. All start and look towards
it. The door quietly opens little by little. A line of light
comes in through it. Two or three faces look round.*]

FIRST FACE. [*Looking curiously at everyone in the hall*]. Has
the show begun? The Living Courtroom?

[*Everyone is startled to the realization. Consciousness dawns
afresh. Samant puts on the lights. Everyone quickly returns
to normal.*]

SAMANT. [*Getting up and going forward*]. Oh? No, no, not

now—but it will, soon. But plesae wait outside. Come on
—five minutes—come on. [*He takes them out somehow.*]

KARNIK. Well ! It's really late, you know.

MRS KASHIKAR. Goodness, I just didn't realize the time !

PONKSHE. What's the time ? It's quite dark.

KASHIKAR. Rokde, it's your job to look after the timing of
the show. What were you doing all this time ? Useless
fellow !

SUKHATME. Let him be, Kashikar. We had some good fun !
Felt just like fighting a real case !

KASHIKAR. Come on. Get ready quickly, everyone...come
on...

PONKSHE. I am always ready—

[*He points to Benare. They are all arrested. Silent, serious.
They gather round the motionless Benare.*].

MRS KASHIKAR [*Stroking the garland in her hair*]. She's
taken it really to heart. How sensitive the child is !

KASHIKAR. You're telling me. She's taking it much too much
to heart. After all it was—

SUKHATME. Just a game ! What else ? A game ! That's all !

PONKSHE. A mere game !

KARNIK. Benare, come on, get up. It's time for the show.
The show must go on.

MRS KASHIKAR [*Shaking her*]. Do get up, Benare. The show
must start on time. Come on now. Look, it was all untrue.
It would hardly be true, would it ?

[*Samant has entered.*]

PONKSHE. Samant, please arrange for some tea. The lady
needs some tea.

SAMANT. Yes.

KASHIKAR. [*Taking off his wig as he gets up. He notices the
bottle of* TIK-20 *in front of him on the table. For a moment, he stays looking at it with staring eyes. Then, removing his gaze, to the others*]. Come on... Come on—come
and wash and dress up—enough playing about ! Now to
business ! Come on.

[*All withdraw with silent steps into the next room, in a
herd behind him. Benare on the stage, motionless. Samant*

*by the door watching her. Embarrassed, he comes diffi-
dently in from one side and quietly picks up the bright
green cloth parrot that he had put there earlier, from the
luggage on the dais. He starts going back towards the door.
Then, unable to restrain himself, he stops some distance
from Benare. Looking at her, he is overcome by feeling.
He can't think what to do. He calls out indistinctly,
'Miss...' but she does not hear. He is even more embarrassed. Since there is nothing else he can do, gently,
affectionately, and with great respect he puts the green
cloth parrot in front of her, from a distance. Exit.
Benare feebly stirs a little. Then gives up the effort. The
bright green cloth parrot is near her. From somewhere
unseen, her own voice is heard singing softly.]*

> The parrot to the sparrow said,
> 'Why, oh why, are your eyes so red?'
> 'Oh, my dear friend, what shall I say?
> Someone has stolen my nest away.'
> Sparrow, sparrow, poor little sparrow...
> 'Oh, brother crow, oh, brother crow.
> Were you there? Did you see it go?'
> 'No, I don't know. I didn't see.
> What are your troubles to do with me?'
> O sparrow, sparrow, poor little sparrow ...

[Light on Benare only. The rest of the stage in darkness.]

CURTAIN